A WINDOW ON
RED SQUARE

A WINDOW ON

HOUGHTON MIFFLIN COMPANY

Red Square

BY FRANK ROUNDS, JR.

BOSTON The Riverside Press CAMBRIDGE ★ 1953

The Riverside Press
CAMBRIDGE · MASSACHUSETTS
PRINTED IN THE U.S.A.

To my mother and my brother,
and the memory of my father

A WINDOW ON
RED SQUARE

☆ ☆ ☆

THE RUSSIAN BORDER. 8.05 A.M. A bleak, lonely, snow-white landscape. Then, a little further, the cold country in which the war of 1939–1940 against Finland was fought. The train is creeping along at a few miles an hour. It is still quite dark and the only thing I can see are low hills barely visible in the gray-black dawn — with tall, peaked evergreens in groves and a few bare birches loaded with snow.

Occasionally we pass a small log cabin with a light burning in it. And from the chimney of one or two of the cabins spreads gray smoke. Once or twice I see guards along the track. The radio amplifier next to my compartment is blaring forth the news throughout the corridor. Now we have music.

Our passports were taken first by black-uniformed control officers (Finns, I think) at Vainikkala — and then the papers were returned. About one half-hour beyond Vainikkala two officers (one in a long coat down to his ankles, the other with a jacket and gold shoulder boards — and both in black boots and green caps) took my passport again. And these were the Russians.

Nearing Vyborg, we pass pillboxes, smashed with shell holes, and broken brick walls of houses (still left over from the war). Now we go by a few lakes frozen over and flat with untouched snow. This stretch between Vainikkala and Vyborg is single track. I now see a silhouette of a house in ruins against the skyline, with a skier standing in the broken arch with his arms outstretched like a scarecrow, leaning on his ski poles.

Outside of Vyborg we pass a squad of troops marching on the road, and I see scattered troops in the railway yard. Women are shoveling snow with wooden shovels, tossing the snow away from the tracks into empty flatcars.

All the tall buildings in Vyborg are still in ruins. We wait here in Vyborg for two hours and a light snow falls. There are many warmly dressed kids playing on the platform.

A Russian passenger, an extremely pleasant (but serious) middle-aged woman, speaks good English and she quietly asked me about Dreiser, Jack London, and Byron. She was most fond of London, she said. "But I think Oscar Wilde's *The Picture of Dorian Gray* is really powerful." I asked her if she had read Faulkner and she replied, "Yes, of course" — but she had not heard the forbidden news that he had just been awarded the Nobel Prize.

Outside on the platform the radio loudspeaker continues to screech and it can be heard all over the railway yard. But nobody seems to be listening.

There is no dining car on this train, throughout the day-long ride to Leningrad, so soon I shall have to start to eat the box lunch of heavy ham sandwiches prepared for me by the waitress at the Klaus Kurki Hotel in Helsinki.

As I think back of last night, my most vivid impression was the familiar train sound of creaking cars as we rolled slowly up to the Russian border ("rolled" is not right — we jerked and bumped, and stopped and started). All the doors

. . . . **now this fear seems mad**

and windows and fixtures made their own peculiar noises all night long. In addition, there was the sound of the two Russians snoring in the next compartment. The electric lights in my compartment would grow bright one minute, and then dim out the next, as the electric power wavered. I didn't get much sleep, I must admit. The fear was still with me, the incredible fear I had felt even in Helsinki, when I wondered whether or not Russians were following me in the hotel corridor and hiding behind closet doors. And sometimes I had wondered during the blackness of the Helsinki night whether or not an F.B.I. agent also might be hiding there.

Now, in the broad daylight of the same old world (even though this particular bit of earth is a new, hostile world), after my first friendly conversations with Russians, this fear seems mad and unreasoning. Maybe all fear is difficult to analyze — but my particular brand, I am sure, was based as much on the conditioning I received in Washington, on the months of secret security checks and the months of black McCarthy headlines, and the months of whispered suspicion in my own small home town, as it was on the dread of all the real evils and ever-present dangers in the Soviet Union.

The tea served all night long and all day long by the girl attendant in the corridor, however, has made up for the lack of sleep. She is young, blond, polite and pleasant — and in her rough white apron, spread over the skirt and blouse of her uniform, she does an efficient job.

Now out the train window I see the white frozen lace of birch boughs and a few yards farther stone fortifications.

A few miles outside of Vyborg we pass a large, but inactive, factory — a wooden building surrounded with piles of bricks

Approach to Leningrad . . . .

and building material and cement blocks. As we approach the district of Lake Ladoga (the largest lake in Europe), I see two woodsmen carrying a big log on their shoulders as they tread along the path in the undergrowth — but aside from these men there is hardly any activity or sign of life in the frozen horizon.

Now the train is creeping at fifteen miles an hour through long low flat country with stands of tall thin evergreens, and at the moment we are crossing a series of marshes.

At Vyborg the customs inspector said that the temperature was minus seventeen (about zero Fahrenheit).

This train leaves every other day (the odd days of the month) from Helsinki. There are only nine cars (one "International Sleeper" dating from the turn of the century, on baggage car, one mail car, and assorted coaches).

Children seem to be everywhere, shuffling along on skis.

At 2.30 in the afternoon we make a ten-minute stop at a new station, with very fancy yellow and white walls and a high-domed center, with glass in front and back — but I have difficulty seeing the details of the station as the frost has gathered on the outer window of my car, making visibility very low.

Now, in midafternoon, the sun comes out in a blue sky. We are beginning to approach Leningrad — and I see the first motor vehicles I have seen all day long. So far, also, we have passed only one train, going north in the opposite direction. Everything remains unbelievably white: there is no soot, no mud. Now it is 3.30, and the yellow sun already is beginning to sink behind the ice-covered trees low on the horizon.

In a few minutes we shall be in Leningrad and I shall leave this compartment which has been my home for a day.

There are about eight or nine compartments just like mine in this ancient "International" car. The chief characteristics are a high-domed ceiling, very dark brown polished paneling everywhere with green and white moldings, and stained-glass windows from the bathroom into the corridor (red flowers and green stem and leaves). The carpeting is red with an oriental rug design. The sheets and pillowcases are clean but extremely rough, and there is only one blanket, but it is very heavy.

Throughout the night and day the car was kept very warm. During the day the electricity was turned off. Thrown on top of my berth blanket was one white linen hand towel, but there was no soap at all.

We creep into Leningrad's Finland Station, the celebrated station where Lenin arrived after his long exile to take over the Russian Revolution.

As I took a taxi to the Astoria Hotel, I made my first forlorn attempt at conversation. Trying to appear as gay and self-assured as possible, I asked the driver, *"Kak dela?"* (How are things with you?)

"Bad, very bad," he said.

My confidence, for some reason, returned with a rush. I felt that I was a human being again, and that I was in the company of other human beings too.

JANUARY 11, 1951

I wake up early in the dim light of Room 125 at the Astoria in Leningrad — and this is what I see:

Blue painted walls; white woodwork and ceilings; old red carpet; high windows and narrow balcony (with fancy lace

Red curtains and brass . . . .

curtains and red silk draperies); big, gold-framed oil painting of fruit; an inner alcove (with heavy red curtains on brass
rod and rings) with brass bed and bedside table filling most
of the alcove (and on the bed are a red quilt, two enormous
pillows, a lace cover and next to the bed is a brass bedside
lamp which has to be plugged in and out of the wall socket
to turn it on); the rest of the room is filled with "Leningrad"
furniture — big, heavy, blue upholstered couch against the
wall under the fruit still life, round table in center with
white tablecloth draping it to the floor, four chairs, chest,
dressing table, corner cabinet with oval full-length mirror;
plus a second painting on the wall (a dismal Russian snow
landscape, with two sledges and two horses pulling two peasants across the fields); a desk with a telephone, heavy Victorian black and gold writing equipment, and a desk lamp,
which is a half-nude bronze woman on a big base holding a
huge orange silk lampshade with three-inch fringe; push
buttons for chambermaids and waiters (with directions in
Russian, English, and German) but the push buttons don't
work and the ordering is done by telephone; a narrow red
carpeted corridor with closets and a white-tile bath with lukewarm hot water; a modern flush toilet, tub and hand shower;
one long narrow bath towel with even longer fringe; sheaf of
large soft sheets of crinkly toilet paper; one small piece of
orange soap.

I have spent most of the day in the Hermitage, which in
many ways is still the greatest art collection in the world.
For hours I have been standing in front of Titians (7),
Rembrandts (25), Leonardo da Vincis (2), Raphaels (2), El
Grecos (2), Velásquezes and Zurbaráns by the score, and so
many paintings by Rubens and Van Dyck that it is impos-

. . . . **The Hermitage**

sible to count them. As I walked along the dark, empty corridors of the Hermitage, which is an endless part of the endless Winter Palace, I looked out into the courtyard of the
former home of the tsars. And the sight I saw must have
been similar to the scene on the night of November 7–8,
1917, when the Winter Palace finally fell to the onslaught of
the revolutionists. The courtyard walls were chipped and
broken, and the leafless frozen stems of dead weeds stood
stark against the snow.

JANUARY 12, 1951

*On the overnight four-hundred-mile train trip between
Leningrad and Moscow.*

Dear Mother and Dad:

This is a hurried note to let you know, immediately, that
my first two days in Russia (en route from Vyborg to Moscow) have been among the happiest in my life — certainly
the most fascinating. Nothing has gone wrong, everything
has gone right. My language has worked like a charm (much
better than in the classroom at Cambridge — maybe I've
lost my Harvard accent!), and I have been talking constantly,
or listening constantly, for the last forty-eight hours, so interested that I have barely slept. But most wonderful of all
is the discovery (completely contrary to all the gloomy pre-
dictions and warnings) that I can get along with the Russian
people, closely touch them, get them to like me. And the
method so far has been so good and simple: a smile, a joke,
a friendly gesture.

Of course all this may change in Moscow, and soon I may

First letter home . . . .

laugh over this early enthusiasm, but right now I am sure I am right — and it is a wonderful feeling.

Now that I have arrived safely, I can tell you that I quickly shook off the American courier "guards" in Leningrad. On one of my last days in Helsinki I telephoned the Embassy in Moscow, and asked for permission to stay for an extra day and night in Leningrad. That meant that I would be there alone, and make the rest of the trip to Moscow unaccompanied. Moscow said O.K., if I was positive that I could take care of myself! And so I have been a free agent for the last two days.

Then something very good happened at once, which I should have known would happen: I hadn't been in Leningrad more than a couple of hours before I met two people I knew! One was a friend whom I had known in Hong Kong (he's now a State Department courier, and was on his way out from Moscow back to Helsinki); I bumped into him in the Astoria Hotel almost upon arrival. The other was a French correspondent with whom I worked a great deal in China after the war, and the surprise on his face was indescribable when we met in the Hermitage yesterday morning. Last night I had supper with him and his English wife, and a member of the British Embassy in Moscow who happened to be with them. It's such a big, big world.

We have just stopped at a station on the outskirts of Moscow, and the red-faced, mitten-clapping platform attendant reported that the temperature was 25° below zero (13° below, Fahrenheit). At the present moment the train is beginning to slow down. It is with quite a bit of difficulty that I believe the words which I am about to write down — but there, as I scratch a view in the frost-covered window-

. . .   **"Here it is then at last, that famous city!"**

pane, straight ahead, shining in the yellow-white light of the low eastern sun, is Moscow. But I do believe these words which I add: I miss you, and love you now, more than ever before.

JANUARY 13, 1951

Tolstoy, I am afraid, is a greater writer than I am. What better description could there be of one's first arrival in Moscow, and of one's attendant feelings, than the words the novelist put into the mind and mouth of Napoleon?

> The view of the strange city with its peculiar architec-ture, such as he had never seen before, filled Napoleon with the rather envious and uneasy curiosity men feel when they see an alien form of life that has no knowledge of them. This city was evidently living with the full force of its own life. By the indefinite signs which, even at a distance, distinguish a living body from a dead one, Napoleon from the Poklonny Hill perceived the throb of life in the town and felt, as it were, the breathing of that great and beautiful body. . . .
> "That Asiatic city of the innumerable churches, holy Moscow! Here it is then at last, that famous city! It was high time," said he, dismounting. . . .

And so I dismount.

JANUARY 14, 1951

I ran into trouble with the police my first day in Moscow — in fact, my first hour.

As I left the American Embassy, immediately after check-

First adventure — Red Square . . . .

ing in, I started to head for Red Square across the street, in a high state of excitement to see the Kremlin walls at close hand, and Lenin's tomb, and St. Basil's Cathedral.

There, straight ahead of me, rose the pyramidal spires and chaotic cupolas of St. Basil's, some moss-green in color, some mustard-yellow, some faded red. And I could see, as I approached, a dash of blue tile and mauve on the drums of the bulbous cupolas, and the grotesque designs of the cupolas themselves, all different, some ribbed and spiral, some with tiles like aspen shingles, some like a honeycomb, some with facets like pineapples.

Then, suddenly, I realized I was all alone. Indeed, there was nobody within a quarter of a mile of me. I was certainly all by myself in the middle of the square. But not quite all alone, because there was a tap on my shoulder, and turning around, I saw a big Russian militiaman in a long blue coat standing behind me, and breathing white vapor down my neck. "What are you doing here?" he asked. "I am going to look at St. Basil's Cathedral," I replied. "But you cannot walk across this square," he insisted. "No, no, no."

His manner was friendly and polite, but his tugs at my arms were firm and persistent, to put it mildly. As we trudged the long way back to the sidewalk, his face showed a little flash of amusement that anybody could be quite so stupid.

JANUARY 15, 1951

First impressions — especially when gained from such an experience as one's initial entry into the Soviet Union — have, it seems to me, their strong points as well as weak

. . . . . . **The viciousness and the goodness**

points. They are important, I am sure — and so I feel justified in writing this down in my diary after only a few hours in Moscow:

The Soviet regime seems much more depraved (and efficient) than I had expected — and I had expected the worst. And the Russian people seem much finer and friendlier (and more approachable) than I had expected — and I had expected the best.

After nearly three years of remote, textbook study of the U.S.S.R., I did, as I say, anticipate the viciousness, on the one hand, and the goodness, on the other — but I am surprised by the high degree of both.

JANUARY 23, 1951

The U.S. Navy doctor at the Embassy today issued a bulletin which has been distributed in mimeographed form to all hands — a bulletin that reflects the strange, strained living conditions of Americans in Moscow, the conditions of an isolated bivouac, with all kinds of enemies — a few of them imaginary, but most of them real — ready to attack:

"It has been learned from three different sources that there is an epidemic of typhoid fever in Moscow at the present time and that city authorities are taking certain precautionary measures against it. . . . It is recommended that: (*a*) drinking water be boiled for five minutes; (*b*) milk purchased be boiled for five minutes; (*c*) sour cream, cheese, butter and other dairy products purchased in the market be avoided, even though they may be labeled 'pasteurized.' "

But typhoid fever, it seems to me, is not the only poison in this sick city. The disease of the spirit is worse.

They play "Anchors Aweigh" . . . .

Tonight I had my first dinner outside the hotel in a Moscow restaurant. The restaurant was in one of the outer areas of the city, in a rather poor factory district — but nonetheless, as I found out, it was a wonderful restaurant.

As soon as I entered, the waiter asked me: "Are you by any chance a Czech?" At once I replied, "No, I am an American." A few minutes later, when the small orchestra came in, the first number they played was "Anchors Aweigh."

JANUARY 30, 1951

Here is a small observation but, it seems to me, it has considerable significance. Discipline is such in Moscow, and maybe pride too is involved, that every automobile in the winter has to have the snow and ice scraped off of the roof, hood, and mudguards. If your car has a bit of snow on it, a militiaman is sure to stop you and force you, there and then, to get out in the middle of the street and clean it off. All of this means that you always carry with you not only the usual flat-tire tools, but also a dustpan and brush.

FEBRUARY 2, 1951

One of the first — and most unpleasant — facts of life you learn in Moscow is the official exchange rate.

As of today, that rate is four Russian rubles to one American dollar. I stress "as of today," because the rate has been lowered (in a sense unfavorable to foreigners) several times in recent years — and all Westerners in Moscow fear that

. . . . **Room and bath — $4000 a year**

any day the Kremlin will make the official rate even less realistic, and less defensible, than it is today.

When I say "unrealistic," I am sure that all American taxpayers would agree if they were to learn that at this rate they are paying more than $4000 a year just for my small hotel room and bath in Moscow. The annual charge for this tiny setup at the musty Metropole is 17,385 rubles — and to get that amount at the current four-to-one rate the U.S. dispersing officer at the Embassy must hand over to the Russian State Bank exactly $4346.25 beautiful American dollars.

Such figures have been staggering me ever since my arrival. So that I might have a better idea of what a fair and meaningful exchange rate would be for me, I asked an economist at the Embassy today how many rubles an American Embassy officer should get for his dollar to be able to live in the same way he would in the U.S.A. That, at least, is one way of looking at the question of the exchange rate — and it seems to me to be a valid test, certainly as far as my own problem is concerned.

The answer was: "If you take food and clothing prices, for example, and then draw up an average retail price index, I don't think it would be far wrong to say that on the basis on such an index you should get from twenty to twenty-five rubles for one dollar. If you take into consideration the quality of the things you buy, then, perhaps, as much as thirty rubles would be fair."

I have already mentioned here the question of retail prices — and this might be a good opportunity to put down at random some of the prices I have noted so far during my first few weeks in the U.S.S.R. with the dollar equivalent at the *official* rate:

Some local prices . . . .

An order of bread and butter at the best hotel in Moscow —
2.5 rubles (63¢).

Pressing a two-piece suit — 16 rubles ($4).

A bottle of Russia's best beer (in the buffet of a Moscow
theater) — 5 rubles ($1.25).

A glass of tea, without sugar or lemon (in the same theater)
— 20 kopecks (5¢). (100 kopecks to a ruble.)

Opera and ballet tickets — 20 to 35 rubles ($5 — $8.75).

Movie tickets — 5 to 10 rubles ($1.25 — $2.50).

A small pot of black coffee (two cups) in a Moscow restaurant
— 3 rubles (75¢).

A coarse, ready-made suit in the men's department of a
Moscow clothing store — 1800 rubles ($450).

A small second-hand (and empty) flowerpot — 4.25 rubles
($1.06).

A luxurious thirteen-tube short-wave radio — 1215 rubles
($303.75).

Books — 1 to 40 rubles (25¢ — $10).

A small child's doll (wooden, hand-painted) in a Moscow
peasant-goods shop — 8.65 rubles ($2.16).

The fare for one subway ride (whether short or long) in
Moscow's celebrated Metro — 50 kopecks (12½¢).

A first-edition (1842) copy of Gogol's *Dead Souls* — 75 rubles
($18.75).

A haircut (for some reason, the biggest bargain in Russia)
— 2 rubles (50¢) but the tip to barber should be three times
that much; and many additional rubles should be added
for a shampoo, shave, and finally and inevitably, "Eau de
Cologne," the name given by Russians to all tonics and
hair dressings, all of which the modern Soviet male considers indispensable on a visit to the barbershop.

One lemon — 6 rubles ($1.50), in winter; reported to be 2
rubles in summer.

Airmail postage (for a letter from Moscow to U.S.A.) —

1.40 rubles (35¢); 40 kopecks (10¢) for regular postage.

Four-minute telephone call (from Moscow to Hanover, Massachusetts, U.S.A.) — 48.20 rubles ($12.05).

A small Palekh box (a popular luxury article, uniquely Russian, made of papier-mâché material by a special process, lacquered and hand-painted by expert craftsmen) — 88 rubles ($22).

A large Palekh box (the size of a five-lb. candy box), with a hand-painted portrait of Stalin standing on the Kremlin wall — 3000 rubles ($750).

An old icon (found on a shelf in a country monastery) — whatever I wanted to put in the collection box.

You can see what these prices mean to me — with every ruble I spend worth twenty-five cents. What do these prices mean to the average Soviet citizen? One way to arrive at an answer to this question is to take the average monthly wage, and then figure out the portion of the month's earnings represented by such expenditures as those I have just listed. The basic problem here, of course, is to make an accurate estimate of the average monthly wage in the U.S.S.R. today. I find that most foreign experts in Moscow come up with the figure of 600 rubles. That, at any rate, is the generally accepted total. It is probably about 20 per cent higher than that in Moscow itself — but on the whole the estimate of 600 is not unfair, as it represents approximately what the first postwar Five-Year Plan aimed at. It is important to remember, however, that from the 600 rubles at least 10 per cent should be deducted for income taxes, state loans, union dues, and such — leaving about 540 rubles of "take home" pay. If one allows 40 rubles per month for rent and utilities (it is fairly well known, I guess, that a Russian worker who has housing provided by his factory pays much less than an

the worst play ... the most beautiful theater .   .   .

American or French or British worker might pay), then that
means the average person must clothe and feed himself (and
do whatever else he wants to do) on 500 rubles ($125) every
month. And that is taking a most generous view of the situation.

Henceforth in this diary, when I quote prices in rubles, the
calculations and considerations mentioned above should be
borne in mind.

FEBRUARY 10, 1951

Tonight I witnessed the worst play I have ever seen in the
most beautiful theater I have ever seen.

The theater was the Maly (Russian for "little" or "small"),
which is located on the east side of Sverdlov Square, formerly
Theater Square, one of the big central plazas of Moscow, not
far from the Kremlin. In this square — which, by the way,
is about the only spot in Moscow to boast formal gardens
and a fountain — the Maly is catercorner to the Bolshoi
(Russian for "big" or "great"), where the highly publicized
and praised, and justly so, ballets and operas are given.

The Bolshoi, with its pretentious musical productions, is
more celebrated than the Maly, with its repertoire of more
modest comedies and tragedies. Nor is the Maly so well
known in the West as the Moscow Art Theater, founded by
Stanislavsky and Nemirovich-Danchenko in 1898, which is a
few blocks away. But among Moscow's large total of some
twenty-seven theaters now in operation, the Maly ranks, in
my opinion, close to the very top.

Certainly as a building the Maly is one of the most interesting structures in Russia. Built early in the nineteenth century (authorities seem to disagree on the exact year, the

. . . . **a pretty frightening experience**

dates ranging from 1824 to 1841), it is the oldest theater in
Moscow — the Bolshoi having been destroyed by fire in the
middle of the century — and it is probably one of the oldest
theaters in the world still staging performances every night.
Then, as I have said, the interior is an architectural master-
piece. The inconspicuous exterior is noteworthy only for
an impressive monument put up by the Soviets in 1929, a
bronze statue of Ostrovsky, whose realistic middle-class
satires were first presented here. The building is designed to
hold as many as a thousand spectators, but through a unique
and arresting arrangement of boxes, stalls, balconies, *bel
étage* (the Russian equivalent of a dress circle), and an
unusual amphitheater, the total impression is one of inti-
macy. And I shouldn't forget to mention here the large oval
"buffet," reached by a pair of long staircases, descending in
a wide curve to the tables and chairs and bar spread out
below. The décor of the interior is in the traditional Empire
style, with a rich crimson, cream, and gold as the colors —
all in perfect taste and of great beauty.

The play, however, had little taste or beauty. It was a
drama in four acts and five scenes called *People of Good
Will,* by the Soviet playwright Georgi Mdivani. It was the
first anti-American play I have seen in Russia and, I must
admit, a pretty frightening experience. As far as I know, nobody in the Embassy here has reported on the content of the
play or the reaction of the audience — and that is something
I cannot understand, because here, if anywhere, is a direct
clue to Kremlin thinking on foreign affairs, as well as an
opportunity to size up the real response of the average Russian to that thinking.

Printed in the program under the name of the play,
People of Good Will, there is a rather cryptic phrase in

An anti-American play · · · · · · · · ·

parentheses, "Where war is possible." It is not clear to me
whether this phrase refers directly to the title itself, or is
meant to be the author's designation of the scene of action.
But by the end of the evening it is certainly clear that actually the scene of action is Korea. I say "actually" because
seemingly the locale is European, with the stage sets and
costumes indicating a Balkan background. But it is Korea
all right.

To prove this, all I have to do is report that the theme of
the play consists of the efforts of the United States of America
to push a certain unnamed puppet government into aggression by instigating an attack northward across a carefully
defined geographic parallel. And then all I have to do is add
that the leader of the armed forces in the execution of this
unprovoked attack is an American general named John
Arthur. All of this, of course, corresponds to the Kremlin's
explanation of the outbreak of the Korean War — and I am
afraid that most Russians, hearing and reading nothing to
the contrary, do believe that South Korea, shoved and sup-
ported by the U.S.A., was the aggressor in the first instance;
and that U.S. troops, in springing to the offensive against
North Korea, have committed unheard-of atrocities against
the local population.

Aside from General Arthur, the cast of characters includes
an American senator named Brown; Simon, a United Press
correspondent; a Luxemburger named Peter Lubin, who is
chairman of a United Nations Commission; the Interior
Minister and the War Minister of the puppet government;
an American pilot, an American courier, and several American officers and enlisted men. Arrayed against this unholy
team of conspirators are the kind, simple people of the nation

. . . . **I too was stunned**

across the border to the north — a peasant and his wife and son; a woodcutter; a schoolteacher and his daughter — and a host of fiery partisans.

As the plot thickens, the action centers around Haigh, the wounded American pilot. (The crash of his plane offstage, incidentally, provides an opportunity for one of the most spectacular and realistic sound effects ever heard in any theater — the kind of technical effect at which the Russians excel and of which they are so fond, an effect typical of all kinds of mechanical tricks which are such an important part of the Soviet stage today, particularly at the Bolshoi.) Thanks to the tender care given to Haigh by the local peasants and thanks to the indoctrination passionately given by the partisans, this American finally sees the light, and realizes that he and his countrymen are murderers of innocent people, that the U.S.A. is bent on world conquest. The curtain falls as one of the victims crawls painfully along the floor, and with a dying gasp paints the word *MIR* (Peace) on the wall of the peasant hut.

Throughout the play, all the Americans onstage (with the exception of the pilot) behaved as though they *were* determined to conquer the world — either as slick and slimy plotters or as plain jungle beasts hot for blood. In one scene, for example, the U.S. Army officers and men madly machine-gunned everybody in sight — and everybody was unarmed. And throughout the play the Russian audience responded audibly and visibly — applauding and cheering every deed of heroism by the brave partisans of "people's democracy," gasping with real shock and horror at every act of brutality by the American imperialists.

I too was stunned by the message of *People of Good Will*

A Russian restaurant . . . .

— but for different reasons. I left the theater in a mood of extreme depression, anger, and fear — but a strange surprise was in store for me. In Russia, as everywhere, not everything is black or white — nor is it wise to jump to easy conclusions.

My theater companion and I suddenly decided to have a midnight supper of Kamchatka crabmeat bisque, a drop of vodka, and a plate of caviar in a restaurant around the corner from the Maly. The place was full — except for one round table with two empty seats. At the two occupied places sat two Russians, one thin and dark, the other very fat and of a sandy complexion. To the best of my memory — I am writing this only a few minutes after the event — this is an accurate transcription of the dialogue that took place in the next quarter hour:

My companion, a girl from the French Embassy, who spoke excellent Russian: "Excuse me, are these two seats taken?"

The thin Russian: "No — please."

We sat down. Silence.

The thin Russian: "You are foreigners?"

I: "Yes — my friend is from France, and I am an American."

Silence.

The fat Russian: "You are, then, a member of a peace delegation, or of a labor delegation visiting the Soviet Union?"

I: "No, I am a member of the American Embassy here in Moscow."

Silence.

The thin Russian: "Remarkable! Remarkable!! To think

. . "Remarkable! **To be with an American again.**"

I am sitting beside an American. Wonderful!"

My companion: "And where are you from, what part of Russia?"

The thin Russian: "We have both just arrived from Siberia."

I: "By train?"

The thin Russian: "I came by air — but my good friend here has a bad heart, and he took the train."

The fat Russian: "Five days on the Trans-Siberian."

I: "And what do you do back home?"

The thin Russian: "He is a farmer, and I am an engineer." (Pause.) "Remarkable! To be with an American again."

I: "Again?"

The thin Russian: "Oh, yes. I have known many Americans. I was born in the last century — and before the Revolution and after the Revolution, especially during the period of the New Economic Policy in the 1920's, I came to know many foreigners. The Americans I met have always been fine, very fine, men and women."

I: "It's good to hear that — especially because tonight we have just seen a typical anti-American play, and — "

The thin Russian: "Now, let's not discuss that. Fate brought us together tonight, didn't it? And I don't think we should spoil the good luck by discussing politics. We could stay up all night doing that, and get nowhere. Let's just accept the position as it is — I always do that anyway — and enjoy this happy occasion. Let's make it pleasant and have a good time together."

I: "All right, fine. Will you have a cigarette?"

The thin Russian: "Thank you."

I: "And you?"

The map of Moscow . . . .

The fat Russian: "No, thank you. I don't smoke. But maybe, after all, if it's an American cigarette, I might try it."

Later, having finished our supper and paid the bill, we prepared to leave.

The fat Russian: "No, I disagree with my friend about discussing the international situation. I think we should ask you why your governments have changed in their attitude toward the Soviet Union."

My companion: "It is not *our* governments, believe me, but —"

The thin Russian: "Stop. The important thing is for you to remember how much Russia helped the West in the last war, and for us to remember how much you helped Russia. We will never forget. That's the important thing."

As I left the restaurant, my depression suddenly disappeared. It was perhaps, after all, an evening with people of good will.

FEBRUARY 16, 1951

Any map of Moscow, particularly a good street plan, would show that the center of this capital city — indeed, the very center of all Russia — is exactly like a gigantic and perfectly spun spiderweb with the Kremlin in the very middle, the silent spider, patiently lying in wait for its victims. Large highways and avenues radiate out from the center; with a series of concentric rings of walls and boulevards, and a mesh of side streets.

And six million insects are caught in the web, slowly dying, with barely a buzz.

P.S. When I blithely say "any map of Moscow," I should

. . . . **The big and the little lie**

point out, of course, that there are no maps at all. The Soviet regime apparently does not permit the publication of such vital, secret material — and even sightseeing Soviet citizens cannot buy street plans of their capital. Nor is it possible to look down on Moscow from the air — because no civilian planes are allowed to fly anywhere near the city, let alone directly over it. A bird's-eye view is out of the question. No, this impression of mine has been gained mainly through my own wanderings around the encircling boulevards and through the crisscross of connecting streets. However, at the risk of being called a sinister spy, I should admit that once I did see a map, from which I was able to make a sketch — a photostat of a German military map of Moscow, a pre-invasion grid plan published by the German General Staff in 1941 — and there it was, the spiderweb.

FEBRUARY 18, 1951

The thing hardest to take in Russia is not so much the secret police, not even slave labor with all the human cruelty involved, as bad as these things are: to my mind the thing hardest to take, day in and night out, is the lie — the big meaningful lie *and* the glib little lie. More than anything in the world I hate the cool willingness of the handful in the Kremlin to lie about *anything,* any hour; and not only a willingness, but a rare ability to do so. And this willingness and ability seem to be at the root of the whole system.

FEBRUARY 19, 1951

It is now so cold outside — or, rather, indoors — that this morning when I woke up I found that a glass of orange juice

Washington's Birthday . . . .

which I had left on my bedside table in the middle of my
hotel room was frozen solid.

February 22, 1951

Washington's Birthday — it was a great shock and thrill
when, driving to work this morning, I saw the bright red-
white-and-blue of the American flag flying in the slant of
the snow flakes from the façade of the American Embassy,
facing the Kremlin. The Embassy rises straight up from the
sidewalk facing Red Square, and so, many Russians too were
walking under the flag on their way to work. Was it a symbol
of horror and dread or a sign of hope for them?

February 23, 1951

At exactly eight o'clock tonight, while I was putting on dress
clothes for a formal dinner at Spaso House, my mirror gazing
was suddenly interrupted by a terrific blast of gunfire. I
rushed to the window and saw searchlights sweeping the
black sky.

Then, fortunately, I remembered from the morning papers
that today is the thirty-third anniversary of the Soviet Army
and Navy, and so I figured out that the guns were being fired
to celebrate the occasion and not necessarily to do away with
me.

At slow intervals, the artillery rounds continued — twenty
in all. And, while the guns echoed in thunderclaps through
the still city, the searchlights kept on chasing each other
across the horizon. From the angle of my window I could
see that one mobile searchlight truck and crew had been sta-

tioned in the street directly below me, and, as its shaft of light shot up and around, I could make out individual flakes of snow, a few among millions, as they fell slantwise through the beam. The whole effect was heightened by green rockets and Roman candles which, with each gun salute, were set off simultaneously in a great pattern on the perimeter of the city.

All of this gave me a slightly unreal feeling (which is beginning to become familiar), as I returned to the mirror and tucked in my breast-pocket handkerchief and adjusted my silk tie.

FEBRUARY 24, 1951

Dinner at the Ararat Restaurant next to the Maly Theater. This is one of the best and most popular restaurants in Moscow and its low-vaulted room has a great deal of atmosphere. We had very good trout. The service in the Ararat is excellent and the many waiters are dressed in clean uniforms.

The dance orchestra was one of the best I have yet heard in Moscow. This restaurant on the whole is a thousand per cent better than most.

MARCH 13, 1951

At 5.30 this afternoon, I saw a preview (given for the foreign colony) of a new Soviet technicolor feature film, *Bounteous Summer,* described by *Izvestiya* as "a joyous lyrical comedy, telling of the life of collective farm workers of a Ukrainian village and of its foremost people — innovators, who by their labor have achieved great successes in improving yield and developing animal husbandry."

A diplomatic preview . . . .

The film had nice singing, and all the peasant girls were extremely beautiful and attractively dressed. But the picture was very dull otherwise — increasing production by means of consolidating collective farms is not exactly an exciting plot motivation.

The audience in the Dom Kino, a center of the Soviet cinema industry in Moscow, was polite, but definitely bored and very silent. Here, for the first time since my arrival in Moscow, I saw representatives of "friendly" and "enemy" missions together in the same room (a very rare occasion). Nobody spoke to anybody. We were greeted (and closely watched) at every door and stairway landing by uniformed officials of the Ministry of Foreign Affairs, who shook hands with us without a word.

MARCH 15, 1951

Today it rained for the first time since I have been in Moscow — and that has been nine weeks now.

The winter weather here in the middle of Russia strikes me as perfect. The cold is bearable, even during countless weeks of subzero temperature, because, strangely enough, there is so little wind. The minute you step outdoors, your face tingles — but it is an invigorating, not a painful sensation. Furthermore, the sky is either full of sun or full of snow. There are no in-between days, no gray days of drizzle and thaw, no damp days. All of this means that, best of all, there is no slush. For five months now it has been so cold that in spite of days of bright sunshine not a flake of snow has melted.

One effect of this is to make Moscow a beautiful city—

much more beautiful than in the summer, I am told. Except
for the Kremlin itself, there is so much ugliness to cover —
gloomy, dirty courtyards that only Dostoyevsky or Gorky
could describe, unpainted façades, chipped and broken walls,
bleak, treeless stretches of asphalt, rusty cupolas — so ten
feet of frozen snow helps quite a bit.

MARCH 16, 1951

Yesterday, in writing about the weather, I should have mentioned that another — this time, man-made — reason for the
lack of slush in Moscow is that every single particle of snow
is swept from the street the minute it falls.

I am sure that many years from now my most vivid memory
of Moscow will turn out to be the echo of a sound — the
endless, endless scraping and sweeping of snow and ice off
the streets in the still of the night. Many times already I
have been waked in the blackness of three or four o'clock
in the morning by this chipping sound, this shoveling sound,
as the street workers scratch the predawn silence in their
ceaseless struggle against the snowflake.

And who are these street workers? That brings up the
whole fascinating question of snow disposal in Moscow, and
the obviously brutal (but obviously efficient) way in which
the Soviets tackle this problem. The answer to the question
is: women, thousands upon thousands of women. If you
arrive in Moscow for the first time in the middle of winter,
as I did, certainly one of your first exclamations as you drive
into the center of town will be: "And who are those girls in
the street, dressed in white smocks that look like butcher's
aprons, with twig brooms in their hands?" These girls, of

Snow removal . . . .

course, are the street cleaners, and, what is more important in ice-bound Russia, the snow sweepers.

These girls are also something else: they are a daily topic of conversation, as you can imagine, among the handful of American girls working in our Moscow Embassy. Indeed, the sight of them is always such a shock to foreigners that they never quite get over it. And Westerners talk about these women so much that a popular theory has even been developed:

In the eyes of the Kremlin, times have changed since the day when snow in the street was a help to the sleighs of Moscow. Today Moscow, as the so-called show capital of the world, must be modern in every way — and must handle modern transportation problems in a modern manner — so, the snow sweepers.

To us, of course, the obvious solution is the snowplow and a moving belt to load trucks. Moscow does boast about a dozen giant caterpillar belts for this purpose — which, from the expression of admiration on the faces of onlookers standing wide-eyed and knee-deep in the gutter, would appear to be miracle machines, indeed. But most of the work still must be done by hand.

Another solution, not so modern, is more administrative than mechanical: it is an age-old arrangement whereby all householders or janitors or gatekeepers are responsible for the pavement of both street and sidewalk on which their premises face. At one of our Embassy buildings, for example, the *dvornik* — as the Russians call the yardman — spends a great deal of his day, and most of his night, removing the snow to the back fence where, by now, it is piled almost twenty feet high in some places.

· · · · · · ·   **"Only let us go to Moscow!"**

But — according to the theory I am describing — these solutions are not enough. The snow keeps falling — and piling up. And so, every year, the Kremlin "recruits" scores of thousands, maybe hundreds of thousands, of peasant girls from the hinterland. And all these women from the country and provincial towns are only too happy to go to the capital, only too eager to leave their lonely lives, readily volunteering for any kind of work in exchange for the attractions of Moscow, the Mecca of all Russia. That, at least, is the explanation of the foreigners who repeat this theory.

Having seen many of Russia's cheerless farms and forgotten towns, I can easily understand how Moscow appeals to Russia's "outlanders," how the capital draws peasants from remote regions as a light bulb draws frantic moths. It is all exactly like the celebrated curtain lines of *The Three Sisters,* the gloomiest of Chekhov's dramas, which, incidentally, still plays to packed houses every season at the Moscow Art Theater. Fifty years ago, Chekhov had Irina say in desperation (at the end of Act II): "To Moscow! Moscow! Moscow!" — and at the end of Act III: "Only let us go to Moscow! I implore you, let's go! There's nothing better than Moscow on earth! Let's go, Olga, let's go!"

But I often wonder just how happy these women are when they get here. Certainly they do not seem happy — and, most certain of all, they should not be, if they are. Whether seen in small clusters on the street corner next door or in big silent herds stretching down the bleak highway, they look a forlorn lot. For one thing, their clothes are the poorest I have noticed in Russia. Most Soviet citizens seem adequately (warmly — if not elegantly) clothed, but these girls

a girl leaning on her broom, weeping . . . . .

are the exception. In spite of their heavy outdoor work in subzero temperatures, they are dressed for the most part in flimsy cotton skirts, cheap cotton stockings, and low-grade felt boots — and very few have mittens or gloves of any kind. Their hands are all rough and red, chapped and bruised. Further, it is monotonous, backbreaking work — and, since the main function of these labor squads is to sweep the snow away as it falls, thus preventing any coating at all, much of the toil goes on all night long. Somehow they seem most pathetic, not when scraping away in the blackness of the night, but when being carried to or from work, packed like silent slaughterhouse cattle in big open trucks.

These women are after all human beings, and so differ as individuals. Some of the girls are as tough as they come — and independent and self-willed, too. I have seen some beefy brawls on the street corners, with the women angrily throwing shovelfuls of snow and ice at passers-by, at their bosses on the block, and at each other. Others appear gay and carefree. Once I heard wonderful singing during a playful snowball fight. On the other hand, on a few occasions, I have heard real sobs and screams; and half an hour ago, returning home, I saw a girl leaning on her broom, weeping without a sound.

MARCH 17, 1951

As a footnote to yesterday's comments, I should add that these women are also used on the city's garbage disposal trucks.

·　·　·　·　·　·　· **The press quotes Mr. Truman**

MARCH 18, 1951

Silver fox appears to be the favorite fur piece of Moscow's most stylish women. Certainly many big neckpieces — ostentatiously thrown over the left shoulder, always the left shoulder — are seen at the theater. And most of the women who are wearing furs seem to be the wives of Soviet military officers of high rank.

MARCH 19, 1951

The official population figure for the city of Moscow is five million. Probably five and a half to six million is closer, but no more than that is possible on the basis of living-space figures. It is undoubtedly true that Moscow is not being expanded with new industries, etc. The other largest cities are Leningrad, Kiev, Kharkov, and the newly built industrial centers in the Urals, although no population figures are given for the latter.

MARCH 20, 1951

The Russian press is continually quoting a statement which they say President Truman made when he was a U.S. Senator on June 24, 1941, two days after Hitler's invasion of the Soviet Union: "If we see that Germany is winning we ought to help Russia and if Russia looks as though it were winning we ought to help Germany — in this way let them kill off as many as possible."

All this is a beautiful example of how hostile governments can make capital of irresponsible Congressional comment.

The Moscow press . . . .

and of how such remarks do so much damage throughout the world. In this case you certainly can't blame the Russians for using it if the quotation is correct.

MARCH 21, 1951

A few nights ago I heard the "Volga Boatmen" on the radio. It gave me quite a start because always in the past I had associated this song, of all songs in the world, with Russia, and here I was in the middle of Russia listening to it.

MARCH 22, 1951

Since I spend so much of my time translating Russian newspapers, I've thought about them a good deal and am going to set down such conclusions — contradictory, like everything else in this country — as I have been able to reach.

There are eight daily papers in Moscow. By comparison with our morning monsters, they are thin — four pages each. It is interesting, and perhaps significant, to see how different countries arrange their papers. I suppose our system of the most important news of any category on the front page shows that we're in a hurry to skim off the cream. The more leisurely British have time to turn to the middle of their papers for the big items. Generally speaking, the only place in Russian papers where you find "news," in our sense of the word, is the back page. The first three are propaganda of various sorts, and in *Pravda* the first column of page one is what we would call the editorial, and in a government-controlled press it is in this spot of Russia's most "important" paper that you find the most significant official pronouncements.

. . . . **Slanted news**

The two or three pages that are probably read first by a majority of American males — the sports news — are condensed to a small corner of page four. Not only its comparatively full sports news, but also the theater programs and some local items make *Evening Moscow* the most widely read paper in the city.

Generally speaking, the foreign news in all papers is on the back page, and aside from items which can be "slanted" into denunciation of the outside world, there is very little here. The "slant" is usually against the U.S. and they can distort almost any happening into an "exposé" of our "decadent capitalist" society.

I think there is a general impression at home that the anti-American propaganda campaign is very recent over here. The fact is that it was going full blast when I got here, and people tell me it had been about the same, at least since 1948. One theme will be featured for a period, and then there is a shift to another. Nowadays it's Korea, of course, and we are represented as the aggressors who are using all sorts of illegal warfare.

As of today, there are approximately 7500 newspapers in the Soviet Union, with a total circulation (single printing) of more than 31,000,000. Throughout the country the majority of these papers are posted on public bulletin boards, where those who care to do so can read them. You never see very many taking advantage of the opportunity, however, and my guess is that in spite of their long indoctrination, the people are bored by the monotony of "news" which is always sounding the same note. Maybe they even suspect that such monotony may present a false picture — certainly some do, as I have discovered.

Popular reading . . . .

MARCH 23, 1951

I forgot to mention that, unfortunately for me and other Joint Press Reading Service translators, *Pravda* comes out every day of the year — making holidays out of the question for us. The other Moscow dailies are not published on Mondays.

MARCH 24, 1951

This afternoon I verified a general impression I have had here. I rode the subway and took down some data. Approximately one half of the passengers — male and female — were reading books. About one in ten had a newspaper. From the cases I could actually observe myself, I should say that more than half the books being read were non-fiction, and of the fiction the greater part was classical.

Two conclusions: First, the people are after "learning" — factual learning, mostly scientific — like hounds after a fox. Second, the re-establishment of the classical Russian authors is all part of the official build-up of national pride which you notice in all spheres — historical, artistic, musical, scientific, etc.

This afternoon I noticed people reading:

The Battle of Borodino, a popular, paper-bound book on Kutuzov's campaign against Napoleon, and a very patriotic piece, indeed.

Gogol's *Evenings on a Farm near Dikanka,* a collection of short stories on life in the Ukraine — amusing, moving fiction which is currently providing considerable raw material for important ballets and operas.

. . .   **Dostoyevsky gets the official cold shoulder**

An Economic Geography of the U.S.S.R., a high-school textbook.

Moscow, the Heart of Our Native Land, a brief history, published in 1947, on the occasion of the eight hundredth anniversary of the founding of the city.

Griboedov's clever and really funny comedy in rhymed verse, *Woe From Wit,* a Russian classic which has been running in Moscow for one hundred years now.

A textbook on chemistry — much too advanced for me.

A textbook on mathematics, even more advanced, although I confess that I am not a good judge in these matters.

Only Dostoyevsky, among the classics, as far as I can see, is given the official cold shoulder today. This neglect — neglect rather than positive suppression — is of course understandable. Dostoyevsky was certainly much more of a revolutionary than Tolstoy. Shall I ever forget reading for the first time Dostoyevsky's letter to his brother, written in awful simplicity from the Peter and Paul Fortress on December 22, 1849:

Brother, my precious friend! . . . Today . . . we were taken to the Semenov Drill Ground. There the sentence of death was read to all of us, we were told to kiss the Cross, our swords were broken over our heads and our last toilet was made (white shirts). Then three were tied to the pillar for execution. I was the sixth. Three at a time were called out; consequently, I was in the second batch and no more than a minute was left me to live. I remembered you, brother, and all yours; during the last minute you, you alone, were in my mind, only then I realized how I love you, dear brother mine! . . . Finally the retreat was sounded, and those tied to the pillar were led back, and it was announced to us that His Imperial Majesty granted us our lives. . . .

The American Embassy's domestic staff   •   •   •   •

But nonetheless, Count Tolstoy, the rich nobleman, is the hero, and Dostoyevsky, the poverty-stricken exile, is close to becoming a villain. Reason: Tolstoy wrote all his major world-famous works *before* he was troubled by God, and Dostoyevsky wrote all his major world-famous works *after* he was troubled by God.

MARCH 25, 1951

Phenomenon of fear in the State Department and Foreign Service in the post-war years: one half are afraid of Communists and the other half are afraid of Congressmen.

MARCH 26, 1951

The residence of the American Ambassador, Spaso House, has a total of twenty-three Russian servants, and their wages add up to approximately $45,000 a year. Four of these are laundresses for the entire Embassy staff, but the remaining nineteen have duties confined to the Spaso household, as follows: Four upstairs maids, two downstairs cleaning girls, three cooks, one cook's helper, one houseboy, one pantry boy, three telephone operators, one fireman, two yardmen, and one laundress.

MARCH 27, 1951

Tonight my heart beat fast on two occasions, one moment right after the other, as the result of what I saw in front of footlights, and behind footlights, a few feet away.

Actually, I had been in a state of excitement all day —

. . . . **Drama in the streets**

because, for the first time, I was to see Ulanova, the most romantic and most celebrated ballerina in all of Russia, and without doubt the greatest dancer in the world today. And I was to see her in the best Soviet ballet now playing at the Bolshoi, Pushkin's *Bakhchisaraisky Fontan,* with distinguished music by Asafev.

It was time to go. As I rushed across the big plaza in front of the Bolshoi, I noticed a crowd of passers-by gathered in a tight knot on the icy pavement, in the shadow of the theater's portico, with an open truck standing at the curb. Such a street scene anywhere in the world would catch the curiosity of almost anybody — so I elbowed and shouldered my way through the onlookers.

When I got to the center of the silent circle, there lying flat on the sidewalk was a middle-aged man, with a ragged, padded cotton coat, and with no legs at all. Stretched out beside him, leaning over his chest — really all that there was of him — was a woman, who frantically caressed his bearded face, which stared up at the stars. She also was dressed in dirty padded clothes, but she had legs, and they were sprawled at an awkward angle on the pavement. I could see that rough brown stockings covered these legs up to her round, red knees showing under her short skirt, and that coarse felt boots covered her ankles. As she scraped her legs across the cold cement, one of her stockings became torn and the other gathered a light film of snow.

The woman clung to the living torso as tightly as she could. But her strength was not up to the jerks and yanks of three militiamen, who were determined to get her onto the rear of their truck. Her chapped hands were scratched in two places, and beginning to bleed, but she fought back like a lioness. Then, as she huddled over the half of a man lying motionless beneath her, she began to sob, once convulsively, once quietly. The man said nothing. Nor did anybody in the crowd speak a word. The only other sounds were the grunts of the police, grunts wreathed in white vapor as they breathed hard in the night air.

Finally, the militiamen loosed her from the embrace, and dragged her, with a thud, into the gutter. Then, as she kicked out in all directions, they lifted her onto the tailboard and shoved her in. Her head hung down, and the last thing to catch my eye was the artery in her neck, blue, and still pulsating from the strain.

It was very close to curtain time, and I didn't have another minute to wait to get an explanation of this small scene.

The scene on the Bolshoi stage, a few seconds later, was bigger. It seemed particularly big to me because I was seated in the very front row of the parterre, and life behind the footlights seemed bigger than life itself, and certainly brighter and a little more beautiful.

Ulanova was all that I had heard, and more. Magic. Her art was not gymnastics, not mere mime, not drama through gesture — but simply emotion through motion. Ulanova's lyricism has been described in detail by all the critics — as has the strange feeling of doom that seems to hang over this frail girl from Leningrad. But, in my opinion, a teacher at the Moscow ballet school has summed up Ulanova's genius better than anybody:

"The thing about Ulanova's.dancing is this — you never see it happen. There is a movement, something wonderful happens, but you never see the intervening stage. You never see it done."

. . . . dances *Bakhchisaraisky Fontan*

Although only a few feet away, I, along with everybody else, didn't see the wonderful thing happen as it happened. But I was so close that whenever Ulanova was in repose, when she was relatively still for a moment (as, for example, when fondling the harp of her dead lover as she lay heaped on the floor of the harem, carefully caressing the strings as she hid the harp in the folds of her nightgown; or when perched high on the shoulders of the Khan, after the strange, breath-taking leap to the neck and head of the very man who was trying to seduce her; or when, in the last moments of her life as Maria, after the quick, silent stab of the Khan's wife, she slowly twisted around the curve of the column against which she had thrown herself, finally to face her murderer in death), I could see everything. I could see the pink silk ribbons of her dancing pumps, tightly twisted around her ankles; the perpetual frown, the look of worry, on her pale forehead; the highlights of her chestnut hair; her thin, hunched-over shoulders; her flat, fragile chest; the tissue-paper texture of her white skin, ready to break over her sharp shoulder blades. And I could see in the end, as she lay with her head thrown back at the foot of the pillar, that Ulanova, like all human beings, had a great beating artery under her chin, under the tight, milk-white skin of her throat, and that it too was blue and bulging from the strain.

APRIL 2, 1951

This noon, in the middle of Moscow beside the Kremlin wall, our car was abruptly stopped in the street by a militiaman directing traffic at a considerable distance from us. After wildly whistling at us, the policeman waved our car

A visit to a Russian in his home . . . . . .

(an American make, and so quite conspicuous) to the curb
with his black-and-white traffic baton, and then sauntered
over. This is what he said to the driver, as haughtily as he
(or anyone) could:

"Don't you know it is forbidden to talk when you operate
an automobile? Never do it again! Is that clear? Is that
clear?"

April 3, 1951

Before I came over here, I had the general impression that
it would be almost impossible to talk to any Russians at all,
and entirely impossible to enter a Russian house. Of course
both are difficult to achieve compared to anything we know
outside this world of secrecy, but not impossible. In fact,
in my experience, it is the Russians themselves (of course I
am not now talking about government officials, each of
whom is surrounded by his own iron curtain, but the Russian people) who must be protected by us from indiscretion.
In violent contrast to the fog of fear and mistrust in which
the official world here operates, the people at large don't
seem to be aware of the danger they run in associating with
Americans.

Today I visited a Russian in his own house. I did so after
warning him several times that it was not safe for him to
entertain me. However, he insisted, and the opportunity
being almost unique, I went. The family of six live in two
rooms, but in spite of this crowding, and (for the space) an
enormous amount of furniture, the house was spotlessly
clean and neat. One of the rooms was a bed-sitting room;
the other the kitchen, in which there was one of the great

stoves over which Russians always sleep to keep warm.

I don't know whether I'll get into another Russian house, so I shall treasure this experience which very few foreigners have had in recent years.

APRIL 12, 1951

Most of the world is familiar with many of the inhuman policies of the Soviet Government, but few people seem to recognize how unhuman, as well as inhuman, is the atmosphere in which these policies are made.

By now we should know all about the surroundings and trappings of dictatorships. World history has provided enough cases. Start, for example, with Pisistratus during the Age of Tyrants in sixth-century Athens, and go on to Caesar in Rome, Cromwell in England, Napoleon in France, and finally to dictators of our own day, Mussolini and Hitler in twentieth-century Italy and Germany.

But the totalitarianism of Stalin is completely different from these previous examples. No predecessor of Stalin ever lived in such an unnatural atmosphere. No other despot ever designed such an abnormal way of life, either for himself or his people. As evil as Hitler was, he was, nonetheless, understandable and recognizable as a man, as a fellow human being — even in his madness.

And so, I say, the secret secrecy and the silent silence surrounding the beautiful Kremlin walls are something new in history. I am sure that thousands of people in Athens knew exactly where Pisistratus lived, thousands of people in Rome knew all the details of Caesar's private life, thousands of people in London knew the daily comings and goings of

The façade of the Bolshoi at nightfall   . . . .

Cromwell, thousands of people in Paris knew the personal habits of Napoleon, thousands of people in Rome knew the family affairs of Mussolini, thousands of people in Berlin knew that Hitler attended a performance of *Götterdämmerung* the night before last — but not one of these things is known about Stalin and his circle by anybody in Moscow, or by anybody anywhere else. *Nothing is known.*

If I read history correctly, there has never before been anything like this on earth.

APRIL 14, 1951

One of the best hours of the day is at nightfall in the spring just before eight o'clock. The lights go on under the vast Ionic portico of the Bolshoi Theater, softening the yellow and white effect before the evening performance. The lighting shows the dark forms of people hurrying across the square and up the portico steps to get to their seats before curtain time, and it throws into black shadows the huge bronze statue of Apollo in his chariot which flies out from the pediment.

The view of all this from my hotel window is superb: the whole façade of the Bolshoi, and a corner of the hundred-year-old Maly Theater with its old yellow walls and red roof jutting into the right foreground.

APRIL 19, 1951

I have great difficulty in understanding and in being understood on the telephone when speaking and listening to Russians. On the telephone, the Russians seem to scream unnecessarily loud and to talk even faster than usual. That is all probably because I can't see their lips and gesticulations, or at least that is the explanation given me.

When answering the phone, the equivalent to our "Hello" is *"Slushayu,"* which means "I am listening."

APRIL 20, 1951

Bright orange, really a tangerine color, sems to be the favor-ite shade of lipstick among Moscow womenfolk.

Another color, seen everywhere on the streets, has also been catching, and hurting, my eyes — a raspberry hue that doesn't go very well with khaki, but with khaki it goes, on the cap-cover, ribbons and shoulder boards of every other Soviet soldier in sight. "Raspberry" is not quite the right description and today I asked a fashion-conscious (and knowledgeable) American girl in the Embassy for the exact word. "Fuchsia, of course."

APRIL 29, 1951

It is now 2.00 A.M. Easter Sunday in Russia. I am writing this in my notebook as I lie on a rough wooden bench in the Troitse-Sergievskaya Lavra — or the Trinity Monastery of St. Sergius (in a town presently called Zagorsk) — the second most holy place in Russia, and, in many ways, the most historic. Beside me sleeps a beautiful Russian girl, with long dark hair, which almost reaches the floor from her bench.

Outside the monastery wall I can hear thousands of pil-grims chanting and singing as they march under the great trees, carrying their candles in their hands. The bells near

"Christ Is Risen" . . . .

the Cathedral of the Trinity, built by St. Nikon in 1422, clang in the night air, and when the bells are silent, I hear the cawing of the rooks in their nests high above me. A few feet away Boris Godunov sleeps in his 350-year-old grave, a strange little mound rising above the grass. All is dark and quiet in the old building next door, where one August midnight in 1689 young Peter the Great took refuge, still dressed in his long white nightgown, after frantically flying from his palace on the first horse he could find, with those who wanted to murder him not far behind.

The girl beside me moves a bit in her sleep. Perhaps she is trying to escape the glare of the single electric light bulb which hangs directly above us — and which she insisted should be kept burning. The girl is the person assigned to shadow me on this trip of mine to the monastery — and, since there was no place else to sleep and I insisted on staying overnight, there was nothing for her to do but sink down in exhaustion on the adjoining bench.

Now the singing becomes louder, and I can hear distinctly the words· "Christ Is Risen."

MAY 1, 1951

May Day. The biggest day in all the Russian year and the entire Communist world. And likewise for different reasons, the big day in the American Embassy, because here on May Day we have to entertain the entire friendly foreign population of Moscow from 7.00 A.M. to 5.00 P.M.

The reason for this is that our location is the best from which to watch the celebration. A fantastic location, looking out over the Kremlin walls, past the towers, into the cobble-

. . . . . . May Day — the American Embassy

stone surface of Red Square, flanked on the one hand by Lenin's tomb and beyond by St. Basil's Cathedral. All this we can see from our balcony windows.

The reason we have to begin to entertain so early is that all the streets of downtown Moscow are cleared throughout this day, starting at 7.00 A.M. Since all traffic stops at that moment, all foreigners have to get up early and rush to the American Embassy by seven o'clock. That means that the entertainment is both long and varied.

Beginning at 7.00 A.M. all Western foreigners start their descent upon the Embassy with their children and nursemaids, secretaries and assistant attachés. The entertainment consists of coffee, cup after cup after cup, during the morning hours, and then cocktails, glass after glass after glass, until the middle of the afternoon, and then a buffet lunch.

It is a very elaborate arrangement. For weeks beforehand the entertainment schedule is arranged. That means that the ambassador asks all the ambassadors in Moscow, the minister asks all the ministers, the counselors ask all the counselors, the military attachés ask all the military attachés, and down along the line. Under this arrangement several friendly Westerners are left out, and I am afraid that lots are drawn for those lowest on the diplomatic list.

A list of nationalities present in one apartment of the Embassy where I made a count at one moment during the day: Turk, Swiss, Iranian, French, English, Finn, Dane, Swede, Austrian, Italian, Burmese, Afghan, Norwegian, Luxemburger, Mexican, Argentine, Indian, Pakistani, Siamese, Egyptian, Australian, Canadian, Greek, Israeli, Lebanese, Syrian, Yugoslav, American.

Several apartments in the Embassy are set aside for the

Preparations for the "spontaneous celebration"   .   .

children, and American wives arrange their day in such a way that each one has two or three hours' charge of the nursery, where Egyptians and Pakistanis, Yugoslavs and French, Swedes and Afghans, all mix together.

The noise and hubbub in the streets outside the windows start as soon as the guests arrive. In fact, from 7.00 A.M. on there is a roar in the air and I really mean a roar, from one half to one million people in one small spot. In this connection, it should be borne in mind that the parades on May Day and on November 7 (the anniversary of the 1917 Revolution) are certainly unique. They differ from parades in the West in that instead of having onlookers on the curbstones, as you have with us, in Moscow everybody is in the street, and the only onlooker is Stalin, on top of Lenin's tomb.

The Soviet press speaks of the spontaneous celebration, year after year, but actually the whole performance is rehearsed and staged for several days in advance. In fact, the streets are lined with whitewash for at least a week before the parade, with complicated arrows showing which factory, which school, which club, is to go where.

The streets are lightly sanded, and the approaches to Red Square, which lies at the top of a slope, are heavily sanded, because at the beginning of the parade there are a few horses, and later in the day many tanks, streaming up the side streets.

At exactly 10 A.M. the parade marshal appears on horseback to see that the troops are ready. "Hoorays" thunder as he inspects them. Then there is a brief ten-minute "hate" speech and after that many "Long Live's" to May Day, to the Communist Party, to the Soviet State, and to

. . . .   **The May Day Parade**

Stalin. Then the military parade lasts for about forty minutes: mostly bottle-green tanks of all kinds roaring up the
grade, while the light blue of their exhaust spills over the
whole scene; weapons carriers, motorcycles (with drivers in
uniforms made entirely of leather); gun carriages, troop lor-
ries, etc. At the same time the air show takes place. At first
there are four-engine bombers, TU-4's (which are the Soviet
version of our B-29's) in groups of three, thundering over the
square at about 220 miles an hour. Then come the jet
fighters with their swept-back wings (the MIG-15), also in
groups of three, whistling and screaming overhead at about
400 miles an hour — almost out of sight to the southeast the
second they appear over the roof of the National Hotel to
our left.

Throughout the day the loudspeakers are on everywhere
in the city. The programs vary from the "Soviet Hymn" and
march music to wild accordion dances, from mass choral
music to high sopranos, and as background to all this loudspeaker noise is the constant roar of the paraders; chanting
and cheering and singing for eight hours in a row. In the
parade itself, there are not many bands.

The costumes and banners and flags are in all colors.
However, the dominant theme is red, though throughout
the city you can see great masses of green, blue, white, yellow, orange, gold, pink.

All day long thousands of Pioneers (boys and girls) carry
sticks of artificial green leaves to mark the spring festival,
and other regimented paraders carry thousands of white
paper blossoms, which they wave in a sea in front of Lenin's
tomb, in front of Stalin's smiling face.

The tomb itself is tightly fenced off by close-packed

"We Are for Peace" . . . .

M.V.D. troops, almost all of whom are officers, and it is
noticeable that when the civilian parade and demonstrations
start, these troops are reinforced immediately. These
M.V.D. troops are placed in elaborate formation, one facing
in, the next out — all of which is a double precaution.
There are many drunks among the paraders, and more and
more as the day goes on, but all these are carefully and
abruptly removed by the militiamen by the time they reach
the slope up into Red Square.

All day long from the early hours before sunrise until late
hours after sunset, the "spontaneous" paraders pour into the
square, coming from all directions along the main boulevards and side streets which converge onto the few thousand
cobblestones which are the center of Russia.

While the thousands of paraders are waiting for their
turn, they dance in the street. Some of the dancing seen
from our window overlooking Red Square is done by individuals and some by small groups. All of it is fast, frantic,
Russian folk dancing. Almost all of the paraders who wait
for hours in front of the Embassy recognize the building as
the American headquarters in Moscow. After all, the stars
and stripes are flying as large as life from the big white pole
over the sidewalk.

Many of the paraders wave to us as they go by — in scorn
or friendship — and some deliberately turn such banners
and slogans as "We Are for Peace" toward us in the windows,
as we look down with cocktail glass in hand.

May 3, 1951

Pattern of the great gold and red (in unfortunate bilious

. . . . **Cripples and beggars**

combination) curtain of the Bolshoi Theater: the main motif of the pattern is made up of the letters "CCCP" (U.S. S.R.) and the date "1917," but also in the pattern are the dates "1905" and "1871" (the latter is presumably for the Paris Commune). Under these dates are Proletarians Unite slogans in small white letters, most in Russian, but the slogan under 1871 is in French.

One reason for the total, faded red-and-gold-and-beige effect of the curtain is that other patterns running throughout are thin sheaves of wheat.

MAY 11, 1951

I have noticed an unusually large number of crippled people and what are presumably war-wounded on the streets, particularly one-legged men with crutches and canes, and many, many one-armed individuals.

I have also seen a few beggars on the street as well as on suburban trains and in the Metro (subway). Many of these are young, and the bandages over their wounds are quite conspicuous.

Almost everybody, and I mean everybody, gives the beggars a few kopecks.

MAY 15, 1951

I have just returned today from a visit to Yaroslavl — my first trip to a city of any size at some distance from "home." We (an adventuresome gal from the Embassy, and I) left by train a little over two days ago, shortly after midnight on May 13, and arrived in Yaroslavl at 6.30 A.M. the same day,

A supervised visit to Yaroslavl . . . .

after traveling a distance of about 170 miles. Again taking a night train, we returned to Moscow early this morning.

There was that lethargy about the city so peculiar to provincial towns in Russia. This sense of deadness was accentuated by the absence of new construction, by the dominance of squat, dilapidated, eighteenth-century Empire-style buildings which gave the impression of arrested growth. The new revolutionary street names — Ulitsa Svobodi, Sovetov, Kirova, etc. — seemed out of place in the old town.

The only smiles we observed belonged to a group of young Soviet Army officers who posed for a photograph on the steps of a maternity hospital on the banks of the Volga.

Our few encounters with Soviet citizens were not sufficient to serve as an absolute basis for generalizations, but it was encouraging to find that in our conversations with ordinary Russians in Yaroslavl they showed no hesitancy in speaking out in our behalf, in defiance of their most immediate symbol of state authority, the militia; and that, despite the poisonous propaganda against the U.S.A., they did not regard Americans as untouchables. Strangely enough, they were also seemingly unaware of possible personal consequences of their association with us. The employees and officials of the government, on the other hand, as opposed to the rank and file, were extremely uneasy, unpleasant, and, at times, under considerable strain on learning that we were Americans.

Although shadows and followers were not always physically in evidence, their ready appearance at crucial moments indicated that they were on our heels most of the time. Our encounter with the militiaman at the approach to the ferry crossing the Volga was the first indication that our movements had someone's close attention. As we happily stood

. . . . **A militiaman intervenes**

with ferry tickets in hand (bought at a booth a short distance from the boat), a militiaman suddenly appeared right out of the ground, like a Wagnerian warrior on the Rhine popping up from the stage of the Metropolitan, and rudely ordered us off the riverbank.

Our attempt to visit the Church of St. John the Baptist was typical of our experiences in Yaroslavl. This church, one of the finest examples of Russian polychrome decoration and the last great monument of the Muscovite school, was at the head of our list of innocent sightseeing projects. Taking a small, ancient, wooden trolley car from the center of town, we misjudged the stop, discovering that the church was still at some distance. The sidewalks were not paved and the rains had left them a muddy ribbon; the street was also muddy with stretches of rough, upturned stones. As the numerous cupolas, faceted apses, and the bell tower of St. John's rose into sight about a block to the right, and it seemed that our tightrope walk was to be rewarded, a militiaman suddenly slipped before us and roughly told us we could go no further, not a step. He demanded travel authorization documents. We told him that our presence in the town itself showed that our trip had been approved by the Ministry of Foreign Affairs, and that we only wanted to see the historic church (the hotel had insisted on retaining our diplomatic cards). In the meantime, a crowd had gathered, and while the policeman repeated that we could not proceed, a bystander, perhaps in his early forties, demanded with determination why we shouldn't be allowed to go on. The militiaman, infuriated by this remark, spat out between clenched teeth: "You as an outsider have no concern in this matter." The stranger spiritedly replied:

The crowd speaks up . . . .

"I do not fall under your authority and can say what I please." As we again said that we couldn't understand the objections of the police, an elderly peasant woman stated that we should be permitted to view the church, which, although closed, was of much interest. The militiaman, by now isolated, shed a bit of his aloof arrogance, seeming to feel a need to explain his obstinacy. He said that his *raion,* on the outskirts of the town, south of the river Kotorosl, had little to offer to sightseers and that the center of the city had many historic churches. Many in the crowd continued to express their disapproval of the militiaman's ruling. Having had the opportunity to hear the people's reaction, we decided to leave, since a further discussion obviously would not turn matters to our advantage and might serve to compromise the sympathetic spectators. Our suspicion that the church grounds were a forbidden area because of large factories in the near vicinity was confirmed in a later discussion at the Executive Commitee of the Oblast Soviet.

Curious as to the reception government authorities might give us, we made up our minds to visit the City Soviet on Krestyanskaya Ulitsa, housed in a building which apparently had once been the old Zemstvo seat. The reason for our visit was to obtain a ruling on what photographs, if any, could be taken in the city. It was Sunday and the building was almost completely empty. As we inquired of someone in the main hall where we could find the Chairman of the Executive Committee of the Soviet, an attendant came out of a side room and asked what we wanted. We replied that we were Americans sightseeing in Yaroslavl, and wished permission to take photographs. He immediately asked us if we were a "delegation" (after the May Day festivities in Mos-

.　.　.　.　.　**We visit the local government offices**

cow, many Iron Curtain delegations had departed for guided tours of the country). On hearing that we were not, his face visibly fell and he looked somewhat distraught. He bounced upstairs, returned shortly, and asked us to follow him. We were brought into a sparsely furnished room — just a desk before the wall opposite the entry, with a photograph of Molotov overhead (aside from Lenin and Stalin, Molotov was the only Russian whose portrait was prominently displayed in the public places of Yaroslavl), and a half-dozen straight-backed chairs on either side. We were left waiting. In a few minutes he informed us that the Oblast Soviet authorities would have to be conferred with in this matter.

The Executive Committee of the Oblast Soviet was located in the pre-revolutionary government offices in Iliinskaya Square. Approach to this square had already been prohibited to us (and to Soviet citizenry in general) a short time before, because of a relay race scheduled for the early part of the afternoon. On the first corner from the City Soviet building a militiaman blocked our passage, demanding a pass or permit called a *propusk*. Soviet citizens were also still denied entry. On our explaining that we had received instructions from the City Soviet to proceed to the Oblast Soviet, he waved us through. The next militiaman, at the end of the same block, declared that the previous clearance did not automatically give us the right to pass *him*. We again repeated our story, and after some discussion, he also permitted us to advance — right into the arms of a soldier with bayoneted rifle stationed on the next corner. The soldier, quite courteously, told us that the Oblast offices were closed that day.

Although the City Soviet representative had obviously given us the run-around, we nevertheless paid a call on the

"Impossible" . . . .

Oblast Soviet the next morning, even more interested in the response at this higher level to our request to see the church and its famous fifteen cupolas. A long line of poorly dressed people, with petitions of some sort, were patiently waiting outside the room toward which we were directed. The girl at the desk seemed a bit tense when we told her we were Americans and wanted to obtain a *propusk* to see the church. She stated that we would have to wait our turn in line. On the other hand, a workingman who had been discussing his particular problem with the girl when we entered was not at all uneasy — indeed, he was most curious. On hearing that we were leaving Yaroslavl that day and could not wait, the girl finally fetched an older woman, who brought us — after a long walk through deserted corridors — to the Section on Cultural and Educational Work. We announced, again, that we were from the American Embassy and wished to obtain permission to visit the Church of St. John the Baptist. The official in charge replied at once that the factories in that vicinity made trips there impossible. We suggested that he have someone escort us. Unfortunately, he said, the special guide was having his day off. We pointed out that there was no need to assign a trained guide as we had already studied the history and design of the church — down to the last line of wonderful blue tiling set in the last red wall in 1687. Any person would do to see that we were kept within bounds, we added. At this point his face was perspiring. Speaking in a sharper (but still civil) manner, he said he would check to see if anyone were free. No one, of course, was available to accompany us. We then asked him to write out a pass. He assured us with extreme conviction that this would be impossible for him to do inasmuch as the

. . . . **In a Soviet plane**

factories in question were under the jurisdiction of the *raion,* and consequently it was quite beyond his authority to issue such a document. "Good-bye."

Very few times in recent years, as far as I know, have Americans found themselves wandering through Soviet Government offices, watching hopeless underlings at their desks, talking to ordinary citizens in the hallways, tackling ever resourceful officials on their swivel chairs. It was a great opportunity, in the middle of the bear pit, to see Soviet bureaucracy at work. In a completely negative sense, I guess you might even say we were lucky. But luckier still will be the American who sees the Church of St. John the Baptist. And he will be later as well as luckier, much later — about two generations after me, I would say.

MAY 16, 1951

My phrase for the day in thinking about Russians as they scurry under the Kremlin walls: the Masses and the Masters.

MAY 22, 1951

I am writing these notes in a Soviet plane, dipping at 1900 meters (so says the dial in the cabin) above the lakes and swamps of the wild country southeast of Leningrad. Most of the view in my window is filled by the left-hand wing, which, in turn, is covered with large black letters, "CCCP" (U.S.S.R.). But I can see that the flight may be rough, as the sky one moment seems black with clouds, and the next moment blue with sunshine. As I turn my look to the right, inside the plane, my eyes take in a strange group of fellow

Trip home and return to Moscow . . . . . .

passengers: some heavily bearded, some completely bald, some slant-eyed, some squint-eyed — and all very silent. And between us, I see, is a fancy oriental carpet stretching along the center aisle — an elaborate bit of furnishing to make up, perhaps, for the absence of safety belts in the seats.

We took off from Vnukovo Airport at Moscow two hours ago, at 8.10 A.M., and are due in Leningrad in fifteen minutes. I understand that we shall spend an hour there, locked up in the airport restaurant, before taking off again for Helsinki. I hope that the delay will not be too long, as I have many close connections to make on this emergency trip home.

I continue writing in this old pocket notebook to keep my mind off the days that lie ahead. . . .

JULY 9, 1951

I returned to Moscow by train this morning, alone and unmet.

The change of scene and emotion on my emergency flight home was abrupt — much too abrupt. I made the plane trip in a little over twenty-four hours — an early breakfast in Moscow one morning, a late breakfast in New York the next. I am sure that no other human being has ever covered the geographical and spiritual space between the two cities in such a short time.

It is a mistake to leave the Soviet Union, for a brief period, in the middle of your tour of duty. While you remain in Moscow, month after month, you seem to forget, little by little, the brightness, the opulence and sleekness, the quick laughter and easy liberty, and the shining eyes, of the other world. And, when you are in America, in your own home (even when your house is hollow and unfamiliar because of the sudden absence of your father), you begin to forget, little by little, the bare, treeless asphalt, the bleak façades, and the sad, set faces of Moscow — and you gradually learn to break the habit of looking over your shoulder.

JULY 15, 1951

Today, almost for the first time since my arrival in Moscow, I had a healthy day — a day outdoors in the sun. Two British friends had persuaded me that it would do me good to get some exercise, and so we left downtown Moscow early this morning for a place called "Silver Woods" on the banks of the Moscow River — a favorite swimming spot for all Muscovites. I had been looking forward to this outing with a mild form of enthusiasm for several days.

Our taxi drive took about half an hour, through the factory outskirts of the city, and then out into the country a little way. Actually the Moscow River twists throughout the city in such a manner that you are never really very far from the Kremlin on its banks.

We got an early start because we wanted to go rowing as well as swimming and my friends told me that there were only a few rowboats and it was necessary to get there early.

Our taxi took us close to the river and then we walked through the "Silver Woods" to the mud of the riverbank. We were told that the best swimming was on the other side of the river so we took, for a few kopecks, a three-minute ferry ride across the river and landed on more mud. Here there was an unpainted shed for changing your clothes but

Swimming at the Silver Woods . . . .

it was so far from our destination that we didn't stop there. The walk went on and on as we tried to find a beach. Finally we found a less slimy place and we began to undress in front of everybody, as everybody was doing in front of us. Being a bit shy and modest, I did my best to hide behind a miserable little bush.

Once in our trunks, we slid down the mud of the bank into the mud of the river. It was still early in the morning but already many Russians were there enjoying the sunlight which began to blaze overhead. We had found on landing from the ferry that all the rowboats had been taken, as my British colleagues had feared, so the whole day was devoted to swimming and sun bathing.

Soon there were people all over the place and I had a chance to study the bathing costumes of the Russian people. In most cases, it was purely a matter of swimming in your underwear. That is, the women had little skirts and big brassieres.

After five hours of this, the sun had moved the distance it usually moves in five hours and we decided to go home. The scene as we left it showed about forty Russians wallowing enthusiastically in the mud.

We crossed the river again on the same ferry and *everybody* on board, with one exception, agreed that it had been a wonderful day.

JULY 16, 1951

On my return to Moscow on July 9, hot weather immediately set in, so hot that the American and British Embassys took afternoons off on particularly bad days. Even *Pravda,* which

. . . . **Of cats and dogs**

never has a word to say about such uninteresting, non-Stalinist phenomena as the weather, broke all traditions on July 15 with the relatively human headline, "Hot Days in Moscow." Then *Pravda* said: "The maximum air temperature in Moscow on July 14 reached thirty-four degrees [94° Fahrenheit]. The Central Institute of Meteorology informed a TASS correspondent that: 'Such a high temperature is a rare event in Moscow. It is only two and a half degrees lower than the maximum temperature observed in July during the last fifty-odd years. A higher air temperature has been observed in Moscow only three times.' "

JULY 19, 1951

Moscow is full of mongrel, parti-colored cats curled on the window sills and crouching in the weeds and overgrown grass of sidewalk plots and back yards, but there are hardly any dogs at all in the city, although the villages of Russia are full of them. The few dogs you do see on the sidewalk are either on leashes or muzzled.

JULY 28, 1951

This has been an historic day — for me anyway, if not for Stalin. This morning, for three hours, I was inside the hardest place in the world to get inside of, the Kremlin.

Here are my first, immediate impressions (scribbled down in my notebook as fast as I could write, during a late lunch immediately after the visit):

Silence.

Peace.

The Kremlin — Silence . . . .

Once I was inside the gate, and after the shrill electric bells had stopped ringing and the red lights had stopped flashing and the big iron entrance doors had stopped sliding back and forth, the first thing I saw in the Kremlin was a white butterfly, settling on a small piece of lawn.

Blue spruces pricking the skyline on the high bluff over the Moscow River. A bed of red and orange dahlias and white snapdragons. Broad, bare, open cobblestone squares, and spotless macadam streets, edged with low evergreen hedges.

A long hose in one of the streets, dripping water into one of the drains in the gutter. The faraway sound of a hammer, echoing across a large plaza.

Another sound: chimes ringing at a distant gate. Then again, silence.

Now another sound: the tramp of a company of Kremlin guards as they cross the cobblestone pavement — troops dressed in black boots, khaki uniforms, and blue caps.

A bread truck goes by.

Two peasant women, in white kerchiefs, tending a bed of tiger lilies.

Towering dark rain clouds rising over the city.

Two more peasant women adjusting one of the shields put up behind a young evergreen on the brow of the Kremlin hill.

Silence.

The view from the crest of the hill — the view Stalin sees every hour: the housetops and chimneys of Moscow, the new University skyscraper going up in the distance, the cupolas of churches, and the fingers of factory smokestacks.

Again the lonely sound of the hammer.

·　·　·　·　·　·　　**The Hall of the Supreme Soviet**

All of the windows in the long stretches of yellow barracks and green-roofed public buildings are open — as well they might be, because it is a hot day. But not a sound comes from a single window.

JULY 29, 1951

Late last night I tried to finish my notes on the Kremlin tour yesterday:

Of all the old buildings now still in use, the Great Kremlin Palace, with the Hall of the Supreme Soviet, proved to be of most interest. In this hall, converted from one of the largest reception rooms under the tsars into the meeting place of the Supreme Soviet, the "law makers" of Russia rubberstamp the decrees of the government once a year, sitting under the very thumb of Stalin. As a matter of fact, Stalin and the Politburo look down on the gathering from exactly the same spot where the tsar used to sit on his throne.

The present-day color scheme of the hall is pearl-pink and white — severe, simple, and ugly. The rows of seats and desks and the rostrum are of dark polished wood, as are all the doors leading into the hall. The south side of the hall is a series of enormous (and celebrated) windows, with light yellow curtains, looking out on the Moscow skyline and the river flowing at the foot of the hill one hundred and fifty feet below.

A row of semicircular boxes protrudes halfway up the north wall, like scalloping — loges for the diplomatic corps. In front, rising at the back center of the presidium platform is a huge statue of Lenin, more than life size. And over Lenin is a utilitarian clock. This stage consists of a half-

The Tsars' thrones . . . .

dozen rows of chairs rising in back of a simple boxlike lectern (with carved insignia of the hammer and sickle superimposed on the globe, and with a microphone). All the seats and desks in the hall have white dust covers, and these remain in place all year, except for the brief annual session, which usually lasts about a week. The carpets are of a tasteless color combination: orange and pink.

From the windows of the gallery corridor along the north side of the hall, I got a wonderful view across the inner court of the Great Kremlin Palace: I could see the strange, shut-in pyramid-like pile of the "Terem" with its rows of tiny, colored windows, where the tsars and their wives and children lived, and ruled over Russia, three and four and five hundred years ago.

Most of the time of the tour is taken up by a visit to the museum — the greatest museum in Russia, which no Russian can see. I could write a book about what I saw, but here are a handful of sights:

One room has all the thrones of the tsars. First in line is the ivory throne of Ivan the Terrible. The most beautiful seat of all, to my mind, is the throne of Boris Godunov — a low square chair of thin gold plate, studded with over two thousand precious stones and pearls. And then there are the thrones of Michael, the first of the Romanovs, and Alexei, and then the ugly, ungainly double throne of the young boy tsars, Ivan V and Peter I (the latter soon turned into the Great). Today this throne remains in tattered crimson cloth and silver gilt — with a tall, straight back (with the fascinating flap through which the boys' sister, Sophia, gave them their orders: an incredibly clear-cut physical example of "the power behind the throne," probably the most vivid illustration in history).

. . the most famous material thing in all of Russia

Nearby is the carriage room, which turned out to be equally fascinating. Of particular interest to me was the big, bulky, awkward coach which Queen Elizabeth of England gave to Boris Godunov (and to which our woman guide pointed with great disdain, saying that it was not, after all very fancy — indeed, quite crude — and that the wheels could not even turn at an angle; this was quite true — but the Russians were the last people to complain at that time, having no such carriages of their own).

And then there is the huge closed-in sleigh in which Empress Elizabeth drove from Petersburg to Moscow for her coronation in 1742 — fitted out as a complete small room, upholstered in green cloth, with a table and divans, two doors, and fourteen tiny isinglass windows.

And also there is a fantastically florid, rococo carriage of gilt (with paintings of cupids by Boucher on the doors), which was a gift to Catherine the Great from one of her favorites (she had twenty-one "official" lovers in forty-four years, if I remember my history). In this case, Grigory Orlov (as I understood the guide) was the giver — or maybe the transaction was vice versa (and now that I think of it, it probably *was* vice versa). And, too, I saw tiny, elaborate, toylike sleighs which once belonged to assorted tsareviches and tsarevnas.

The rooms stretch on and on and on. But the high point of the two hours spent in the museum was the half-hour in the crown room — at least I thought so.

The ancient crowns of all the tsars are there, including the Cap of Monomakh, a little object which is probably the most famous material thing in all of Russia. This is the first crown of Russia, the crown of Grand Prince Vladimir Monomakh of the twelfth century — a delicate gold filigree cap,

To Zagorsk . . . .

studded with a few enormous precious jewels, and lined at
the rim with soft, light brown sable. This little cap, so light
in weight, always has been the symbol of power in Russia
— and it prompted Pushkin, when he was writing *Boris
Godunov,* to say in one of the most significant lines in all
Russian literature (at least the passage was so described to
me by a Russian girl I met one night at the theater):

"Ah! heavy art thou, crown of Monomakh!"

JULY 30, 1951

An extraordinary coincidence marked my life yesterday — a
strange and moving trick of fate which I shall never forget.

It happened on a train trip to Zagorsk, the present-day
name of the small town northeast of Moscow in which is
located the fourteenth-century Troitse-Sergievskaya Monastery. Next to the holy monument at Kiev, this has always
been the richest, most distinguished, and historically the
most important monastery in Russia. I had been to Zagorsk
before — and on that first visit had taken the suburban train
for the two-hour trip, rather than an Embassy car. I was trying to break the bad American habit of using an automobile for every occasion — a habit which is even more pronounced among the handful of Americans in Moscow than
it is among the millions at home. And I had another reason, too. Train travel in Russia is always an interesting
experience — and trips by rail invariably provide surprising
opportunities for close, if brief, contact with the Russian
people. So, again, when three Embassy friends asked me to
take them to Zagorsk yesterday, I persuaded them to make
the trip by train.

· · · · · · · · · · · · · **The train**

Yesterday was Sunday, and the holiday crowds in the Yaroslavl station were larger than ever. Thousands were hurriedly leaving the hot, dusty city for a summer afternoon in the country, for a few hours in the green shade of the *dachas* (small country cottages) which line the railway track for miles beyond the city. The stinking station was full of other kinds of travelers as well: pathetic family groups huddled on the benches, sleeping on their bags and belongings, silently waiting hour after hour for tickets to who knows where; and troops in all directions, dashing off to who knows where.

When we arrived shortly after noon, the Zagorsk train was ready at the track. We started to rush inside, but we didn't rush far. All the cars were full and bulging. Every seat was taken, all the corridors were jammed, and people were packed into the platforms. Passengers were leaning out of the windows, panting for air. Finally, we got a foothold on the carriage steps, and gradually began to work our way inside. As the train began to pull slowly out of the station, I found that our opportunity for close contact with the Russians, on this occasion at least, was much too good. The furthest distance between us was about half an inch. The Russians around us — or rather I should say standing on us, poking into us, and breathing down us — were silent but good-natured. The heat was hot and the smell was smelly. Then suddenly there was a crush and a commotion. Fat peasant women with their market bags, small boys with books, and well-dressed officials with overnight suitcases all began to give way and make place on the tiny platform between the carriages. A drunkard had toppled over unconscious, and lay on the dusty floor at my feet. He was dressed in dirty, ragged clothes and was unshaven. Soon the crowd

Tolstoy said it . . . .

surged back around us and we stepped on the unconscious figure as gently as we could. Through the bundles and boots and skirts and arms and legs, however, I could see that the face of this man was bleeding and there was a little foam on his lips.

After the first few stops, the crowd thinned out and there was room in which to heave one's lungs and move one's elbow. And then took place the coincidence to which I referred at the beginning of this entry. I was carrying with me a pocket edition of Tolstoy's *Resurrection* — the strange novel which he wrote near the end of his life, the novel which is so little known in the West. Still on my feet I started to look for my place in the book. I did this in order to keep my eyes off the man who was still stretched on the floor under my legs (and who, at this point, was beginning to moan) and to make it impossible for the Russians present to think that I, as a foreigner, was staring, either too rudely or too compassionately. Here is what I read — the words used by Tolstoy to describe the thoughts of his hero as another train pulled out of Moscow half a century ago:

> The heat in the large third-class carriage, which had been standing in the burning sun all day, was so great that Nekhlyudov did not go in but stayed on the little platform behind. But there was not a breath of fresh air there either, and Nekhlyudov breathed freely only when the train had passed the buildings and a draught blew across the platform.
>
> "Yes, killed," he said, repeating to himself the words he had used to his sister. And in his imagination, in the midst of all other impressions, there arose with wonderful clearness the beautiful face of the second dead convict, with the smile on the lips, the severe expression of brows, and the small, firm ear below the shaven, bluish skull.

. . . . "No one is guilty, and yet . . ."

"And what seems terrible," he thought, "is that while he has been murdered, no one knows who murdered him. Yet he has been murdered. He was led out by Maslennikov's orders like all the rest of the prisoners. Maslennikov probably gave the usual order, signing with his stupid flourish a paper with a printed heading, and most certainly did not consider himself guilty. Still less will the careful doctor who examined the convicts. He performed his duty accurately, and separated the weak. How could he foresee this terrible heat, or the fact that they would start so late in the day and in such crowds? The prison inspector? But the inspector has only carried into execution the order that on a given day a certain number of exiles and convicts — men and women — were to be sent off. The convoy officer cannot be guilty either, for his business was to receive a certain number of persons at a certain place and to deliver up the same number. He conducted them in the usual manner, and could not foresee that two such strong men as those I saw would be unable to stand it, and would die. No one is guilty, and yet the men have been murdered by these people who are not guilty of their death.

"All this comes," thought Nekhlyudov, "from the fact that all these people — governors, inspectors, police officers, and policemen — consider that there are circumstances when human relations are not necessary between human beings. All these men, Maslennikov, and the inspector, and the convoy officer, if they were not governor, inspector, officer, would have considered twenty times before sending such a mass of people out in such heat — would have stopped twenty times on the way, and seeing a man growing weak, gasping for breath, would have led him into the shade, would have given him water and let him rest, and if an accident had still occurred, they would have expressed pity. But not only did they not do this, but they hindered others from doing it, because they thought not of men and their duty towards them but only of the office they themselves filled, and considered the obligations of that office to be above human relations. That is the whole matter," Nekhlyudov continued. "If once we admit — be it only for an hour or in some exceptional case — that anything can be more important than a feeling of love for our fellows, then there is no crime which we may not commit with easy minds, free from feelings of guilt. . . .

"Oh! I was thinking that all those people: inspector, convoy men — all those in the service — are for the greater part kind people, cruel only because they serve."

He recalled Maslennikov's indifference when he told him of what was being done in the prison, the inspector's severity, and the cruelty of the convoy officer in refusing places on the carts to those who asked for them, and paying no attention to the fact that there was a woman in travail in the train. All these people were evidently invulnerable by and impermeable to the simplest feelings of compassion only because they held offices. "As officials they are as impermeable to the feelings of humanity as this paved earth is impermeable to the rain," thought Nekhlyudov, as he looked at the sides of the cutting paved with stones of different colors, down which the water was running in streams instead of soaking into the earth. "Perhaps it is necessary to pave slopes with stones, but it is sad to look at earth deprived of vegetation, when it might be yielding corn, grass, bushes, or trees like those on the top of this cutting.

"And it is the same thing with men," thought Nekhlyudov. "Perhaps these governors, inspectors, policemen are needed; but it is terrible to see men deprived of the chief human attribute: love and sympathy for one another. The thing is," he continued, "that these people acknowledge as law what is not law, and do not acknowledge as law at all, the eternal, immutable law written by God in the hearts of men.

. . . . . . "governors, inspectors, policemen"

That is why I feel so depressed when I am with these people. I am simply afraid of them. And really they are terrible, more terrible than robbers. A robber might, after all, feel pity, but they can feel no pity; they are inured against pity as these stones are against vegetation. That is what makes them so terrible. It is said that the Pugatchevs and the Razins are terrible. These are a thousand times more terrible," he continued in his thoughts.

"If a psychological problem were set to find means of making men of our time — Christian, humane, simple, kind people — perform the most horrible crimes without feeling guilty, only one solution could be devised: simply to go on doing what is being done now. It is only necessary that these people should be governors, inspectors, policemen; that they should be fully convinced that there is a kind of business, called Government service, which allows men to treat other men as things without having human brotherly relations with them; and that they should be so linked together by this Government service that the responsibility for the results of their deeds should not fall on any one of them individually. Without these conditions the terrible acts I witnessed today would be impossible in our times. It all lies in the fact that men think there are circumstances when one may deal with human beings without love. But there are no such circumstances. We may deal with things without love — we cut down trees, make bricks, hammer iron without love — but we cannot deal with men without it, just as one cannot deal with bees without being careful. If one deals carelessly with bees one will injure them and will one's self be injured. And so with men. It cannot be otherwise, because mutual love is the fundamental law of human life. It is true that a man cannot force another to love him as he can force him to work for him, but it does not follow that one may deal with men without love, especially if one de-

Tolstoy is popular · · · · · · · · · ·

mands or expects anything from them. If you feel no love, sit still," Nekhlyudov thought: "occupy yourself with things, with yourself, with anything you like, only not with men. Just as you can only eat without injuring yourself when you are hungry, so you can only usefully and without injury deal with men when you love. . . . Yes, yes, it is so," thought Nekhlyudov; "it is true; yes, it is true," he repeated, enjoying the freshness after the torturing heat, and conscious of having attained the fullest clearness on a question that had long occupied him.

That is the passage which by strange chance I read as the train passed through the countryside north of Moscow. I quote these words of Tolstoy at length, not only because of the striking prose, but also and especially because they stirred my imagination, forcing me to ask myself what my Russian traveling companions themselves would think when reading this chapter from *Resurrection*. And here I should add that they do, indeed, have an opportunity to read Tolstoy. Furthermore, very prominent among his works is *Resurrection*, which the Soviet public, unlike the Western public, links with *War and Peace* and *Anna Karenina* as Tolstoy's great fictional trilogy. Indeed, a dramatization of the novel has been a hit at the Moscow Art Theater for many seasons now — and I myself have seen it played twice to sell-out houses. All of this does not mean, of course, that Tolstoy's later Christlike views are literally interpreted by the Kremlin as we might understand them. Like Hitler, who admired but missed the point of Wagner's Siegfried epic, Stalin, it seems to me, completely misses the burning message of Tolstoy.

Zagorsk is about fifty miles from Moscow — and so, as our

· · · · · · · · · **"They can feel no pity"**

train crept through the woods of Sokolniki and then on past
Mytishchi and the ancient villages of Pushkino and Khot-
kovo, I had plenty of time to study the Russians by my side
— the peasants and workers, the students and white-collar
bureaucrats and uniformed soldiers, the old and young; time
to wonder how my fellow passengers felt about their present-
day "governors, inspectors, police officers, and policemen."
Did they feel that their Kremlin rulers "acknowledge as law
what is not law, and do not acknowledge as law at all, the
eternal, immutable law written by God in the hearts of
men": that their own countrymen who carry out the orders
of Stalin and Malenkov, Beria and Molotov, are "cruel only
because they serve"? The answer, of course, was not given to
me — but didn't I read in the eyes of the individuals around
me: "I am simply afraid of them. And really they are terrible, more terrible than robbers. . . . They can feel no
pity"?

And I wondered, too, what thoughts we Americans today
might have about ourselves in our new role as rulers of half
the world.

JULY 31, 1951

Last night I had a very revealing time. I dined with a British correspondent, and the other guest was Joe Clark, the
reporter for the *Daily Worker*. He's the first American
Communist, as far as I know, whom I have ever met, and to
meet and talk with him here, in his Mecca, is a weird experience. The facts which he sees around him every day don't
seem to register with Clark, and he is as enthusiastic for
Communism now as he ever was in New York. He writes so

The "Time of Troubles" . . . .

exactly what the regime here wants that they often translate his articles for the Soviet press. Here is an apparently intelligent man who is seeing just what I see all day and yet the evidence of his own senses does not register in his mind. For instance, he even has written (and says) that there is no drunkenness in Russia, whereas anyone here has seen daily the silent, morose, grim absorption of alcohol by the people who, without ever appearing to get any "lift" out of it, will pass out and be carted off by the government ambulances to a "sobering-up station" especially maintained for the purpose.

AUGUST 3, 1951

One of the best known times in all of Russia's thousand year old history (perhaps the best known period) is a time called *Smutnoe Vremya* — a phrase that is quite difficult to translate, although nowadays in all history books it is given as "Time of Troubles."

This period lasted from 1598 to 1613 and took in the reign, chiefly, of Boris Godunov, just before the start of the Romanov dynasty. A more literal translation of the phrase would be the "dim" or "vague" times.

Today, three hundred and fifty years later, I would think that all Russians would feel a shock of recognition on reading the words *Smutnoe Vremya*.

AUGUST 6, 1951

To resume my diary:

A week ago I moved from the Metropole Hotel to "Ves-

·   ·   ·   ·   ·   ·   ·   ·   ·   ·   ·   ·   ·   **"Vesnina"**

nina," the name given by the American Embassy to an elaborate town house which we have been renting for several years as living quarters for Foreign Service personnel. The name "Vesnina" comes from the present name of the street on which it is located, a rather celebrated side street known in the old days as Money Street, because — I have heard — the state silver vaults were once housed here. Built at the turn of the century, "Vesnina" is a very dirty but very fancy late Victorian barn, with a stained-glass window of purple tulips and green weeds over the front entrance, but with no gas and no hot water.

This minor mansion is typical of countless dwellings, gloomy, grotesque alcazars put up by rich Moscow merchants fifty to sixty years ago. An even bigger one, now the Italian Embassy, is across the street from us, a few doors away. It, like ours, is "guarded" day and night by militiamen at a sentry box, and by plain-clothes men pacing up and down the back yard.

I walk past the Italian Embassy every day on my way to work — and today I found out (perhaps) why the militiamen there invariably give me an extra-careful once-over. This spot was the scene, thirty-three years ago, of a world-shaking assassination, the shooting of Count von Mirbach, the first German Ambassador following the Revolution — an assassination which Bruce Lockhart calls "the most dramatic political murder of modern times." In the summer of 1918, a few months after the Treaty of Brest-Litovsk, this mansion on Money Street became the German Embassy. It was guarded in those days, too — and, from all accounts, by a detachment of Bolshevik troops numbering many more than those now protecting the place from people like me. None-

New Quarters . . . .

theless, the assassin had no difficulty in getting inside, empty-
ing his Browning gun into the body of the Ambassador, and
then throwing a hand grenade behind him, for good measure, as he jumped out of an open window. International
affairs — particularly Russo-German relations — have never
been quite the same since that moment.

AUGUST 7, 1951

There is so much to write about, but at midnight my eyelids
fall, and so does my pen. Last night, for example, instead of
spellbinding myself with the details of the Mirbach murder,
I should have described our own living conditions here at
"Vesnina," and made this telling comment at least: only
four Americans live in this one-story town house, and an
estimated forty Russians live in exactly the same area in the
basement beneath us. Thus the ratio is 10–to–1 — and the
cubic ratio must be even higher, if only for the reason that
our ceiling stretches high to heaven, and the basement appears to be a low, dark hole.

I am forced to write "appears to be," because we, the
American inmates, cannot, of course, go into our own cellar
to see who our "neighbors" are, and how they live. The
Russians living half a foot below us have a separate sidewalk gate and a separate house door (I assume so, because
they must get in and out somehow) — and so the Iron Floor
is complete.

Our only contact is one of smell. Some of our Soviet
housemates have to leave their garbage and hang their
laundry in the black alcove under the long marble staircase
of our ceremonial entrance. A nice comparison, a fitting

commentary: here, in these few square feet, it seems to me, is a perfect microcosm of the world today — scores of decent Russians silently (and sometimes drunkenly) dumping their refuse in the dark; a handful of decent Americans noisily (and sometimes drunkenly) leaning over the rich, wrought-iron balustrade above the garbage cans; and through the front-door window the ever present outline of the Soviet militia-man, watching now the Americans, now the Russians.

Needless to say, all this points to the acute housing short-age throughout the Soviet Union — the greatest postwar problem still unlicked by the Kremlin, an open sore for all to see.

It must have been a prewar problem, too — because, from the looks of things today, housing for the great majority of the people has never been a strong point in Russia. Then came the war itself, with its destruction of much of the little that was standing in the first place. In 1947, Nikolai A. Voznesensky, as Chief of the State Planning Commission and a Deputy Premier of the U.S.S.R. at that time, had this to say about the damage done to housing during World War II:

Of the 2,567,000 dwelling houses located in cities of the U.S.S.R. which were occupied by the Germans, 1,209,000 homes were destroyed or ruined. (In terms of dwelling space, this number of houses comprised more than 50 per cent of all urban dwelling space of those cities.) Of the 12,000,000 rural dwelling houses in the occupied regions of Russia, 3,500,000 were ruined or destroyed by Hitler's occupying forces. Further, over one half of the household property of the population living in areas subjected to occupation was either destroyed or looted.

The Hate America campaign . . . .

Today, housing remains a very weak spot indeed in the Soviet economy. There is an awful lot of uncontrolled talk in the controlled press about postwar progress in housing — but I have noticed hardly any new scaffolding on the skyline. My forty Russian neighbors in the basement deserve better than this. When will they, and the rest of the civilian population, wake up and really complain about the lack of house-building? There are some signs of open grumbling among the consumers of Russia, who have so little to consume, but the day has not come (and perhaps never can come) when the people will say: "We are living in a roofless paradise."

AUGUST 10, 1951

I have been trying to figure out an effective way to give all fellow Americans (my mother and brother, President Truman and Secretary Acheson, Senator Taft and Senator McCarthy, General Eisenhower and General MacArthur — to name a few) the sight and sound, the smell and feel, of the anti-American campaign.

Certainly one way (rarely tried) is to give *in full* — not in snatches, not merely in scattered phrases in quotation marks under the Moscow dateline of a foreign correspondent — a typical article from the Soviet press. And that is what I am going to do here — present a specimen, complete in itself, and representative of the whole. And I hope that those eight Americans mentioned above, and any others who might eventually come upon this diary, will in turn do their part and read these words *in full*.

Here is how I made the selection. A few minutes ago I

. . . . **"The businessmen are praying."**

spread out in front of me the newspaper articles I had translated at work this morning, and then, with my eyes shut, let
my hand fall. My finger pointed to a piece entitled "The
Businessmen's Prayers," a feuilleton filling an entire column
in yesterday's *Literary Gazette,* a paper, incidentally, which
comes out three times a week, and performs a great deal of
the preliminary hatchet work for such better-known dailies
as *Pravda* and *Izvestiya.* The author uses a pseudonym,
"Man of Letters." Here are the letters of this man:

> The businessmen are praying. They lift up their hands
> to heaven, make pious faces, and ask:
> "Oh, God, help us to tear their soldiers to bloody pieces
> with our shells; help us to cover their flowering fields with
> the corpses of their patriots; help us to destroy their peace-
> ful dwellings with a hurricane of fire; help us to break with
> inconsolable grief the hearts of their widows who are guilty
> of nothing; help us to deprive them of shelter and to force
> them, with their children, to wander over the devastated
> earth without refuge, in rags, suffering from hunger and
> thirst."
> In these words, so murderously accurate with respect to
> their striking irony, Mark Twain expressed, more than fifty
> years ago, the "morals" of the American imperialists. Today,
> as never before, one should understand this "prayer" of mur-
> derers and man haters in the most direct and literal sense
> possible.
> Sometimes, it is true, they pray differently. In such cases
> Congressmen and Senators bedeck themselves in the togas of
> peacemakers, and the word "peace" is present in the utter-
> ances of highly placed American figures. It is met more than
> once, for example, in the message of President Truman of
> the U.S.A. to the President of the Presidium of the Supreme

The Russian press looks at Kaesong . . . . .

Soviet of the U.S.S.R., Shvernik, which was published yesterday. However, as a result of this, the policy conducted by the American government in no way becomes peace loving. This is explained by the fact that, as it is said in the answer of N. M. Shvernik to Mr. Truman, "there exist in some states forces which are striving to unleash a new world war, in which the circles in question see the source of their own enrichment." Is it surprising that the policy and actions of the government of the U.S.A., which are dictated by these very circles, are divorced from its verbal declarations on the preservation of peace, as well as from the peace-loving aspirations of the American people? Between the words and deeds of the U.S. Government, one can say, there is a distance of enormous extent.

Armistice negotiations are taking place these days in the region of the 38th Parallel, at Kaesong, destroyed and demolished by war. This is where, it would seem, there is a complete opportunity for peaceful efforts from the American side! What, however, is taking place in actuality? The prospect of an armistice in Korea is provoking gnashing of teeth on Wall Street. And immediately, at the command of the Wall Street bosses, the venal pens begin to scribble about the "peace slump" which is threatening America.

"The greatest danger," writes Lindley, a commentator of the magazine "Newsweek," "will arise after the agreement on an armistice in Korea." What then does this mouthpiece of Morgan, Harriman and Co. fear? He fears, it appears, the slackening of the arms race, and, consequently, the reduction of military orders, a decrease in profits.

The fears which have seized the bosses of the industrial companies and banking houses in connection with the negotiations at Kaesong are easily explained. Wall Street in 1950 "earned" 22.4 billion dollars of pure profit on the Korean

. . . . **and American policy**

war. This exceeds by more than two times the profits of the most "profitable" year of the Second World War and is one third more than the profits of 1949!

But those who "should be in the know" are hastening to calm the agitated businessmen. Recently Truman presented to Congress the midyear economic report. In this curious document, the President of the U.S.A. made haste to assure, not so much, naturally, the Congressmen as the financiers and businessmen, that "independent of whether or not peace is established in Korea," war production in the U.S.A. will grow, and the armed forces will be increased. So the gentlemen from Wall Street should not be especially upset.

And one must say that the ruling circles of the U.S.A. are disturbed by another problem; the cessation of bloodshed in Korea can provoke a slump in the war hysteria in the U.S.A., the hysteria which has been fanned with such diligence in recent years. An armistice in Korea, confirming the rightness of those who appeal for a peaceful solution of international problems by means of negotiations, and not by the method of force, can inflict a blow on the policy once officially proclaimed by John Foster Dulles — to hold the American people in a state of "artificial tension." This most of all is now feared in Washington and on Wall Street. This "psychological problem," writes the "Washington Post," "is provoking the same worry among American military leaders" as the possible slowing down of the pace of military preparations.

This is why the American imperialists are hastening to pour oil on the flames of war hysteria. Not without reason did Marshall, the U.S. Secretary of Defense, state at one of the meetings of a subcommittee of the House Appropriations Committee that one should consider the appropriations of 60 billion dollars for military requirements only as the

The Russian people do not hate you and me — yet.

first "large capital investment." Korea, in the words of Marshall, is only "an incident in the world situation"; therefore, one should concern oneself with Europe in a speedier and more thorough fashion. Pace, the U.S. Secretary of the Army, recently elaborated the hidden meaning of Marshall's statements. Speaking to a subcommittee of the Senate Appropriations Committee, he announced the possibility of a repetition of a "Korean incident" in Iran, Yugoslavia and other regions of the globe.

The businessmen and financiers are appealing to God as they dream of new wars and new profits. But the dreams of the businessmen from Wall Street are not destined to be fulfilled. After all, those times when Mark Twain wrote down their bloodthirsty prayers have irretrievably passed.

As I wrote at the beginning, this piece is typical of what the Russians read and hear every minute, and they have no chance to read or hear anything else. Multiply these words by *billions* more just like them, and you have the sum total of the anti-American campaign.

AUGUST 11, 1951

As a footnote to yesterday's "exhibit" of the hate-America campaign, I must make this additional — and important — comment:

The Russian people do *not* hate you and me — yet.

When I first arrived in Russia, I, like every other American here, was stunned by the ferocity and scale of the operation. And I could understand (a little, anyway) the fears of some of our Embassy people that they might be attacked on the street, that they might be assaulted by individual

. . . . the Party line has been shifted so often

Russians maddened by hate and fear. But I now know that in judging the reaction of the Russian people to the Kremlin campaign, newcomers to the U.S.S.R. must always remember that the Party line has been shifted so often, that propaganda has been switched in so many directions throughout so many years, that the average Russian by this time is often quite immune to poison. And so, really, I shouldn't be too surprised that the Russians do not, indeed, act as though they hated me in the prescribed manner.

Put it another way: If the Russians really did believe in their hearts what they read and hear all day long, they certainly would show personal animosity in one way or another — and I wouldn't blame them. The point is: they don't.

AUGUST 12, 1951

This morning I saw the tennis championships at the courts of the Red Army Club. There are no grass courts in the U.S.S.R. and the courts at the Red Army Club, which are supposed to be among the very best in Russia, seem to me to be of poor sand. All during the championship matches the loudspeaker system throughout the grounds was playing and all the time I could hear either a review of the latest news from the North Korean front or very loud band music or high sopranos or *Pravda's* "International Review," while the finals were going on.

Sometimes the radio was so loud that you could not hear the scorekeepers, and how the players could concentrate I do not know.

These were the Moscow City Championships — the

Tennis championships . . . .

women's and men's finals. The players took very long rests between sets. The language of the scoring was half traditional
and half Sovietized. That is, once in a while they would say
"Nol" (meaning zero), and the rest of the time they would
say "Love."

Both women players were "dead pan" throughout and
showed no expression or personality whatsoever. They wore
silk shorts of a cream color and white T-shirts. When the
women's matches were finished, the court was swept up by
an old peasant woman in a white kerchief wielding a twig
broom.

The ground strokes of the Russians seemed quite good but
their serves, volleys, overhead smashes, and network were
poor.

The women's finals started at 11.00 A.M. and the men's
at 12.45 P.M. Bright blue sunny day, very hot, and no shade
whatsoever. Factory surroundings, in spite of the fact that
the court was in a park. Old red brick factory buildings and
red tin roofs and unpainted board fences. However, all the
fences were covered with small red flags fluttering in the
breeze. The umpire, who was dressed in his shirt sleeves,
folded a copy of *Pravda* into a cocked hat and put it on his
head for protection from the sun.

There were two small ball boys who were quite casual
about their jobs and several times they left balls in the
middle of the court during play.

The players' club and dressing room was directly behind
the backstop and over it was a big red star.

Only three or four hundred spectators sitting on the six
rows of the wooden stands. The big thrill of the day for me
was that I sat directly behind Lepeshinskaya, technically the
most perfect dancer in all of Russia, and in many ways consid-

ered a greater ballerina than Ulanova. I sat directly behind
her and my knees kept nudging her back. She is small, and
"firm" and now has henna-colored hair in strong contrast
to her blue eyes. The high instep of her foot arched over
her fashionable red shoes as she crossed her legs. She wore
a French-looking silk scarf, low on the back of her head,
and the scarf matched her skirt. Seeing Lepeshinskaya in this
way was a real treat because none of us now has a good opportunity to see any of the ballerinas or artists except across
the footlights.

All in all, the skill of the Russian players does not approach that of Western players. In fact they seem quite
amateurish.

The spectators appeared quite a bit different from the
average Russian you see on the street. They were all dressed
with a little more style and somehow the whole atmosphere
seemed rather cosmopolitan. I found out about these
matches by reading the most popular paper in Russia,
Evening Moscow, which gives relatively more sports news
and relatively more local news than any other Moscow paper.
The tickets were very inexpensive and I had no trouble in
buying them at the gate early this morning.

AUGUST 14, 1951

Rough drafts of a series of picture postcards sent home:
  Dear Mother and Brother:
  This is a photograph of Tchaikovsky's home at Klin, which
I visited recently. Klin is one of the very few places outside
of Moscow we are allowed to visit by car — and so I have
always been especially anxious to make the trip.
  I organized the party: an extremely attractive British girl

A trip to Klin . . . .

who is an Oxford graduate and one of the Joint Press Reading Service translators; the only British correspondent here (*Sunday Times* of London); and a First Secretary of the American Embassy — a very select crew.

Every moment of our visit to Tchaikovsky's home was fascinating. There is so much to write that — since I bought a package of postcards — I think I shall send you a series on the subject.

So I leave you now as we streak out of Moscow, down the Leningrad Highway, to the countryside of Klin, eighty-five kilometers to the northwest. . . .

On our trip to Klin we took the correspondent's car (rented by him from the British Embassy), a tiny, broken-down British Humber — and his wild Russian driver (as you probably have been reading in the papers, no American here can get a driver's license).

The car was the correspondent's contribution; and the British girl provided a picnic lunch, and the First Secretary and I brought along beer and wine.

In the usual picnic fashion, everybody had a different idea about where to stop for lunch by the side of the road, but the driver was going so fast it was always too late to stop. Finally, a few miles this side of Klin, we managed to halt — in a spot almost exactly like the one on this card (which is a photograph taken in the environs of Klin).

We had just started to cool our beer and wine in a muddy cow-pasture brook, and to settle down on the edge of a hayfield, when a uniformed militiaman, heavy with revolvers, suddenly appeared over the hill and silently walked toward us. *(To be continued).* . . .

. . . . **An interrupted picnic**

At the end of the last chapter, a sinister and silent militia-man was walking up the path (almost exactly like the one pictured here). For a moment his outline was black against the hilltop horizon, and then he came up to us, and asked, politely but firmly: "What are you doing here?" (As a matter of fact, we had really expected him, as the Leningrad Highway is completely closed to foreigners — except for the special trip to Klin, about which, incidentally, we have to notify the Soviet Foreign Office forty-eight hours in advance — and the great favor of traveling to Tchaikovsky's house does not include stopping by the side of the road, even for a minute.) We replied that we were foreign diplomats having a picnic in a cow pasture — and would he like some beer which we were cooling in the brook. He declined with an extremely formal "thank you," gave us five minutes in which to leave, and then disappeared behind us in the undergrowth.

In four and one half minutes we had picked up every eggshell and beer-bottle cap and were on our way. The only other incident of the journey was on the return trip — *three* flat tires. . . .

Late in the afternoon we arrived at this gate to Tchaikovsky's home, and drove up the short drive to the house itself (as pictured in the first card I sent).

It was here that Tchaikovsky spent the last two years of his life, 1892–93 (and it was here, in this spot, that he wrote among other major works, the Sixth — or "Pathétique" — Symphony; in view of all this, you may want to play it, right now, in honor of my visit).

Tchaikovsky moved to Klin because "he wanted to have peace, to be alone — removed from the uproar of Moscow

Tchaikovsky's nephew . . . .

and St. Petersburg." These words are in quotation marks because they were told to me that afternoon by — of all people — Tchaikovsky's nephew, a fascinating seventy-seven-year-old gentleman named Davidov, who acted as our guide. And he will be the subject of my next card. . . .

You will remember that in my last card I was telling you about Tchaikovsky's nephew, Davidov, who served as our guide at Klin. I am sending you this photograph of Tchaikovsky (taken in 1893, the year of his death), not because it looks like Tchaikovsky, but because it looks *exactly* like Davidov. The resemblance is fantastic (even down to the last white hair of the beard and mustache, the style of which Davidov obviously affects).

Since Davidov, the son of Tchaikovsky's younger sister, was nineteen when the composer died in 1893 ("indeed, he died in my own bed, in my quarters in St. Petersburg"), he must be seventy-seven years old now. He was dressed in an unpressed white summer suit, without a tie, but with Soviet ribbons on his coat!

His eyes were young and bright blue; his manner worldly (quite a phenomenon in Russia these days); and his English was without accent (although, as he said, "the words themselves are forgotten — because of lack of practice"). What he told us in that perfect English I shall pass on in the next chapter. . . .

More *re* Davidov, who has his office on the ground floor of the house, behind the garden bushes which you see in this photograph:

"When Tchaikovsky lived here," Davidov said, "his rooms

. . . . and the composer's bedroom

were all on the second floor, with the windows of his bedroom, where he did all his composing, looking out on the
garden." Then Davidov told us, "Tchaikovsky got up at seven
in the morning every day, and started to work at eight-thirty;
he worked steadily until two, and then had dinner; after
that, he took a walk for two hours or so, far into the country
and back — always alone; he never worked at night."

My next cards will show you the interiors of the simple
upstairs rooms, where the composer spent most of his hours,
and where I spent one of my hours — and one of my best. . . .

This is a picture of Tchaikovsky's bedroom, which I mentioned in the last card. As you can see, it is a bare room for
mid-Victorian days — and to me it seemed lonely and lamentable (particularly if you imagined Tchaikovsky climbing into that hard, narrow brass bed, and then dreaming
away). The most interesting object in the room, in fact,
in the whole house, unfortunately is not visible in this shot
— and that is the simple rough wooden kitchen table at
which he did all his composing (apparently he heard everything in his head, and he did not write at his big grand
piano, which fills the adjoining living room).

The kitchen table was simply a stripped-down workbench
— Tchaikovsky even had the flat middle drawer removed
for convenience's sake — and it was here that, in twenty-
seven hectic days, he wrote the entire "Pathétique." "And,"
Davidov added, "the composer dedicated it to my
brother." . . .

We now pass on to Tchaikovsky's overstuffed living room
and study. In the foreground you see his big Victorian desk,

Unsung notes . . . .

which he used only for letter-writing. The biggest — and most important — object in the room you cannot see: Tchaikovsky's piano (which is to the right, behind the desk).

One of the high points in our visit took place in the far corner, in front of the bookcase, when Davidov pulled a book of Russian poetry from the shelf and showed us pages of music which Tchaikovsky had scribbled in beside the lines of verse as he read them — unsung notes on old, yellow paper. But I thought "unsung" too soon — because, almost immediately, Davidov began to sing them to us, in a quiet, mournful high-pitched voice.

"I used to be an opera singer," he said with some pride, "but now I am an agronomist."

AUGUST 18, 1951

9.30 P.M.   Exactly half an hour ago I set sail on board the *Mikhail Kalinin* for a weekend excursion trip to the so-called "Moscow Sea." We departed from Khimki, the "River Station" on the outskirts of the city, and tonight we shall steam along the Moscow-Volga Canal. This important canal, linking the capital with the Volga River, was built in the 1930's, reportedly by slave labor. The canal runs almost due north of Moscow, and is a little over 100 kilometers in length, a large part of the course being made up of a chain of small lakes immediately after you leave Moscow — and we are sailing through one of those lakes at the moment. The Moscow Sea itself, located in Kalinin Oblast, is really a part of the Volga system, and the canal runs into this large body of water at the east end, just south of the point where the Volga flows out. Since this is now the only boat trip of any

. . . . . **Overnight on the Moscow-Volga canal**

length which we are permitted to take within the borders of the Soviet Union, I am going to try to make every minute count, and, in doing so, will keep a running account, an hour-by-hour log.

10.00 P.M. Not much excitement so far — except for a terrific bump a few minutes ago, when we hit a huge raft floating free on the canal.

10.30 P.M. I have just returned from a tour of the *Mikhail Kalinin,* during which I noticed, on a bulkhead placard, that the ship was built in 1937. I also noted that this excursion boat has three classes (and once again I reflected, with wonder, about Stalin's classless society). We, incidentally, are traveling second class (and the cost of this weekend trip is 109 rubles per person). One other observation: the promenade deck is called "the terrace."

11.00 P.M. Heavy fog is beginning to drift low over the canal banks and surrounding meadows. As a result, our arrival at the Moscow Sea early tomorrow morning will probably be delayed.

11.30 P.M. The ship doesn't seem to be very crowded. Aside from our group, the only other foreigners on board are two families of Pakistanis. The Russian passengers (including children) are keeping to themselves, as usual — and are far from frolicsome. Indeed, the entire atmosphere of the ship is oppressive. I am writing this note on a dirty food-stained cloth on a table in the dining salon, where we are now having a little vodka and caviar to cheer ourselves up — but this room is turning out to be the most deadly place of all. In fact, it is just about the ungayest spot I have ever been in. The food is bad, the silence is worse.

Midnight. Time to go to bed. Perhaps my dreams will be

The Moscow Sea . . . .

pleasant. I have just heard the lonely blast of our boat whistle echoing over the endless, flat countryside — and it matches my mood.

AUGUST 19, 1951

7.00 A.M. I got up early to watch our entrance into the Moscow Sea — but it was too early, as we have been delayed by the fog last night. The dining room, unfortunately, will not be open for another two hours — and so, to pass the time, I went into an adjoining cubicle a few moments ago to have a shave. The ship's barber enticed me onto his chair while I was arguing, in vain, with a waitress for a cup of tea. The barber reeked of garlic, and now I reek of Russian "Eau de Cologne."

8.00 A.M. We arrive at the Moscow Sea.

9.00 A.M. We stayed at the Moscow Sea for only forty minutes. The "Sea" turned out to be a desolate, flooded area — with absolutely nothing of interest in sight. Most of our time here was spent tied up to a bleak barge landing called "Bolshaya Volga." Some of us did go ashore, and we walked as far as we dared through the meadows. When we returned to the landing on hearing the blast of the whistle, we saw that some peasants had gathered on the bank with baskets of food for sale: a few fresh eggs and some cans of milk and four or five tomatoes. And so the excursion ended.

10.00 A.M. Returning along the canal during daylight hours, I now have a better idea of what the countryside looks like. It is beautiful at times, but very monotonous, made up mostly of long, low fields, with green undergrowth, and with a few dark evergreens and white birches on the distant horizon. In the immediate foreground, three or four feet of

. . . . the blare of loudspeakers

rocks line the canal from the edge of the water to the top of the bank. And here the only sign of life is an occasional skinny kid, in black trunks, swimming in the canal.

11.00 A.M. The *Mikhail Kalinin* continues to creep along at a rate of about seven or eight knots — although the engineer's assistant reports a speed of "eighteen kilometers."

12.00 Noon. We are now passing Dmitrov, on the east bank. This is the only town of any size on our route, and it is supposed to have a population of close to 10,000 — but it doesn't look like much more than a large village to me. I hear that Dmitrov has iron and metal and cellulose factories, but few of these are visible from our low level. The town dates from the twelfth century and it still has a twelfth-century aspect. As far as I know, Dmitrov is mentioned in Russian history books at least twice — and in both of these instances the occasion is an invasion. In the first case, the city suffered damage from the Tatars in Russia's Middle Ages — a fact which shows how far west hordes from the East have swept across Russia. The second case is more recent: Dmitrov, which is only forty miles from Moscow, was reached by the Germans in December, 1941 — a fact which shows how far east hordes from the West have swept across Russia.

1.00 P.M. I am getting so accustomed to the constant blare of loudspeakers everywhere I go that I forgot to mention that here, too, on board ship, Moscow Radio has been trumpeting at us every single minute of the excursion. Speakers are strategically placed in all public rooms and along the deck — and the only way to get away from the sound is to bury your head in a pillow, and that is just what I am about to do.

2.00 P.M. The Moscow-Volga is certainly not a crowded

Landscape . . . .

canal. In fact, it looks very deserted — and that is strange, because it must be one of Russia's most important waterways. The only traffic I have seen so far has consisted of a few long flat river barges, and one or two small excursion boats. We have just passed close by one of the latter, and there did not seem to be much gaiety there, either. The bright red flag, with hammer and sickle, flapping on the sternpost, was the only flutter of activity and the only spot of color.

3.00 P.M. During our trip today we have gone through four small locks — and they did boast a remarkable feature. Each one was lined with flower beds. But even these flowers, as bright and carefully tended as they were, seemed, somehow, pathetic.

4.00 P.M. At this moment I see, through the starboard rail, a ferryman sitting alone in his rowboat, patiently waiting by the canal bank, at the edge of a dirt country road, which drops abruptly to the level of the water. He doesn't stir an inch, but just looks straight ahead. Behind him, neat stacks of yellow hay are piled along the bank, and beyond, three farm horses stand absolutely motionless, three black statues in the green fields. It is as though the whole countryside were posing for a photograph, with every living thing standing still, expressionless as well as motionless. In looking at this static scene, at this cheerless solitude, I have to smile when I think of a passage from Gogol which I memorized last year during my Russian studies, the passage from *Dead Souls* which goes like this:

And, Russia, art not thou too flying onwards like a spirited troika that nothing can overtake? The road is smoking under thee, the bridges rumble, everything falls back and is left behind! The spectator stands still struck dumb by the divine miracle: is it not a flash of lightning from heaven? What is the meaning of this terrifying onrush? What mysterious force is hidden in this troika, never seen before? Ah, horses, horses — what horses! Is the whirlwind hidden under your manes? Is there some delicate sense tingling in every vein? They hear the familiar song over their heads — at once in unison they strain their iron chests and scarcely touching the earth with their hoofs are transformed almost into straight lines flying through the air — and the troika rushes on, full of divine inspiration . . . . Russia, whither flyest thou? Answer! She gives no answer. The ringing of the bells melts into music; the air, torn to shreds, whirs and rushes like the wind, everything there is on earth is flying by, and the other states and nations, with looks askance, make way for her and draw aside.

5.00 P.M.   I have just been watching a poor old woman, dressed in coarse, greasy clothes, carefully carrying out one of her duties for the fatherland. Can she be a member of the crew? Squatting on the fantail, she was holding the red Soviet flag of our stern post in her rough hand, and was trying to trim the torn, shredded edge with a pair of scissors. Perhaps she, too, had seen the bright, new flag on the other excursion boat. Occasionally she lifted her eyes from her lap to look at the white sails of the sport boats on the lake through which we are now steaming.

6.00 P.M.   We arrive back at Khimki — with the Moscow skyline dark against the evening clouds. As I leave the ship, I notice that the old woman is still sitting on the deck, patching her flag.

a very pleasant dinner at the Kirks' . . . . .

SEPTEMBER 5, 1951

I'm just back from a very pleasant dinner party given by the Kirks. They are wonderful hosts, as well as perfect official representatives of our country. During an evening like this you can forget — almost — where you are. It's the same wonderful almost-entire escape you used to feel in the war when you got to some dream-world Officers' Club after a disagreeable time. You don't quite forget the overwhelming Thing that's going on near at hand, but that fact even adds to the luxury of knowing you don't have to cope with it for a while.

After dinner some of us inevitably got talking about Americans and Russians — the people, not their "systems." Someone pointed out an interesting thing. There is absolutely no outlet, here, for the urge to "join" — to be a member of an organization which will outlast the individual.

I say there is no outlet for this urge in Russia, but the important fact, of course, is that there *is one* — the Communist Party. You can't join anything that would correspond to the Rotary Club, or the Elks, or any purely social club either. There is no "Russian Legion," no political party (except the one); no social service "activity." You can't even be a "member" of the Church — though you can go to its services. What would an American "joiner" — male or female — do in this situation? Probably just about what the average Russian does — concentrate on becoming a member of the one and only organization — the Communist Party. It's not an easy ambition to fulfill; which adds to membership some of the thrill of exclusiveness.

To get into the Party, the easiest way (and it is not easy), is to start in childhood and climb through the grades of the

· · · · · · · · · · · **Party membership**

youth organizations. If you get into the Komsomol (Young Communist League), you have a chance to graduate into a local "cell" of the Party. It's impossible to tell just how many party members there are. The last official figure was six million members in 1946 — about 3 per cent of the population. It fluctuates with changes of policy. For a while there will be a drive for membership, and then a "purge" will take place. This alternation keeps the exclusive appeal of Party membership, and also makes pretty sure that only the most Simon-pure believers are "in" for any length of time.

One other thing I haven't mentioned. There are a good many privileges for the Elect; some, at least, of the daily petty irritations of life are partly ironed out. On the other hand, as one of the elect, the members are, of course, under closer observation, and probably are expected to show forth a purer "Regularity" than the average citizen. Rank here, as elsewhere, hath not only its privileges, but its perils — and in Russia the perils are ultimate.

SEPTEMBER 6, 1951

At Spaso House, a few days ago, the Ambassador asked me to give him any suggestions I might have for the speech he is going to make in New York on his return to the U.S.A. a few weeks from now. Here are two or three of the ideas which I typed out for him today — ideas which to me are all-important:

1. The words "freedom" and "liberty" and "democracy" are now so soiled and shopworn, as a result of political demagogy in the U.S.A., or so perverted, as the result of deliberate

truth is more explosive than atoms . . . . . .

double-talk in the U.S.S.R., that, in the usual platform context, they are without meaning. They are still, however, the most important words in our world of time and space — and somehow they must be used. I personally find a solution to this problem in the phrases of the second paragraph of the Declaration of Independence, the power and beauty of which hit you so hard that I think we should repeat them every day and hold them in front of us, whether we are living in America or Russia: "We hold these truths to be self-evident, that all men are created equal, that they are endowed by their Creator with certain unalienable Rights, that among these are Life, Liberty, and the Pursuit of Happiness." When one lives in Moscow, one realizes that these simple words are dynamite — more revolutionary than anything ever said by Marx or Lenin or Stalin. If we really believe that truth is more explosive than atoms, and that truth is on our side, we should pay more attention to these thirty-six words, it seems to me, and should accept them literally, boldly, and without qualification. But even more important than that: we should practise at home what we preach abroad — boldly and literally and without qualification.

2. This brings up the question — and I think it is one of the most pressing questions in our life — of whether or not the desire for freedom is self-generating. Although this problem may seem somewhat academic, belonging either to the realm of history or metaphysics, it is, in my view, a most practical matter — particularly with regard to our relations with the U.S.S.R. In other words, is our policy — either short-term or long-range — going to be based on the theory that the Russian people (especially the younger generations) no longer know about freedom, and so do not care about it

. . . . mortally sick in spirit
and will not fight for it (that is, the assumption that human
freedom is not self-generating, and can be completely eradi-
cated in a society forever); or is our working policy going to
be based on the theory that the more the Russians themselves
are restricted, the more powerful will be their desire for
liberty (that is, the assumption that freedom generates itself
as a reaction to imprisonment, and so does not necessarily
have to be handed down through the generations as a sacred,
unbroken tradition, from fifth-century Athens to twentieth-
century Washington)? We must select one belief or the
other, and I, for one, choose the latter.

3. As you can see from the above, I believe that in approaching the Russians, we should emphasize universal
spiritual values rather than American material advantages.
Aside from many other factors, this choice of emphasis is
based on two down-to-earth observations: (1) it is impossible to impress the Russian people with such statements, for
example, as the fact that we have twenty million washing
machines (or whatever the figure is) when they do not know
what a washing machine is; (2) it is impossible to impress
the Russian people with such figures, even if they do comprehend them, when they can see with their own eyes that
their own standard of living is *improving*, although slowly,
year by year (and this is a process we should never discount).
By the same token, I believe that it is relatively less difficult
and much more essential to convince the Russians and other
Iron Curtain peoples that they are mortally sick in spirit —
if not in body. From our own experiences here, we should
be able to give countless examples of this sense of constant,
silent fear, this feeling, secret and unexpressed, but all-
pervasive, that the great experiment has failed. The police

"irreconcilable hatred" . . . .

state itself — with all its evil manifestations — is the most eloquent proof of this. What better proof does one need?

SEPTEMBER 7, 1951

While working on my suggestions for the Ambassador's speech, I also handed in two quotations from the works of public figures in Soviet life — passages which seem to have been overlooked by students of the Russian scene, but which strike me as being extremely enlightening, and extremely frightening.

The first is from a Soviet textbook for teachers of elementary schools (*Pedagogy* by B. P. Yesipov and N. K. Goncharov), which was published and approved for general use in 1946:

> The pupils of the Soviet school must realize that the feeling of Soviet patriotism is saturated with irreconcilable hatred toward the enemies of socialist society.
>
> Hatred gives birth to class revolutionary vigilance and creates a feeling of irreconcilability toward the class enemy; the weakening of such vigilance undermines the cause of the socialist revolution. It is necessary to learn, not only to hate the enemy, but also to struggle with him, in time to unmask him, and finally, if he does not surrender, to destroy him.

Thus, formally and officially, hatred is now a virtue, an ideal, something toward which Soviet children must stretch their hands and hearts.

The second quotation is from Stalin himself — a passage from a "Talk With Metallurgists," which was published in *Pravda* in 1934. Here are Stalin's words, on the surface so sweet, underneath so menacing:

. . . . **merely vegetable matter**

"People must be grown carefully and tenderly, just as a gardener grows a favorite fruit tree."

Thus, in Soviet terms, indeed in Stalin's own words, the Russian human being is no longer thought of even as an animal, but merely as vegetable matter. Stalin's simile of a tree is, I think, very apt — particularly when you watch the Great Gardener bending human boughs and plucking the fruit at will.

SEPTEMBER 12, 1951

Newcomers to Moscow — especially Americans — are always surprised to find that there is now television in the Soviet Union. The industry certainly is very, very far from the proportions which it has attained in the U.S.A., but progress is being made here in Russia.

The Soviet authorities must clearly see — as Lenin quickly understood with respect to the motion picture — that television affords tremendous possibilities in the field of propaganda and indoctrination.

There are varying estimates as to the number of television receivers in the Soviet Union today — but, in my opinion, the best guess is approximately 17,000. You might be interested in the strange method used to reach this figure — the only method possible. As far as I know, the latest official statistics on the subject were published about a year ago, and the total given then was approximately 8000. The only way to measure the increase since the fall of 1950 is to make a rough estimate of antennas now visible in city blocks of Moscow, and then compare that impression with the roof-line view of a year ago. Since there now seem to be a little more than twice as many antennas, the amateur statisticians arrive at the figure of 17,000. Such are the rough-and-ready calculations of foreign economists in present-day Moscow.

Of this total number of receivers, the overwhelming majority are located in Moscow (with probably two or three thousand in Leningrad, and a few hundred in such large cities as Kharkov).

According to the latest information I have, there are two models: a small, six-inch size which costs 1275 rubles — or $319 at the official, meaningless, exchange rate; and a larger model, with a screen of nine or ten inches which costs 2500 rubles.

As far as quantity of programs is concerned, I should point out that there is only one channel, and that programs on this channel are televised only in the evening for about four or five hours, on the average. The output is further cut by the usual practice of not scheduling any programs at all on at least one night a week.

On the whole, the technique of the television producers, directors, and photographers strikes me as being extremely unimaginative.

In regard to content, I must say that the programs are far different from ours — and, as far as they go, much better. None of us, of course, has an opportunity to watch television shows in a Russian home, but night after night I look at Soviet programs on an American receiver in our own quarters. And every program, without fail, consists of one or more of the following items: newsreels, documentaries, feature films, a full-length opera or ballet direct from the Bolshoi Theater (and by "full-length" I mean four hours at least), a symphony concert, a full-length musical comedy or variety show televised from one of the Moscow theaters,

. . . . **Flowers and chipped paint**

or a program of folk dancing and singing. Propaganda, indeed, is indirectly involved in many (if not most) of these programs, but the *cultural* level is invariably far, far above our own. And so is the standard of taste. That I shall maintain even, if necessary, before Messrs. McCarran and McCarthy.

SEPTEMBER 13, 1951

Moscow yards and windows in the spring and summer and fall are full of a favorite plant, called *vyunok* in Russian — a kind of bindweed, or morning-glory, with pale white and pale pink flowers. You see these most of all on the rails of sagging balconies of Moscow apartment houses and also growing straight up vertical strings, row after row, from tiny weed-smothered plots off the sidewalk, climbing to the first-floor windows, where their leaves help a bit to cover the chipped frames and peeling paint.

SEPTEMBER 27, 1951

This evening, once again, I saw Tchaikovsky's great romantic opera, *Eugene Onegin,* at the Bolshoi (with Kozlovsky singing Lensky) — and, once again, I decided (in spite of the fact that Moscow's teen-age bobby-soxers rushed screaming and pushing down to the orchestra pit to cheer Kozlovsky, faint and frail, during his curtain calls), I decided, I say, that there is not one good dramatic tenor in all of Russia. And that is strange for a nation of two hundred million singers.

Leave . . . .

SEPTEMBER 30, 1951

A few minutes after midnight last night I left Moscow for Leningrad — and for two weeks of leave in London.

I am still on the "Red Arrow" express train as I write this, sipping tea as fast as the good-natured car attendant can bring it from her ancient charcoal samovar at the end of the corridor. She seems incredulous when I gravely decline the neatly wrapped lumps of sugar she carries on her plate every time. And, all the while, I am looking out the window at the sad autumn scene: the fast-falling leaves, yellow and orange, and the brown, weather-beaten haystacks, so soon looking old and stained as they stand against the solid gray sky.

Outside my compartment door I can hear the last tremendous bars of Musorgsky's *Pictures at an Exhibition,* as the loudspeaker in our car penetrates every corner and every Soviet ear. And, although the composer was describing "the great gate at Kiev," his music now is putting me in the mood for St. Petersburg. And I am looking forward to another afternoon in the dark, dirty, icebox depths of the Cathedral of St. Peter and St. Paul, where, once again, I shall stand beside, and touch, the simple marble slabs (with their gold imperial arms) marking whatever dust remains of Peter the Great and Catherine the Great, and the bones of Alexander I and Nicholas I and Alexander II. And then, I think, I shall walk out the cathedral door, into the cobblestone courtyard of the fortress, where, thanks to the few men and women whose tombs now sink into the stone floor a few feet away, so many noble Russians once hung from the gallow posts, adding their swaying shadows to the still, thin strip of

· · · · · · · · · · · **The frontier again**

shade made by the golden needle of the church spire high above.

NOVEMBER 1, 1951

Back again in Moscow, arriving at the White Russia Railway Station early this evening in the first snowstorm of the winter.

I made the gruesome three-day train trip alone (a mistake), through Berlin, Warsaw, Brest-Litovsk, Minsk, Smolensk, and Borodino — thus tearing a five-foot, seven-inch gap in the Iron Curtain at a series of terror-stricken places on the map of Europe, one right after the other, as I moved deeper and deeper into the heartland: first the eastern sector of Berlin, then the eastern zone of Germany, then the Polish border, then the Russian border — each frontier progressively a little more lonesome, and a little more smothered with barbed wire and silence, than the last.

NOVEMBER 2, 1951

I should mention without fail, in connection with my description of yesterday's train trip, a rather remarkable incident that took place in the dining car just outside Brest-Litovsk, en route to Minsk.

At Brest I had been shut up for two hours in a dark windowless room of the station, as I waited for the "courier" express train to Moscow. The Intourist and station officials would not let me out of the room even for a cup of tea in the station buffet. Perhaps they were afraid that if I were outside, I would have one more look at this critical frontier point between Poland and Russia — another look at the

a ticklish situation . . . .

Bug River, with its iron latticework bridge, and with its
countless concrete dugout fortifications rising in rows from
the sandy bank, at the lonely high wooden watchtower overlooking the scene (the scene which consisted mostly of pigs
and cattle browsing peacefully in the mud and grass and
purple cabbage plants at the foot of the dugouts) — all of
which I had noticed in passing on the local daytime Polish
train I had taken from Warsaw in the morning.

So I was extremely hungry when I got onto the Moscow
express. And, to my surprise, I found that it had a dining
car (the only diner I have seen so far on my travels in the
Soviet Union). As soon as I had put my bags into my compartment, I rushed into the diner just as the train was pulling out of the station at 6.30. The car was already full —
except for one lone seat — and it was full of troops, Soviet
officers and soldiers presumably on their way back to Russia
from duty in one of the Eastern European satellite nations.
And the car was noisy — in fact, the noisiest place I have yet
seen (or, rather, listened to) in Russia. And the reason for
the noise was obviously all the vodka and beer and wine
which was spilling from bottles right and left — and perhaps
another reason was just high spirits at the prospect of returning home.

I took the only free seat, and was immediately mobbed by
at least a dozen soldiers. Naturally I was conspicuous — because I was the only civilian in the car, in the first place, and
because I was clearly a foreigner, in the second place. And
when everybody present found out that I was an American,
to boot, their confusion, and at the same time their curiosity,
turned the scene into an uproar. It was a very ticklish situation for me because some of the officers were sober and some

were extremely drunk and some were in-between — and so
it was hard to talk sense to all of them at once. Further, some
of them obviously feared and hated me, and others wanted
to put their arms around me in friendship. The scene, I
thought to myself, could easily get out of control. I drank
two quick vodkas at their invitation (and at their expense),
and left in a hurry, in spite of my hunger, and in spite of this
wonderful opportunity to see Russia in the raw. If I hadn't
done so, a great new international incident might have been
splashed on the front pages of *Pravda* the next morning, or,
perhaps, in the secret files of the State Department or a Congressional investigating committee.

NOVEMBER 5, 1951

Notes on drinking in Moscow, the mores of Muscovites: the
most interesting aspect of the drinking problem, at least in
Moscow, is an institution called the *vytrezvitel*. That is a
Russian word that has only one meaning, only one dictionary
translation. It seems to me very significant that the language
has to have a particular word for this one purpose — and the
translation is "sobering-up station" — that, and nothing else.

As far as I can see, it is a sort of Turkish bath and apparently the Russians have had these institutions for centuries.

Right next to our house is Vytrezvitel No. 3, and the sign
hanging over the sidewalk says that the building is operated
by the Moscow militia.

No American, to my knowledge, has ever been in one of
these establishments, but as I pass along the sidewalk I can
see the furnaces going day and night through the gutter-level
window and grating. And these furnaces go in the summer

The "Sobering-up Station" . . . .

too because all year long the steam comes out from under the sidewalk.

The Moscow militia have a sort of "Black Maria" vehicle (except that all these trucks have red crosses on them) and several roam through the city throughout the night. I would say that one of these trucks arrives at our "sobering-up station" on the average of every half-hour and when they stop the victims inside are the most passed-out people you have ever seen. The bodies are rolled out over the tailboard, thrown onto a stretcher, and carried past the wooden gate, into the depths of the vytrezvitel.

We do not know for sure, but I have heard that the fee is 30 rubles a night. Apparently the patients have a steam bath, a cold shower, and then they sleep it off.

The main reason for the deadly results of Russian drinking, of course, is that the intoxication comes primarily from vodka, although wines and beers of various qualities are served in the same cafés and working men's bars. The Russians do not have whiskey or gin.

I do not know whether Russian drinking habits are significant or not but they must have some bearing on present-day social problems. The Russians, to put it simply, drink differently than we do in the West. There is no loud boisterous drinking, no gay drinking. There are no crowded cocktail parties with people standing with martinis in hand, chattering at the top of their lungs.

Rather, here there is a kind of sullen, deadly drinking. People, it seems to me, drink to get drunk and pass out and they do that all over the street. Many nights I have seen pathetic cases of unconscious huddled figures crumpled on the sidewalk next to a barroom door.

In all this I certainly do not want to give the impression that Moscow is a drunken city. Actually, I don't think there is as much drinking here as in our cities. For one thing, most of the population does no mass drinking at all. For example, women do not drink in public places. Fewer people drink, but with more disastrous results. These results are so spectacular that they catch your eye, and if you are not careful to analyze the situation, you will come away with a false impression.

All this brings up the question of the famous state banquets about which we have read so much in recent wartime memoirs. Those days, of course, are all over with as far as Westerners are concerned. We have no way of knowing whether ten or twenty or thirty toasts "bottoms up" in vodka go on night after night at state banquets given by the Kremlin for the Eastern European satellites and the Chinese, but my guess is that these banquets *are* going on and that there are many hangovers behind the Iron Curtain.

NOVEMBER 19, 1951

As of now, the celebrated Moscow Metro has thirty-five stations, and the underground lines cover more than a hundred kilometers.

Metro construction started about twenty years ago under the direction of British engineers and was continued even during the war. In January, 1944, the third line was put in operation, and the fourth, the "Big Underground Ring," was started.

The first sector of the latter was put in operation on the

Thoughts while shaving . . . .

first day of 1950, and the second sector will soon be ready for service.

NOVEMBER 23, 1951

Stray thoughts (including one or two world-shaking observations) while shaving this morning:

I don't want to go to work today — one more hour of carefully translating carefully written lies, and I shall blow my cupola. . . .

The British here certainly think the Americans behave like fools in Russia. One minute they say our Embassy people don't get out and around enough, and just spin from one cocktail party to another. Then, the next minute, they say that when we *do* go out, in Moscow or other cities, we do too much, and we do it too conspicuously. In many ways, the British seem more worried about us than about the Russians. Now I sound exactly like the Soviet press, which is constantly playing up what they call "Anglo-American contradictions" (one of their favorite phrases) — so maybe I had better think about something else. . . .

Think, for example, about my good luck at having a beer with Bogolyubskaya, one of Russia's most beautiful ballerinas, in the buffet of the Bolshoi a few nights ago. Bogolyubskaya has been awarded the awkward (but prized) title of "Honored Artist of the R.S.F.S.R." (Russian Soviet Federated Socialist Republic), a typical Soviet honorific — but actually this young ballerina, with her small pale face and lovely limbs, seldom dances. When she does, her best role is that of Maria in *Bakhchisaraisky Fontan,* and there she has a chance to show the rare, sensitive quality of her dancing.

· · · · · · · · **A beer with Bogolyubskaya**

The phrase, "having a beer with," is boasting a bit, I admit. In fact, it's boasting quite a lot. Bogolyubskaya was at the same table with me, yes, and when she leaned over to drink her beer, our elbows almost touched, and I could see the perfect part in her reddish hair and the restless look in her eyes, as she searched for something way in the distance. But she was escorted by somebody else (a short, fat, greasy Russian), and the only reason I was sitting there at all was that it was the only vacant seat when I entered the buffet during one of the Bolshoi's endless intermissions. (Probably all the other Russians present had recognized her — or at least they had sensed the *presence* of somebody important, somebody unusually stylish and a bit special — and had been decent enough, or frightened enough, to give her a little privacy.) Tonight I am going to see *Swan Lake* again (for the fourth time), and I hope that she will dance in the *pas de trois* of the first act — one of the most perfect moments in the most perfect of ballets. . . .

What Moscow needs most — aside from a flood of freedom, wild, abandoned freedom — is a tidal wave of paint, with wild, abandoned splashes of clean color, on every door and window, on every wall and roof. But maybe, if freedom is far away, bleak, chipped, weather-beaten walls are more appropriate houses for hearts still in chains. . . .

We have been having wonderful weather — tingling temperatures, bright shiny days, clean, clear air, a pure sky. But the atmosphere is *toxic*. . . .

What a scene that was yesterday, at the swinging door of the main entrance of Moscow's most fashionable hotel, the Metropole — the only swinging door in Moscow. A peasant family just in from the country — a cotton-padded farmer,

still shaving . . . .

his wife, and three children — stood outside on the sidewalk, transfixed in astonishment, trying to figure out how the door worked. (What were they doing there, anyway?) Then, as they all screwed up their courage, they attempted to get inside, not taking turns, but in one body. Clearly they had never seen a swinging door before, and their bewilderment at getting bumped in the plate-glass partition as the door whirled around was heartbreaking. Do I, as an American looking at the possible future enemy, laugh or weep at this? . . .

No, I don't want to go to work today.

NOVEMBER 24, 1951

Still shaving, still thinking:

Today (even though it is Saturday) I want to go to work very much — because, as I keep saying to myself, the work is important. The Soviet press, as poisonous as it is, is, nonetheless, our main source of information about the Communist world — and so it must be translated every day with care, and with speed. The fancy Ministers, Counselors, and Military Attachés at the Chancery, many of whom don't know a word of Russian, may look with diplomatic disdain down their noses at such grubby, low-paid work — but it is reassuring to remember the fact that the words we feed them every hour form the bulk of their day-by-day reports, and so serve, indeed, as the basis of most of their decisions. Already this year our Joint Press Reading Service has put out, at breakneck speed, close to five million words (with a very small number of errors among them) — and I, for one, am proud to have contributed my half million (even though most of the errors were mine) . . . .

· · · · · · · · · · · **"pogrom" is Russian**

I can't get out of my head the beauty of Bogolyubskaya. Yes, she *did* dance in *Swan Lake* last night. In the *pas de trois* of the first act she whirled forth, straight out of a Fragonard painting, all elegance and delicate sparkle. And she was as supple and frail, and as expressive, behind the footlights as she was behind the bottles of Zhigulevskoe beer. . . .

To forget Bogolyubskaya for a minute, and get back to translating work: I learned last week, while tearing through my tattered dictionary for some phrase or other, that one of the very few — in fact, one of the half-dozen — purely Russian words that have become a permanent part of the English language (as well as every language on earth) is the noun *pogrom*. That is a true Russian word, meaning "massacre," and it undoubtedly comes from the Russian verb *gromit,* meaning to "raid," "smash up," "sack," "loot," "annihilate." It must be that this little fact has large significance. . . .

The snow on the window ledge of my bedroom is already half a foot deep, and it will remain that way, pure and untouched, for the next five months. And that reminds me that I should begin to measure the length of the icicle hanging over the back door in the courtyard of our office. Last winter, in the last week of March, it had dripped into a gigantic, five-foot stalactite before finally breaking off. I'll check this on my walk to work this morning — to such innocent interests, and simple joys, do we here in Moscow resort, Kremlin charges to the contrary notwithstanding. . . .

It is strange what little things stick in my memory during my life in Russia. I can't forget, for example, the sweat pouring down the face of David Oistrakh, as he played the Tchaikovsky *Violin Concerto* in an all-Tchaikovsky program in Tchaikovsky Hall one night three weeks ago. Now, for

a little brown net . . . .

more than ten years (ever since he won the International
Violinists' Competition in Brussels in 1937, at the age of
twenty-nine) Oistrakh has been considered the foremost
concert violinist of modern Russia, and many praise him as
the greatest violin virtuoso in the world today — and so I
should have listened every moment to the music he made,
and studied his technique as he made it. But, instead, I
watched in fascination, with the help of opera glasses, as the
beads of perspiration gathered on his forehead, and then
slipped down his fat cheeks and heavy chin, finally splashing
onto the shiny surface of the violin itself. . . .

Another little image I can't get out of my mind's eye (in
fact, I keep telling myself to make a note of it in my diary,
thinking, for some reason, that it is important) is the most
ordinary of material things, a very cheap, and rather pathetic,
household article — the little brown shopping net carried
by all Moscow housewives. Almost invariably the contents
are one or more of the following, but nothing else: six or
seven potatoes, half a cabbage, a dirty green bottle of milk,
a loaf of bread, and maybe a carrot or two sticking out one
of the holes. I don't know whether I call this object "rather
pathetic" because of the cabbage and carrot, selected after
so much thought and calculation, after so much fumbling
with rumpled rubles and kopecks in a dirty pocket, or because of the look on the face of the woman who carries this
bundle with such care. . . .

A Russian girl told me yesterday that, according to an old
Russian tradition, a woman would wear flowers with the
blossoms pointed up if her heart were free, and with the
blossoms turned down if her affections were "engaged." I
would like to verify this custom — but that, I know, is im-

. . . . **ash trays on the sidewalks**

possible for many reasons, and chiefly because, after nearly
a year in Moscow, I have yet to see a corsage, or a real flower
of any kind, worn by a Russian girl. I also learned from the
same woman that, in Russia, the colors of flowers have significance: red — love; white — purity; blue — fidelity;
yellow — farewell; green — treachery. . . .

That's quite an idea the Soviet authorities have of fixing
little metal ash trays on the sidewalk walls of public buildings along the main streets of downtown Moscow. The only
trouble is that the trays are not placed frequently enough —
and, if you don't time your smoking accurately, you'll burn
your fingers before you get a chance to crush your cigarette
butt in the ash tray on the next block. But it is better to
burn your finger tips than to stamp the cigarette out on the
sidewalk or street. Will I ever forget one of my first days in
Moscow when I did just that — that is, stamp out my cigarette stub on the pavement — and a militiaman rushed over
and, as haughtily as he could, told me to pick up the
mess? . . .

In describing Moscow, a writer or artist should paint his
picture not in black or white, certainly, nor even in black
and white — but in chiaroscuro. That's the word. . . .

I wonder how many Christians throughout the world pray
for Stalin and Malenkov, Molotov and Beria, every night.
My hunch is that maybe one or two (if that) in several millions do so — and yet these few men, of all people on earth,
need their help the most. . . .

I do, as I said, want to go to work today — particularly
with such a clean, smooth face.

A state funeral . . . .

NOVEMBER 25, 1951

I attended a public funeral yesterday. I saw the lying-in-state of a prominent Soviet official, named Efremov. All this took place in the fantastically beautiful Hall of Columns of Dom Soyuzov, which used to be the most fashionable place in Moscow, the Club of the Nobility, where all the big balls were held.

Private funerals can be held in Greek Orthodox churches if the family wishes, but all public funerals take place in secular buildings with no church connection or sponsorship whatsoever. And that reminds me of the first private funeral I saw in Russia — quite by accident.

I was attending the morning mass in the old cathedral in Novodevichy Monastery, the floor of which was packed with Russians crowded elbow to elbow. I nudged my way gradually toward the center altar in order to see better what was going on and to listen to the wonderful singing.

While I was making this progress toward the front I bumped into something and leaned my elbow on a wooden shelf in the middle of the floor. The shelf of course turned out to be an open coffin, lined with satin, and I found that my arm had slipped inside beside the corpse of a pale, old woman. I naturally withdrew as fast as I could, particularly when I saw that clinging to the edge of the coffin were five little children whose hands were held high on the edge of the open casket in order, I suppose, to get a last look at their mother or grandmother, whichever she was.

The atmosphere of the Efremov funeral was completely different. I stood on the sidewalk for several minutes at the end of a queue which slowly wound its way in through the various halls and staircases of the old Club of the Nobility.

. . . . **The Hall of Columns**

Finally, we reached the Hall of Columns, a large rectangular room lined with shiny white marble Corinthian columns with an interior balcony running along all four walls at a second-story level.

The chandeliers were of delicate gold and crystal — a large one hanging between each pair of columns, with a smaller one above at the balcony level.

As I entered the room in the black, silent line, I could see that the coffin was at the far end, banked with hundreds of square yards of artificial flowers. Perhaps it was the color of the flowers that made the face in the coffin look so milk-white. The citizens in line moved without noise, slowly and coldly, past the bier and the mourning family and friends who sat for hours in front of everybody, seated on old wooden folding funeral chairs. The most striking part of the scene, however, was the full symphony orchestra, which was playing over and over again the first movement of Tchaikovsky's "Pathétique" Symphony.

After viewing the corpse the line filed down another series of stairs and hallways, this time in the ancient servants' quarters, and then we ended up out a back door down in a dark, dismal courtyard, and then onto the streets of Moscow.

Who were all these people and why did they come? I do not know. The fact that I do not know is typical of the millions of little things that we are not permitted to know here in Moscow.

NOVEMBER 29, 1951

I have just returned tonight from watching the Russians doing something they enjoy almost more than anything else in the world, and something which they do better than any-

What the Russians enjoy most . . . .

body else in the world. I watched them playing chess.

I have noticed chess-playing everywhere, on trains, in public parks, through windows of private houses. Even Stalin takes a personal interest in the chess championships of the U.S.S.R.

The match tonight was between Botvinnik, the world's champion before the war — the last time that Russians played abroad — and Keres, the U.S.S.R. champion — both of course, Russians. The match took place in the Soviet Army Club in Moscow — and I had a terrible time getting tickets. For three days I tried unsuccessfully. Finally, after dinner this evening, I decided to take a chance and go to the box office of the club and talk my way in.

When I arrived, I found at both windows that all tickets had been sold for days and that there was no hope of getting one this late. I decided to brazen it out and passed through a door, walked along a long corridor, and entered a small reception room, where on a large board the diagram of the game, as it took place, was posted. This room was full of Russians standing in front of the board, quietly watching every move. I still had no ticket and of course could go no further.

I returned to the box office and had another long conversation with the girl behind the ticket window. She was firm — but I thought a little less so. I went back to the board and watched one more play (watching one more play means standing for twenty minutes with nothing happening, and then the move is posted on the board). Then, once again, I returned to the box office and had a third talk with the blonde behind the counter. Again she was firm — but, again, she seemed even less so.

Once more I returned through the silent crowd, watched

one more move, and then went back for a final talk at the box office. This time the girl slipped out of the back door, came around the corner, took me by the hand, and we walked through several corridors, up a long ceremonial staircase, past three militiamen, and into the room where the championship was being played. She left me without a word.

About three hundred men were crowded into this room, which was like a small theater with a stage at the end. No women were present. All the chairs were taken so I walked through those standing, up to the stage, which was outlined with a row of potted white plants. Behind the plants there were eight tables, with sixteen players playing at once. But all eyes were on the table at which sat Botvinnik and Keres. On the wall behind the platform were enlarged chessboards of the eight tables so that everybody in the audience, even in the back row, could follow the matches as they progressed.

I remained for close to two hours. The match between Botvinnik and Keres was stopped after forty moves and will be continued tomorrow. The thing that struck me most about the evening was the sense of excitement, and the noise. The noise from the audience, particularly the uproar of comment after a move had been made, was particularly noticeable, because everything else in Moscow has been so silent, and it was ironic really, because here of all places silence was desired — and requested. In fact, there was an official "husher" who went up and down the aisles from row to row telling everybody to be quiet.

Except for the potted white flowers lining the footlights on the stage, the surroundings of this Soviet Army Club were dismal indeed. Unless you consider several full-length portraits of Stalin decorative.

When it was announced that the match was to continue the

Communism makes people selfish . . . . .

next day, there was a crush for the door and everybody rushed down the dirty staircase to the cloakroom. (In Russia everybody has to check his hat and coat before entering any public place.) And while I was waiting in the queue, the only unpleasant episode of the evening took place.

Several Soviet Army colonels asserted their rank and instead of waiting their turns went immediately to the head of the line and demanded their long coats and fur hats. Standing patiently thirty or forty persons behind the colonels in question, I mumbled something about "democracy in the Soviet Union" — but really I should not have been too abusive, because, after all, I myself had short-cut the rules and got to the front row of the auditorium, led by a gentle hand.

DECEMBER 3, 1951

As I look at and listen to the Russians in their daily life, as I watch them when they do not necessarily realize they are being watched, I am always struck by this thought about Communism as it is practised, hour by hour, on the streets, and in shops, and on buses, and in homes — and not as it is theorized about in textbooks. The thought is this: Communism seems to make people more selfish and self-centered as individuals. It looks to me as though in the end it makes people live for themselves. And the question is, why shouldn't it, based as it is on materialism?

One explanation of the way it works in practice on this large scale which we see in the Soviet Union is, I think, that individuals spend so much of their day working officially for the all-powerful and ever-demanding state, and for "the good of all," that in their private lives, in their free time, in their

· · · · · · · · ·   **Evil exists as a Thing**

precious off-hours, they quite naturally exist only for themselves and deliberately ignore everybody else, following old
animal instincts.

DECEMBER 25, 1951

In Moscow, you feel that Evil exists as a Thing, as a Presence.
That is my thought this Christmas Day.

JANUARY 6, 1952

This entry in my diary I want to write with care, because it
describes an incident which, although simple and small,
makes clear to me so much that I have studied in Russian
history. With such a goal, I know I shall fail, but I have got
to try.

The story starts at 4.30 this Sunday morning. At that hour
I got out of bed in the pre-dawn darkness, and rushed to
the kitchen to get breakfast for three American friends who
were to show up at five o'clock. I had persuaded these friends
— a young couple in the Embassy, and a girl in the Embassy
who had accompanied me on past adventures — to go to the
Lenin Hills with me to see the sunrise.

I had read somewhere, many months ago, that in the old
days it was the thing to do to watch the sunrise from the
Sparrow Hills (as they were then called), after a night on
the town. And I had read how much the hills had meant,
for so many reasons, to so many Russians in Moscow's past.

We had had our own celebration the night before, but
gave up soon after midnight, and therefore we decided to
make a fresh start after a few hours' sleep. As it turned out,

Sunrise on the Sparrow Hills . . . .

we picked about the worst day of the year. At least I have never seen such a snowstorm as swirled down this morning.

The Embassy car, which we had chartered after much planning and haggling, showed up shortly before six — and we set off in the morning blackness streaked with snow. As we did so, we could see that another small sedan, which had been parked across the street, started up after us.

Because of the weather conditions it took us almost half an hour to reach the hills, which, actually, are only a few miles out on the outskirts of Moscow, just beyond Gorky Park, looking down over one of the great bends of the Moscow River.

Our Embassy car finally made the grade of the last hill. We got out into the blinding snowstorm and stood on the high cliff overlooking the river, with Moscow somewhere in the distance. As the sun began to rise (or at least we assumed it was rising), the whole scene became gray rather than black. And soon, far below, we were able to see the bell tower of Novodevichy Monastery, and, far in the distance, the bulk of the Kremlin walls.

We stood on an historic spot. Here, on the second of September, 1812, Napoleon stood at the end of his invasion, and looked out, for the first time, on the city of Moscow. Tolstoy, in *War and Peace,* takes us back to that moment:

> "A town captured by the enemy is like a maid who has lost her honor," thought he . . . From that point of view he gazed at the Oriental beauty he had not seen before. It seemed strange to him that his long-felt wish, which had seemed unattainable, had at last been realized. In the clear morning light he gazed now at the city . . . and the assurance of possessing it agitated and awed him.

. . . . "this capital at my feet"

"But could it be otherwise?" he thought. "Here is this capital at my feet. . . . A strange, beautiful, and majestic city; and a strange and majestic moment! . . . One word from me, one movement of my hand, and that ancient capital of the Tsars would perish. But my clemency is always ready to descend upon the vanquished. I must be magnanimous and truly great. But no, it can't be true that I am in Moscow," he suddenly thought. "Yet here she is lying at my feet, with her golden domes and crosses scintillating and twinkling in the sunshine. But I shall spare her. On the ancient monuments of barbarism and despotism I will inscribe great words of justice and mercy. . . . From the height of the Kremlin — yes, there is the Kremlin, yes — I will give them just laws; I will teach them the meaning of true civilization, I will make generations of boyars remember their conqueror with love. I will tell the deputation that I did not, and do not, desire war, that I have waged war only against the false policy of their court; that I love and respect Alexander and that in Moscow I will accept terms of peace worthy of myself and of my people. I do not wish to utilize the fortunes of war to humiliate an honored monarch. . . . But can it be true that I am in Moscow? Yes, there she lies."

And in that same year, 1812, a few months before Napoleon's occupation of Moscow, a boy was born in the city, not far from the Kremlin walls. His name was Alexander Hertzen. He was to turn out to be the first great liberal of Russia, and, in many ways, his life could be described as the starting point of the Russian Revolution. And he was also to turn out to be the writer of perhaps the greatest autobiography ever put on paper.

In these memoirs, written in London in exile, he included a celebrated chapter, "Nick and the Sparrow Hills." And

"vowed in sight of all Moscow" . . . .

here he describes how "the Sparrow Hills . . . soon became our 'Holy Mountain.' "

One hot day after dinner Hertzen, at that time still in his early teens, drove with his father and with his friend Nick (Ogaryov) out to the Sparrow Hills.

> Flushed and breathless, we stood there mopping our faces. The sun was setting, the cupolas glittered, the city lay stretched further than the eye could reach; a fresh breeze blew on our faces, we stood leaning against each other and, suddenly embracing, vowed in sight of all Moscow to sacrifice our lives to the struggle we had chosen.
>
> This scene may strike others as very affected and very theatrical, and yet twenty-six years afterwards I am moved to tears recalling it; there was a sacred sincerity in it, and that our whole life has proved. . . .
>
> We did not know all the strength of the foe with whom we were entering into battle, but we took up the fight. That strength broke much in us, but it did not crush us, and we did not surrender to it in spite of all its blows. The wounds received from it were honorable. Jacob's strained thigh was the sign that he had wrestled in the night with a God.
>
> From that day the Sparrow Hills became a place of worship for us and once or twice a year we went there, and always by ourselves. . . . Ogaryov . . . wrote to me afterwards from his country house: "I have come away and feel sad, sad, as I have never been before. . . . Write," he concluded, "how on that spot, on the Sparrow Hills, the history of our lives, yours and mine, developed."

The lives of Hertzen and Ogaryov developed in such a way that less than one hundred years later, on this same spot, the guns of the Russian revolutionists poured shell on the Kremlin walls in November of 1917.

. . . . . **Can Russians buy automobiles? Yes**

But their lives as lived and their ideals as thought were not such that they would be pleased at the scene which I saw, standing on their "Holy Mountain" in 1952.

As we returned to our sedan parked behind a pile of snow by the side of the road, there was the other car which had followed us. And four plain-clothes men were outside in the snow, pretending they had a flat tire. We walked up to them and asked whether we could help.

JANUARY 9, 1952

While translating an article in this morning's issue of *Trud* (the daily newspaper of the Soviet trade unions), I was reminded of a question asked so frequently by Americans: Can Rusians buy their own private automobiles? The answer is "Yes" — they do buy the smaller models, the four-cylinder Pobeda and the tiny Moskvich. But, as yet, only one person in thousands owns a car.

In fact, so few Russians have their own automobiles that it is considered news when individuals do buy them. And so Russian newspaper editors periodically devote columns of their precious propaganda space to articles on such purchases — a type of "human interest" story which is very rare indeed in the Moscow press.

Here, for example, is the piece I translated this morning, under the headline, "Automobiles for Personal Use." It is a dispatch from Krasnodar, one of the most important industrial and cultural cities of the Caucasus region, with a population of more than 200,000. I quote the story in full, because, word for word, it reveals so much:

"In the Auto Store" . . . .

January 8 (*Trud* Correspondent) — The demand for automobiles, motorcycles, and bicycles increases every day. Only today, several orders for automobiles by the working people of Kuban were received in the Motor and Tractor Sale Store. In the past year, the store sold 400 motor vehicles to workers and employees. The following acquired Pobeda machines: Comrade Buchinsky, department head of an agricultural institute; Comrade Velichko, deputy director of the same institute; Comrade Biramov, combine operator of the Yuzhno-Khutorskaya Machine Tractor Station and a Hero of Socialist Labor; and many others. In the same time, 213 motorcycles and 951 bicycles were sold.

A few months ago, I translated a similar article from *Moscow Pravda,* entitled "In the Auto Store." This piece, likewise, speaks for itself — and, in itself, tells so much, not only about the automobile situation but also about the entire pattern of Russia's economic, social, and cultural life:

Each day the postman brings scores of letters to Building No. 21 on Bakuninskaya Street. Here is located the specialized store of the Chief Administration for Automobile and Tractor Sales. . . .

The number of purchasers of automobiles and motorcycles is growing from month to month. There are already thousands of them. And this is striking evidence of the steady growth of the material prosperity of our people.

The customers are served in an exemplary manner. In the store there are 42 workers — three engineers and specialists who have come here from the plants. They help the purchasers choose the motor vehicle and give technical advice.

Workers, engineers, collective farmers, teachers, doctors, and artists purchase the automobiles. Inhabitants of Moscow

. . . . **there are no "police"**

and the working people of the capital oblast buy many machines.

Recently A. Shtyrova, a distinguished weaver of the Trekh-gornaya Manufaktura Combine named after F. Dzerzhinsky, N. Gribachev, the poet and People's Artist of the R.S.F.S.R., and P. Lisitsian, a soloist of the Bolshoi Theater, bought Pobeda automobiles.

In June and July alone a collective farmer from Kimov-sky Raion, a collective-farm chairman from Mytishchinsky Raion, a turner from Orekhovo-Zuevo, a coal cutter from Uzlovaya, a woman teacher from a Moscow secondary school, and others purchased their own Moskvich automobiles.

No comment is necessary. In these few words I have, I hope, conveyed the "feel" of things in the Soviet Union to-day. It's not that I want to ridicule the individual Russians mentioned above — indeed, I hope they are happy with their new acquisitions. Rather, we should mock the regime for the maddening smugness with which it reports such pathetic accomplishments. On the other hand, I feel that it ill be-comes us, as the richest people on earth, to speak smugly because so many millions of our citizens own automobiles. No, instead we should pay a little more attention to the other two billion people in the world who cannot possibly afford to buy a personal car (of whom, as it happens, I am one). If we don't look at these two billion human beings, the Kremlin will.

JANUARY 12, 1952

In Russia — the biggest and most efficient "police state" ever created — there are no "police." This paradox is easily ex-

The Statue of Liberty sovietized   . . . . . .

plained — and, in fact, throws a great deal of light on the Kremlin's approach to everything.

With respect to the internal situation, the Reds shy away completely from the word "police." The time-honored Russian word *politsiya* (police) has such unpleasant connotations, carried over from tsarist days, that the present rulers of Russia use what they obviously consider a more euphemistic term, *militsioner* (militiaman). Thus, all the thousands of uniformed stalwarts standing around — in their black boots and ankle-length greatcoats, bound tight by leather belts and a crisscross of straps, and heavy with revolvers — are just nice members of the local militia. And, naturally, there is no public mention at all of the secret police — nor of the plain-clothes men lurking in the shadows.

With respect to external matters, it is just the opposite. The adjective *politseisky* is used every other sentence in the press and on the radio when reference is made to the Western world, particularly the United States.

JANUARY 13, 1952

Speaking of "cops" (and that, really, is what I was speaking about in yesterday's diary entry on the "police state"), I shouldn't fail to mention the Soviet propaganda poster that is causing so much comment in Moscow these days. This anti-American cartoon of the Statue of Liberty now hangs on the walls of the Tretyakov Gallery — Moscow's greatest art museum — as a part of the 1951 All-Union Art Exhibition (almost half of which, incidentally, consists of Stalin portraits of one kind or another). The poster is one of a series of hate-American drawings by B. I. Prorokov, a young

Moscow-born artist — and it received a Stalin Prize last year.

A few minutes ago, on a visit to the Tretyakov, I had a good long look at this clever cartoon, the most effective (I'm not speaking here of truthfulness) propaganda drawing I have yet seen in the Soviet Union. At first glance, you see the head of the statue, the familiar classic face of the goddess, beautifully drawn and in bronze-green colors — and then you notice that she is weeping, with a long teardrop hanging from her left eye. On closer inspection, you see something somewhat different: a New York City cop is peering out of each eye of the face (each policeman's head forming an eyeball of the statue). And the teardrop turns out to be a policeman's billy hanging from the wrist of one of the officers.

And, speaking of the Statue of Liberty, I likewise shouldn't fail to mention that I have seen her here in Russia in another form — a tiny, tarnished replica of the statue on a dusty shelf in Tchaikovsky's home at Klin, not far from Moscow. Tchaikovsky obviously received this cheap tourist's model during his trip to America, and, just as obviously, he kept and cherished it as a souvenir of his visit. Everything else in the house — from Tchaikovsky's Bukhara dressing gown to the rough wooden kitchen table on which he wrote the "Pathétique" — is described in scholarly detail, page after page, in the museum catalogue — but there is not a word about the Statue of Liberty. (Nor, for that matter, is there any mention at all these days of Tchaikovsky's trip to the United States.) Soon, I am sure, the statue's presence, revealing criminal negligence on the part of somebody, will be noticed — and the days of this pathetic but wonderful little curio in the cupboard at Klin will come to a junk-heap end.

"Shadowing" and "Plants" . . . .

JANUARY 15, 1952

Naturally all of us wonder and talk about the "security measures" to which we are subjected here. Aside from the obvious and official regulations which control our movements and the equally obvious, but not admittedly official, isolation from Russians, there is the question of "shadowing" and "plants" or, as would have been said in another era, *agents provocateurs.*

It is fairly apparent that we are followed almost always when we are outside of Moscow; and it's equally easy to spot the trailers within the city at least half the time. Of course often — or perhaps always — when we think we are not shadowed, it may just be that it is being done cleverly. For instance, after I moved from the Metropole Hotel into "Vesnina," I'd often get home thinking I had not been followed, but within a few minutes of my return, the telephone call box outside the house would ring for one of the militiamen who were always stationed there. The only thing I could figure out about it was that it was someone checking to see if I had got home.

As to "plants," as far as I can see, they can't be too hard to dodge. At the theater you can always arrive at the last minute and get a seat next to people who are already there. And you can do the same in trains and restaurants. Anyway I *think* this system has worked for me so far, but you never *know.*

JANUARY 23, 1952

Most of my life I have dreamed during my sleep but here in Moscow I dream *every* night — and I haven't had a pleasant dream yet, only wild, blanket-kicking affairs.

. . . .   **Fashion show**

JANUARY 30, 1952

Today, having persuaded an American Embassy girl to accompany me, I went to a women's style show. I hasten to
add that I made this rash move for two reasons: (1) to make
my own personal study of the Soviet Union as complete as
possible; (2) to see with my own eyes what a Soviet model
looked like.

And now, to get my report over with as quickly as I can,
I am just going to copy down verbatim the notes I took at
the time — as follows:

Show held in "All-Union House of Models" on Kuznetsky
Most. . . . Performances take place every day (except Saturday) at 1, 2, and 5 P.M. (admission 10 rubles) . . . . Russians
call these style shows "séances" (!) . . . . Only 30 Russian
women in audience when I was there: majority were peasant
types, spinster types, and elderly white-haired women — all
dressed in worst possible style, even by Soviet standards. . . .
After much whispering backstage, models appeared from
behind gold (more exactly: cocker-spaniel brown) velvet
curtains, and walked down a narrow platform between two
marble pillars, their shoes squeaking — in spite of old red-
and-blue oriental rug on the raised dais. . . . Three models
the day I attended: one brunette, one blond, one "full figure" (the brunette the best — terrific) . . . . Russian models,
I found, behave like models all over the world — that is,
they step and hesitate, and twist and turn, and squirm, like
little children who have to go to the bathroom at once. . . .
We saw the spring styles for 1952 — the "new look," as even
the Russians call it, in coats, suits, dressing gowns, housecoats, pajamas, etc. . . . I learned that this year style in the
U.S.S.R. dictates a distance of from 35 to 38 centimeters (14

Children skate, troops salute . . . .

to 15 inches) "from floor to hemline." . . . I also learned
(from my American escort) that Soviet housecoats are "not
shadow proof" (that is, we could see the legs). . . . The
finale was a blue polka-dot maternity dress, also designed for
breast feeding — the model, who was not pregnant, demon-
strated by holding this practical dress way out in front of
her, and then ended up by opening the blouse for the feeding operation. . . . In spite of all this excitement, most of
the Russian spectators present stared the whole time, not at
the models, but at my American friend (who *is* stylish —
there is no doubt about that) and, I must admit, at me.

FEBRUARY 1, 1952

Typical winter street scene: Little children trying to skate on
the rough ice and packed snow of Moscow's crowded sidestreet sidewalks, off the main thoroughfares, in the unswept
areas of the city.

FEBRUARY 7, 1952

There is much saluting on the streets and that is because
there are so many troops everywhere, in their long gray coats
and black boots.

One day recently I stood on a Moscow street corner and
counted the number of soldiers and sailors who passed me in
a period of ten minutes. The count was very high — about
four passed every minute, on the average. But this does not
mean, necessarily, that all of Russia is an armed camp. I
am sure that if I stood on a street corner in Washington, the
number would be almost as high.

· · · · · · · ·   **the squeak, squeak, squeak**

FEBRUARY 12, 1952

In looking for the Russian word for "appreciative," I have
thumbed through many dictionaries, and I have asked many
literate Muscovites for suggestions — but with no success.
Apparently, in the Russian language, which has more words
than any other language in the world except English, there
is no single word equivalent in meaning to our very meaningful adjective "appreciative." Maybe that is significant.
But again, maybe not — because, even in this city of Russian robots, I have met many "appreciative" men and women
and children.

FEBRUARY 15, 1952

As a rule, I am not — or, better, I try not to be — unduly
conscious of differences in standards of living, of the material
things in life. But here in Moscow one thing I can't get out
of my head, or, more accurately, out of my ears, is the
squeak, squeak, squeak of Russian shoes.

This noise, so seldom heard in the other world, is noticeable everywhere in Moscow — and particularly on the stages
of the theaters, where even the most renowned actresses, who,
quite naturally, wear the best and fanciest clothes available,
have some difficulty in making their own voices heard above
the various voices of their footwear. Sometimes I think the
Russians are completely unaware of this telltale sound. But
at other times I am sure that they are aware of this, if only
because their eyes are invariably and instantly drawn to the
shoes of foreigners. Many times on the streets of Moscow I
have tested this observation: walking along a block, I

I get mad . . . .

have watched the Muscovites coming toward me, counting the percentage of times their eyes have dropped instantaneously to my feet — and the rate has always been seven or eight times out of ten. It is incredible.

Now, the point of all this — the important thing — is not that we should mock the Russian people, or feel superior and self-satisfied, because their living standards are below ours, because style in any form is nonexistent in the Soviet Union. Working as hard as the Russians do for the almighty, all-demanding state, and living as they do in a half-hell, they are entitled, as far as I am concerned, to have the best shoes in the world, if that is what they want. I get mad, I must admit, at many of the Americans here who constantly laugh at the Russians because of the poor quality and minute quantity of their worldly goods, privately ridiculing the women, for example, because their skirts are too short or their lipstick is the color of a ripe tangerine. They should be able to find more vital targets for devastating criticism in other walks of life in a country which is full of political and intellectual and spiritual weaknesses and deficiencies which are more deserving of attention and more worthy of scorn. But I get much madder, I should add, at the Soviet leaders who, with straight faces, tell their subjects, and the rest of the world, that the Russians are the best-shod and the best-everything-else people on earth.

FEBRUARY 23, 1952

I spent most of the afternoon today in the Lenin Library. As far as I know, I am the only American here who has applied for a card to the library and who has used it. The busi-

. . . . **The Lenin Library**

ness of getting admitted was really quite simple — I just walked up to the window and asked for a card. I filled it out right there at the desk in front of the librarian and she stamped it. I was then given a very fancy pass which I keep in my billfold and flash whenever I am asked to.

I am finding that my hours here are not very productive as far as my own studies are concerned but they are productive as far as my observations of the Russian people go. The difficulty about my own studies is that I do not have access to the stacks — nor, in fact, do the Russians either. Furthermore I am not allowed to use the entire card catalogue of the library. In one small room there are two or three shelves of cards and those are the only ones I am permitted to see. So far I have requested about eight books and not one of them was available.

The atmosphere of the library is incredibly serious. It is filled mostly with young people, and I assume they are students of Moscow University, which is just around the corner. The library is open every day of the week including Sundays from 9.00 A.M. to 11.30 P.M. and for many hours during the day there are long queues of students patiently waiting to get in.

Since I have the card of a graduate student I am permitted to pass to the head of this line.

The building itself is one of the few impressive modernistic structures in Moscow — eighteen sheer stories of concrete and glass. The Soviet regime maintains that the Lenin Library is the largest in the world with some fifteen million volumes — about twice as many as our Library of Congress, the British Museum, the Harvard Library, or the New York Public Library.

the liveliest spot in the library . . . .

The liveliest spot in the library is physically the most gloomy, and that is a little room down two or three wooden stairs in the basement where tea and light refreshments are served on rough wooden benches. You order what you want and pay your few kopecks.

In the reading rooms, which are always packed, the students sit at long bare tables in complete silence. There are one or two small smoking rooms upstairs. In one of the smoking rooms there is a telephone booth, a dial pay station. Since there is only one telephone for this large group of people there is usually a line of students waiting for it.

The procedure for getting a book is quite complicated. You fill out a slip and submit it to the girl behind the desk and then you have to wait, usually two days, before you are notified on your return whether or not that book is available. If it is, it is brought to you and you sit down at the nearest table and take notes from it. It is impossible to take any book out of the library and there is a very careful check through a series of guards when you leave.

FEBRUARY 25, 1952

Before arriving in Russia for the first time, I had a definite picture in my mind's eye of what Moscow must look like. This kind of mental projection, with very little foundation, is a common experience with me — and, I imagine, with most human beings.

The central object in this image was, quite naturally, the Kremlin and the Red Square, with the nightmare, neurasthenic cupolas of St. Basil's rising against a stormy sky. In the past, whenever I thought of Moscow, I always saw those red brick walls and towers of the Kremlin — and very little else. All of these familiar features have turned out to be pretty much as I had imagined them — but there have been many surprises connected with sights and scenes I hadn't visualized at all.

Take, for example, a business street, part of a shopping area in downtown Moscow. It just hadn't occurred to me that Moscow would have such a normal, mundane thing as a crowded thoroughfare lined with stores, which in turn would be lined with long queues of shoppers. The illustration I have in mind is the Arbat — a short, narrow, rather crooked street radiating from a large, open square near the Kremlin. By way of comparison, I would say that it reminds me, as much as anything else, of Washington Street in Boston.

I go along this street quite often — mostly on trolley bus No. 2, which runs through the center of Moscow. After paying my 40 kopecks to the sharp-voiced amazon at the rear door, and after finally getting a seat, I usually lose no time in beginning to scratch a peephole in the frost coating the bus window. If I don't do this, I don't know where I am — or, more correctly, where the bus is. And not knowing where you are can lead to calamity, or, at best, to the bus stop ten blocks beyond the point where you want to get off. All Moscow autobuses and trolley buses — like public vehicles in every major city throughout the world — are so crowded, particularly in the center aisles and at the entrance and exit doors, that you have to prepare your debarkation with care (and with several good pushes) — and the peephole in the frosted window is indispensable for a head start.

Shops . . . .

Well, as a result of all of this — all this peering through my
deep-freeze Judas — I have become quite familiar with the
Arbat — so familiar that I have begun to make a list of the
landmarks en route. In itself this list paints a pretty good
picture of a typical business street in the middle of Moscow.
Within a distance of five blocks, and a time of five minutes,
this is what I see:

> Post office (and telegraph counter)
> Three movie houses
> One theater
> At least a dozen bookstores (of all kinds)
> Chemist shops
> Flower shops
> Dentist's office
> Furniture stores
> Meat and fish stores
> Fruit and vegetable stores
> Watch-repair shops
> Photographers' studios
> "Culture" goods (stationery stores)
> Hardware stores
> Ice-cream stores
> Four or five cafés and restaurants
> Cigarette and tobacco shops
> Liquor stores
> Clothing stores
> Bakeries
> Shoe store
> Dry-cleaning shop
> Phonograph record store
> Perfume shops
> "Zoo" store (pet shop)

· · · · · · · · · · · · · · **The Arbat**

Branch of Moscow City Bank
Azerbaijan wine shop
Second-hand stores (commission shops)
Electrical equipment store
Art-goods store
"Diet" shop
Store of preserves and canned goods
House of Pioneers (local headquarters of Communist
   Party organization for children and adolescents be-
   tween the ages of ten and sixteen)
A new 27-story "skyscraper" (government offices)
"Avtomats" (public telephone booths)

In the daytime, in business hours, silent, black-clothed,
purposeful Muscovites swarm the Arbat, like silent, black,
purposeful ants — lonely crowds spilling over from the narrow sidewalks into the gutters. They pack all the stores and
shops mentioned in the list above — buying everything in
sight. But, actually, there is very little to buy in this entire
array of retail trade establishments. It is a brave front, this
façade of the Arbat, with its neon signs and shop windows —
but a hollow shell. But the Russian, resigned as he is, always
has hope that there will be a little more available on the
shelf on his next visit — and there usually is. There is always just enough progress to keep him plodding on.

Late at night the picture of the Arbat is completely different. Surely it is the most deserted street on earth in the
early hours of morning. And it is in those hours that you
can best see the skeleton of Moscow life, a living skeleton
made up of police, militiamen, and plain-clothes men. After
midnight there are no busy crowds in fat flesh to conceal
these grim gentlemen. There they are — alone, exposed, and

Fifty-eight militiamen in six blocks . . . . . .

countless. Actually, there is a special reason for their presence on the Arbat. This street is one of the most heavily guarded in the world simply because it is along this thoroughfare that Stalin and his top ministers and generals, as well as his closest cronies (whoever they are at the moment), pass on their way from the Kremlin to their country *dachas*, and back again. They are driven at top speed down the very center of the street — and all traffic, particularly in the rush hours, is carefully controlled in order to prevent the slightest interference with their passage. Through an elaborate system of block-by-block warnings and red-light signals, all pedestrians and vehicles are cleared out of the way minutes before the big black limousines, with their passengers hidden behind carefully drawn curtains, whiz by, while trailing touring cars, loaded with guards, roar in pursuit.

When I say the police on the Arbat are "countless," I should amend that statement by saying that once recently they were counted. A few weeks ago, I missed the last bus home, and since the Metro had already closed and there was not a taxi in sight, I had to walk through the night from the Embassy to my residence, which is just off the Arbat. It was about 3 A.M. I plowed my way through the falling snow — absolutely alone, except for "the others." And here is where the count comes in. I noticed so many militiamen that I decided to keep a tally of them as I went along. Within six blocks I counted fifty-eight in all — two or three at every corner, two or three standing in the center of the street in the middle of every block, four or five at the bigger intersections. And under cover in more than twenty dark doorways plain-clothes men stood silently in the shadows and watched me pass.

. . . . I buy a short-wave radio

FEBRUARY 27, 1952

I used to wonder, at home, whether the Voice of America broadcasts are ever really heard by Russians. Now I know that they are. I have today bought an excellent Russian short-wave radio from its owner. Having failed to buy such a set in a regular shop, I was as delighted as I was surprised when a bystander in the shop offered to sell me a set which belonged to him. In spite of my warning him that it might be dangerous for him to deal with an American, he brushed all this aside, and I now have a magnificent thirteen-tube short-wave set — one of three types made in Russia. The circumstances of my purchase were such that I feel fairly sure that the man who sold it to me was not a "plant."

The fact is that reception is completely jammed in Moscow and good elsewhere. People have told me that they listen to the Voice programs, and by and large I think the material they hear is excellent and the programs competently chosen. If this were not so, the press here would scarcely spend so much time attacking the Voice.

MARCH 1, 1952

Here is what an anti-American play is like:

The play in question, which I saw last night at the Moscow Theater of Drama and Comedy, is called *Under the Golden Eagle*. Russia's most popular newspaper, *Evening Moscow* (which, incidentally, is the only afternoon daily published in the capital), recently had this to say about the playwright: "The author of the play is Yaroslav Galan, the remarkable Ukrainian writer and publicist, who perished in 1949 at the

An anti-American play . . . .

hands of foul murderers, the hirelings of the American-British imperialists." Another Russian publication has given its readers the following background information: "The tragedy, 'Under the Golden Eagle,' was written by Galan in 1947, after he had served as Soviet correspondent at the Nuremberg trials. Traveling through the Western zone of occupied Germany, Galan visited a number of camps for so-called 'displaced persons.' What he saw served as the basis of his play."

This is the cast of characters:

Andrei Makarov (the hero, a Russian sailor wounded at Sevastopol during World War II, later a prisoner of war in the zone of Germany liberated by the Americans).
Anna Robchuk (a Ukrainian girl).
Norma Fancy (an American woman serving as a correspondent in postwar Germany).
Lieutenant Edwin Bentley (an officer in the U.S. Army).
Major Peterson (the villain, a U.S. Army officer apparently serving as head of a local military police unit).
Sergeant Bob Fober (an American M.P.).
Tom (another American enlisted man serving as an M.P.).
Herr Arkady Belin (a German, with a cigar).
Herr Zupovich (a German, with pince-nez).
Frau Milch (a German innkeeper).
Duda (a Russian friend of Makarov).
Maltsev (another Russian friend of Makarov).
Willie (a blind boy).

The action of the play (in the course of four acts and seven scenes) takes place shortly after the end of World War II in an unidentified town in the Western occupation zone of

Germany. The play is built around a dual theme of American efforts to prevent a group of Soviet prisoners of war (previously liberated by American forces) from returning to their homeland, and the countermoves of the internees to return to the "freedom of the East." Major Peterson and his adjutant, Lieutenant Edwin Bentley, are the villains, major and minor, who execute the American plan to prevent the repatriation of the Soviet citizens. Leading the former Russian war prisoners in their attempts to communicate with the Soviet Repatriation Commission and thus return to their fatherland is the Soviet sailor Makarov, who soon succeeds in enlisting the sympathy of the American foreign correspondent, Miss Fancy.

Recognizing Makarov as the *bête noire* of their plans, the American army officers, through a German stool pigeon, do away with a barmaid employed in the tavern "Under the Golden Eagle," a favorite meeting place for the former Soviet war prisoners. (The name of the tavern, as of the play itself, furnishes a symbol of the U.S. occupation — because, as we learn in the play, the traditional Prussian eagle has been painted over to represent the American species.) The scheme of the Americans is to make Makarov the victim of a frame-up, to charge him with the murder, and then to offer him leniency in exchange for a switch of allegiance and his pledge to undermine the efforts of his fellow citizens to reach the Soviet Repatriation Commission.

In spite of the torture methods of Peterson and his M.P. henchmen, their plot is frustrated by Makarov's valiant refusal to play their game — and so the hero is marched off to his execution shouting, "It is better to die in honor than to live in disgrace," while the drums in the orchestra pit (which,

the depravity and grotesqueness . . . .

incidentally, make sinister sounds, like a Wagnerian leit-
motiv, throughout the play) beat a death march. The U.S.
Army is also thwarted by Miss Fancy (who, by the way, lives
up to her name — dressed as she is in a glamorous cape, a
snappy garrison cap, and a necktie of red and white stripes).
In the beginning of the play Miss Fancy is in love with
Lieutenant Bentley, but as soon as she discovers that he also
is an evil accomplice of American policy, she launches a campaign to expose the aims and methods of the U.S. authorities. It is during a conversation between these two that the
audience learns of the motivation for the American attitude
toward the Soviet citizens: the goal of the United States is
to use the Russians as conscripts in a huge army of merce-
naries to implement the American design for world domina-
tion by force of arms.

During the performance, in the dark, I scribbled notes and
impressions on my program — marginalia which will do
much, I think, to give the tone of this particular play, as
well as the feeling of the entire hate-America campaign now
raging. They will show the depravity and grotesqueness of
this campaign, which now vilifies not only our policy on
paper but also our people as individuals. Here is what I
find on my program:

One of the scenes in the major's quarters takes place at
Christmas time. . . . The walls are decorated with blue and
silver banners, one of which reads: "Marry Cristmas" (mis-
spelled, but not deliberately, I am certain). . . . Beside these
decorations are pictures of pin-up girls and large photographs of lynchings and men hanging on gallows. . . . The
Christmas carol "Silent Night, Holy Night" (translated into
Russian words) is played several times in this scene by means

of a radio onstage, and in subsequent scenes the carol becomes, in effect, the ironically pointed theme song of the play, with the small orchestra in the pit taking up the melody as background music, and various characters — both Americans and Germans — humming and whistling the song onstage while engaging in murder and blackmail and lovemaking. . . . Also prominent in this scene is a Christmas tree, and the decorations and baubles hung on the boughs by the Americans are not silver stars and angels and candy cornucopias — but toy tanks and miniature bombs.

Wherever possible, all the other stage sets and props contribute to the anti-American theme. . . . In the tavern, for example, the word BAR, in English, is blocked in big, black letters on the front door, and when this door swings open and shut, great shadows of these three letters fall with considerable effect across the walls of the interior. . . . Next to the bar itself are Hollywood movie posters (one reads: "American Film: Murder in the Jungle") and in one corner is another colorful advertisement: "Chew Gum — In America Everybody Chews Gum". . . . Conspicuous in another set, in Major Peterson's office, is a stand with a piece of bronze sculpture, a bust of a man who might be Voltaire or Lincoln or Truman or Hitler (from different angles and in different lights, it resembles each — and I couldn't ever make up my mind which), and throughout the performance the American M. P.'s use this bust as a convenient hatrack, disrespectfully and sloppily tossing their white helmets on top of the honored head.

In attitude and attire, the U.S. Army officers are clearly reminiscent of the worst type of Hitlerite police and German storm troopers. . . . Major Peterson, for example, wears a

American officers — Soviet view . . . .

dark blue, SS-type uniform, with gold shoulder boards, gold stripes on his breeches, a broad, brown leather belt, and black leather boots. . . . To complete the picture, he sports a pair of revolvers on his hips, and a pair of steel-rimmed glasses on his nose.

A large and showy crucifix, standing in the center of the major's desk, and thus dominating the entire military head-quarters, is the very focal point of much of Peterson's ac-tivities, a great deal of the play's action taking place within a few inches of Christ's outstretched arms. . . . If you find it hard to believe this, let me describe two scenes. . . . In the first, the major menacingly leans over the crucifix as he argues about the list of Russian war prisoners, the cross-arms framing his angry face. . . . The business in the second in-stance is over a string of black-market pearls, with Peterson making a deal with the German stooges (the latter, inciden-tally, are traditional caricatures of "bad" Germans — one with flashy rings, a black derby and a black cigar; the other with long blond hair, long knickerbockers, and pince-nez with a long chain): in the course of this episode, the major dangles the jewelry over the arms of the Cross, fondling the pearls as he strings them around the head of Christ.

In sharp contrast to the American officers, Makarov is probably the most heroic hero ever to walk the stage. . . . In the first place, he really doesn't walk the stage, but, as the result of his war wound, limps painfully along, always leaning on his cane — thus arousing the natural sympathy of the audience from the start (it is explained, by the way, that Makarov did not surrender, but was taken prisoner only because he was knocked unconscious during the defense of Sevastopol). . . . In the second place, even the attire of

. . . . . . "Not before God, but as a citizen"

Makarov is designed to kindle sympathy and warm feelings of patriotism — by the time of the criminal investigation, for example, his blue-and-white-striped sailor's jersey has become torn and shredded (an indication, I suppose, that the Americans have tortured him), and the black ribbons of his Russian naval cap hang down over his bare and bloody shoulders. . . . Most important, however, are his noble speeches, typical of which is the following statement which he makes to the major at the beginning of this same investigation scene, his face glowing with glory: "Not before God, but as a citizen of the Union of Soviet Socialist Republics, I speak the truth, and nothing but the truth."

When this play first opened in Moscow, there were reports that one of the American M. P.'s wore a ring through his nose; perhaps even the Kremlin propagandists thought this evidence of American savagery was going a bit far, because I saw no sign of the nose ring. . . . There are, however, countless other indications of brutality: the sergeant looks and moves like a gorilla — and his crony, the second M. P., always enters a scene with a submachine gun on his hip, ready to fire; whether they are saying "Sir-r-r!" (in English) to their senior officers, or mouthing "Merry Chreeeesmus" (also in English, as indicated) to their German flunkies, or brusquely ordering the Russians to stand on their feet when Americans enter a room, the M. P.'s invariably behave as uncouthly as possible; the most maddening scene, however, takes place when the American sergeant rips the eyeglasses off the little blind boy, shoves him across the room, and then kicks him onto the floor.

And now, how does the audience react to all of this? The villains were continuously and audibly hissed and booed.

The audience reacts . . . .

The heroine was often warned of approaching danger by shocked Oh's and Ah's from the spectators. The hero was frequently cheered and applauded by the house when he expressed brave, patriotic sentiments (this constant clapping apparently breaking forth in response to the content of the lines, not the delivery or the acting). The Russian girl sitting next to me quietly wept throughout the evening, nervously kneading the handkerchief in her lap into a wet ball.

All in all, the reaction was much the same as that of an unsophisticated American audience to an old-fashioned melodrama of the Victorian era. Whether this audience participation, this easy response, can be interpreted as merely an appreciation of the dramatic qualities of a "thriller," or as a true sign of personal hatred for everything American, it is hard to say. Modern Soviet dramatists and press propagandists are clever at mixing separate emotions — and it is quite possible, I think, that the audience responded as they did *both* because the villains were villains *per se,* and because they were Americans to boot.

MARCH 5, 1952

An inspiriting time is what I had tonight; the sort of thing that happens occasionally and dispels a lot of the gloom that accumulates in this atmosphere of suspicion and silence. I went to a performance of *Madame Butterfly* at the Filial of the Bolshoi. I took along a biography of Puccini, a fat de luxe edition, with much of the score and libretto of *Butterfly,* and with many illustrations.

At the first intermission I fell into conversation with the fellow who sat in the next seat to mine. As usual, he was curious about my nationality and why I was in Moscow. He

. . . . **A inspiriting time**

was a student in Leningrad, and was agog at a chance to ask me about American jazz. I'm afraid my ignorance of the subject disillusioned him, but I did my best.

At the other intermissions we kept up our conversation and got on to serious music, about which he was well informed. Finally, at the end of the opera, I asked him if I might make him a present of my Puccini book, and when he protested, I said, "Oh, come on — accept it as a present from a typical American warmonger!" His reaction was, to say the least, startling. He got very angry and asked if I thought for a moment that he was the sort of person to believe that all Americans were warmongers. He really was insulted. Finally, after I apologized, he accepted the book very gratefully, and autographed his program and gave it to me with apologies that it was the only thing he had to give me in return.

Well, if one educated Russian can not only fail to swallow whole the picture of Americans his propaganda machine grinds out, but even gets angry at the suggestion that he might do so, there's plenty of room to hope there are many thousands like him, and that's a real light in this darkness.

MARCH 6, 1952

> Deep in the Siberian mine,
> Keep your patience proud;
> The bitter toil shall not be lost,
> The rebel thought unbowed.
>
> The sister of misfortune, Hope,
> In the under-darkness dumb
> Speaks joyful courage to your heart:
> The day desired will come.

A travesty of history . . . .

> And love and friendship pour to you
> Across the darkened doors,
> Even as round your galley-beds
> My free music pours.
>
> The heavy-hanging chains will fall,
> The walls will crumble at a word;
> And Freedom greet you in the light,
> And brothers give you back the sword.

Those are the words of Pushkin — a translation by Max Eastman of verses put on paper by Russia's greatest poet exactly a century and a quarter ago. Pushkin, then a young man of twenty-eight, addressed this great message of encouragement to the Decembrists, the leaders of the unsuccessful coup d'état in December, 1825. Tsar Nicholas I executed the ringleaders of this celebrated conspiracy in the Fortress of Peter and Paul in St. Petersburg — but scores of others were exiled to the East, and it was for these survivors that Pushkin wrote his "Message to Siberia."

The Bolsheviks today idolize both the man who wrote the message and the men to whom it was addressed, claiming both Pushkin and the Decembrists as spiritual, if not political forefathers. But here, as elsewhere, the Kremlin's current interpretation of Russian history is a supreme travesty.

As far as the Decembrists are concerned, it is true, of course, that the conspiracy represented the first attempt at revolt on the part of political opposition to the Tsar — but it was a coup d'état of guards, officers, and the landed gentry, not a revolution of the masses. The Decembrists did serve as an inspiration to all succeeding generations — but that is their only relation to the present-day rulers of Russia. In regard to ideas, organization, and personnel, they had little in common with the revolutionary movement of the Bolsheviks — and so could not possibly be considered the first in an unbroken line of leaders pointing the way to the Revolution of 1917 and the Soviet regime of today. Indeed, the main point is that the Decembrists rose in revolt against the very kind of personal tyranny which is found in the Russia of our times.

As far as Pushkin is concerned, it is a grotesque distortion of his doctrine to describe him, as the Soviets do, as the rebel-laureate of the masses. The whole essence of his liberal teaching was that the Russian people must have freedom under the rule of law — and he raised his voice in anger against any form of despotism, whether royal or revolutionary.

And so it is not hard to imagine what either the Decembrists or Puskin would think of the new Nicholas and the fate of Russia's new victims — this time, millions of them. If living today, the Decembrists and Pushkin would be the first, it seems to me, to recognize that the "Message to Siberia" still rings out, and with even greater force, 125 years later. And they would agree, I think, that the world of 1952 should call these verses the "Song of Slave Labor."

Should not this message — written in the Russians' own language, written by the Russian whom all recognize as the outstanding embodiment of Russia's national genius — be taken over today as the message of America to the prisoners and slaves of the Soviet Union? Indeed, should not this message, in these very words which belong to Russia, be the theme of the Voice of America when we broadcast to those now "deep in the Siberian mine"?

Moscow's theaters . . . .

The experience at *Butterfly* has set me thinking about the theater here. In the first place, there are about twenty-five "legitimate" theaters in Moscow, and the population, as close as it can be estimated in the absence of official figures, is about six million. This is about the same proportion of theaters to the population as in New York. About half of the Moscow theaters give classical productions, including plays, ballet, and the opera; the other half are modern, propaganda pieces glorifying Soviet heroes or vilifying foreigners (mostly Americans). I suppose a third of all the plays at any one time are anti-American.

The houses giving the classics are always packed — noticeably more than those giving propaganda plays. I don't know how significant this fact is, and you have to consider it along with the audiences' reactions, which I would say was about 50-50, in the anti-American plays. There's quite a lot of hissing and booing of the villains, but just how much is due to the same reactions people used to have when the mustachioed villain in gay nineties melodramas was tying the beautiful heroine to the railroad tracks is hard to gauge. Since, to judge by their clothes, every segment of the population, down through the least educated, goes to the theater, there must be quite a number who fall for the propaganda.

The whole question of the effect of the theater on the people's morale is one on which the government is touchy here. There is a considerable feeling in the Embassy that the stage may be the last stronghold of comparative independence in Russia. At any rate the Kremlin is known to have doubts as to its effective control in this so popular field.

. . . . Comrade Rassadin in California

For all these reasons, and because it gives one of the best chances for at least casual contact with the people, I have been going to the theater as often as possible — almost one hundred times so far.

MARCH 17, 1952

Here I am writing down every day my impressions of the U.S.S.R., doing my best in this personal diary to tell the truth about the Soviet Union as I see it — and, curiously enough, much of my own daily work involves translating travel stories by Soviet correspondents in the U.S.A., who are doing their best to tell the truth about America as Stalin sees it.

There is quite a difference between the word "I" and the word "Stalin" — and there is quite a difference, I trust, in the results of these two approaches to reporting. At least I hope I don't sound, for example, like Comrade G. Rassadin, who has just written some travel notes on "A Trip Through California." These notes take up seven pages in the current issue of a Soviet periodical called *Round the World,* which faintly corresponds to our *National Geographic Magazine.* In my translation work yesterday afternoon, I sweated over the efforts of my "colleague," and this is what I read in Russian:

> The bulky, four-motor aircraft began slowly to descend. It was early morning. The passengers, who had just now been peacefully dozing in their narrow armchairs, suddenly came to life and stretched toward the windows.
>
> "Here is the Golden State," one of them said in an undertone.
>
> The rouged stewardess emerged from somewhere. She an-

"the workers' quarters in San Francisco" . . . .

nounced that we were approaching San Francisco, and suggested that we fasten the seat belts, which is always done during the landing and take-off of aircraft.

San Francisco twinkled below us with a multitude of electric lights. A few minutes more, and we landed on the soil of California.

How was such a high-flown name taken on by California — the "Golden State"?

Partly it was called up by the "gold fever" which California experienced in the comparatively recent past. Also the fact that nature lavishly endowed this region with various natural resources has, apparently, a certain significance. . . .

Official American propaganda blows up, in every possible way, the myth of the "Golden State," depicting California almost as an earthly paradise, with an allegedly wonderful life for all of its inhabitants. But you have only to visit California, to become a little more closely acquainted with it, to have it become clear that this is a paradise only for a small handful of rich people, and that for the working population it is a real hell, full of tears, hunger and poverty. . . .

We came down from the hill and passed along the by-streets, where the working people of San Francisco live. This was a sad sight. Just as in all the other cities of America, the workers' quarters in San Francisco are the most neglected. Dilapidated, tumble-down houses, which have not been repaired since the day of construction, serve as the shelter for thousands of working families. The dirt and congestion are terrible. In this district of the slums there is not a single blade of grass. The air here, in spite of the proximity of the sea, is close and stuffy. Packs of little children rush about the narrow, filthy side streets. You can read traces of hunger and poverty on the face of every child.

In still greater destitution live the thousands of Chinese who have settled in Chinatown — the Chinese ghetto of San Francisco. Soon after the seizure of California by the Americans, when the building of transcontinental railroads was developed and the mining industry began to grow, an acute demand for a cheap labor force appeared here. In order to cope with this demand, American businessmen began to transport to California coolies from the countries of the Far East, and, first of all, from China, under semi-slave terms of contract labor. . . .

The descendants of the first coolies have been living in California up to the present time. Great numbers of them are concentrated in San Francisco's Chinatown — one of the most wretched slums of bourgeois cities. They do the heaviest work and are subjected to the most cruel exploitation.

Nevertheless, many white workers live no better. The working people of San Francisco are well acquainted with both poverty and unemployment. Not without reason has the bridge across the Golden Gate strait, the longest single-span bridge in America (the length of the bridge span is 1.25 kilometers), acquired mournful fame as the "bridge of suicides." Apparently, life in the "golden" state was not a "heavenly existence" for those unfortunate people.

From San Francisco we went by train to Los Angeles. . . .

From the window of the train car could be seen miserable huts, knocked together from old boards, broken boxes and rusty pieces of iron; and torn, mended tents and vans, in which the families of farm laborers are cooped up. Many even do not have such wretched hovels, and they live where they have to: in mud huts, and sometimes even under bridges.

Cheerless poverty and hunger are the lot of many thousands of farm laborers and workers in California. "We have

"The shadow of American fascism" . . . . .

among us thousands of people who live on the garbage from rubbish pits," writes a woman resident of the California city of San Diego in the newspaper "National Guardian." "I know many of these unfortunate people personally. They are in the same position as homeless dogs."

Toward evening we arrived in Los Angeles — the center of the industrial and agricultural district of Southern California. . . .

We would have liked to visit one of the film studios. However, the directors of the motion picture association of the U.S.A. did not wish to let us, Soviet correspondents, into the film studios of Hollywood. They were afraid to open for us the doors behind which American cinema poison is made day and night.

Already for a long time Hollywood has been used by the American imperialists for unbridled war propaganda. . . .

The propagation of the cult of violence and murders, the cult of war and robbery — such is the main purpose of the present-day output of Hollywood.

Several months ago Hollywood received a special task from the U.S. State Department — to prepare quickly 400 films glorifying the "American way of life," for exhibition in the countries of Western Europe and Asia. Side by side with cannon and machine guns, American cinema poison is becoming a most important article of export for the monopolists of the U.S.A. . . .

Hollywood is now under the sway of anti-Communist hysteria. The shadow of American fascism has been hanging over the film city, as also over the entire country.

We decided to visit the small town of Virginia City, located on the other side of the Sierra Nevada Mountains, in the neighboring state of Nevada, where Mark Twain, the celebrated American writer, lived and worked in his youth. . . .

. . . *A Yankee in King Arthur's Court* seditious

To tell the truth, we had hoped to see a Mark Twain museum in Virginia City. After all, it was here that the celebrated American writer began his literary career in 1861 as a staff member of one of the oldest newspapers in the Far West of the U.S.A. — "Territorial Enterprise." Later he moved to San Francisco, where he also worked on a newspaper. In this period he began his first outstanding works, including "The Celebrated Jumping Frog of Calaveras County."

Reality, however, disproved our assumptions. The house in which the printing press and editorial office of the newspaper were located had been destroyed by fire. The remains of the printing press and the personal belongings of Mark Twain have been heaped in a rotting, tumble-down building on the corner of A Street and Sutton Avenue. Already for a long time there have been no doors or windows in the premises, and the wind blows freely throughout the building.

The American authorities "have not found funds" to put in order, and preserve for posterity, the place where the talented writer and publicist lived and created. Perhaps the fact that a number of his works, including "A Yankee at King Arthur's Court," are acknowledged as "seditious" in present-day America throws light on the attitude of the rulers of the U.S.A. toward the popular writer.

We read a report in the "Los Angeles Times" that Mark Twain's aged daughter was selling by auction the writer's house in Hollywood, his library, letters and autographs.

We returned from Virginia City. . . .

For a distance of scores of miles, almost up to San Francisco itself, visible on both sides of the road were the results of a barbarous attitude toward natural resources. In a wide area of formerly fertile soil you will not see a tree nor an ear of grain — this is a dead, dismal realm of stone. They

"Neither lying propaganda nor fascist repressions"

explained to us that at one time the dredges of gold-mining companies had passed through these places. The owners of gold plants had bought up the land, and then they had broken up and washed literally every meter of it, and left behind heaps of stones, on which not a blade of grass now grows.

"There you have one of the 'achievements' of American capitalism," our traveling companion remarked, pointing with his hand to the stone desert.

The war hysteria being kindled in America also rages in California. At the railroad stations and airports, and on the docks — everywhere are visible groups of soldiers, who are being sent somewhere, are being transferred. On Sundays the streets of San Francisco are filled with drunken sailors. . . .

Placards with pictures of atomic explosions are stuck on the walls of autobuses, on the backs of benches, and at tramway stations. War hysteria has seized the schools, where "atomic raid alarms" are carried out. . . .

However, neither lying propaganda nor fascist repressions are succeeding in breaking the will of the common Americans for peace, for the struggle for their rights.

More and more often American soldiers and sailors, who have been maimed on the Korean front, clatter along the streets of San Francisco on pairs of crutches. The events in Korea have opened the eyes of many Americans. Thousands of them are beginning to understand that only the monopolists of Wall Street are profiting from the blood of American soldiers.

The movement for the cessation of American aggression in Korea and for the peaceful settlement of the situation in the Far East is including ever wider circles of the population of California. . . .

And so the war of words, words, words goes on. Un-

. . . . **What do they call Stalin?**

fortunately, it is a war to the death — and so I think it's important for me, during *my* stay in Russia, to tell Americans what the Soviet correspondents are telling Russians about *their* stay in America. It's a bit complicated, this business of putting up two mirrors face to face — particularly when one (perhaps both) of the mirrors is cracked.

MARCH 18, 1952

By the middle of March the morale of the Americans and British, and probably all foreigners, as well as Russians, seems to be reaching a new low. Everybody is becoming increasingly irritable, sour and quick-tempered — or at least they seem so to me, who am slightly that way myself. One explanation probably is the added depression of the long, dark, winter months, which we have had for half a year now — quite an accumulation of blackness.

MARCH 20, 1952

Just what do they call him? By "they" I mean the Russians, and by "him" I mean Stalin. I am not referring here to any particular epithets, but simply to the name itself. In other words, does the average Soviet citizen — in the secrecy of his home (or, if there is no such thing even as secrecy in a Soviet home, in the secrecy of a Soviet heart) — say to himself merely "Stalin," or "Comrade Stalin," or "the Boss," or "J. V.," or "dear Iosif Vissarionovich," or "that man Djugashvili," or what?

I have often wondered about this, finding the question of particular fascination. And why fascinating? Because the

"Iosif Vissarionovich" . . . .

question is so simple and normal and innocent — and yet absolutely unanswerable. It is one of those unnatural situations that is so natural in the U.S.S.R. today. Everybody knows, I assume, that Americans in the Soviet Union have hardly half a dozen opportunities in a year to converse with Russians on any subject at any length, but I doubt whether it is fully realized that certainly the last subject ever to come up would be Joseph Stalin himself. As far as I can tell, his name has never been mentioned once in a non-official conversation between a Westerner and a Russian.

There are, of course, clues in this mystery. One possibility is the combination of Stalin's Christian name (he was baptized by a Greek Orthodox priest) and patronymic mentioned above, Iosif (Joseph) Vissarionovich, which proves to be such a tongue twister for Anglo-Saxons. Half formal, half affectionate, this appalling appellation is found on the front page of *Pravda* every day of the year, serving as the standard subhead for a daily letter addressed to Stalin. This stereotyped letter to "Dear Iosif Vissarionovich" is "sent" every day by a different organization or group of workers, peasants, employees, engineers, etc., now from one part of the country, now from another, telling Stalin how hard they work and how happy they are, and how deep is their adoration for their teacher and guide who inspires such work and such happiness. The only time I ever heard a Russian speak these two words was my first day in the U.S.S.R., when the Intourist guide in Leningrad was taking me on a sightseeing tour of the city. Pointing out the various scenes and monuments of the October Revolution, she would say unctuously, with a caressing tone to her voice as she pronounced the name, "Here is where Iosif Vissarionovich took care of Lenin

. . . . . . Safer not to breathe Stalin's name

in the weeks before the revolution," "Here is where Iosif Vissarionovich directed the Bolshevik headquarters at Smolny," "Here is where Iosif Vissarionovich personally led the attack against the Winter Palace." That, as I say, is the only time this form of the name has been spoken in my hearing — and it doesn't seem to me likely that a Russian (in privacy, or in any kind of informal, homely setting) would say, for example: "I wonder how Iosif Vissarionovich is getting along these days?"

Another possibility is what has now turned out to be the *official* name — the name heard and seen everywhere in public: in the press, on the radio, on banners and slogans. And that official name is "the Great Stalin." The adjective "Great" is linked to the noun "Stalin" so tightly that today they are almost one indivisible word. When printed, this name is always in capital letters or italicized; when spoken on Moscow Radio, this name is invariably pronounced after a dramatic pause, and with almost breathless reverence. But, again, that can certainly be disregarded as the popular name, the name used by the private citizen in everyday conversations in the family circle and among intimate friends.

My own hunch is that the average Russian today thinks it better and safer not to breathe Stalin's name at all. And that means, I believe, that he or she doesn't even dare to think about him.

MARCH 21, 1952

While on the subject of Stalin's name, I think it would be fitting to give here a little information on the correct pronunciation and spelling of two other names, two surnames

Malenkov and Beria   .   .   .   .

that are in the minds, if not on the lips, of almost everybody in contemporary Russia. These names are Malenkov
and Beria, and they belong to two of the most powerful men
in the world. Along with Molotov, they appear to be the
most likely successors to Stalin's position — Malenkov now
being Stalin's lieutenant in Communist Party matters, Beria
his lieutenant in secret police affairs.

In view of the hiddenness of everything in the Soviet
Union, it is not too surprising that Malenkov and Beria are
two of the least-known men in the entire country. Here, the
higher the position, the heavier the blackout of information
— just the reverse of the situation in the West. So much
secrecy surrounds these men that very few people in the
world even know how to pronounce their names.

Almost all Westerners mispronounce Malenkov's name.
That is understandable, perhaps, because even in the Russian language the accent could fall on any one of the three
syllables. The only arbiter in such a dispute is Moscow Radio,
which, like the B.B.C., sets the standard in such questions
— and when, on several occasions, I have heard Moscow
Radio pronounce Malenkov's name, the stress has been on
the last syllable. Most Muscovites also pronounce the name
that way. So, if you want to be correct, put the accent on
the "kov" — and the final "v," incidentally, is pronounced
as though it were an "f."

In regard to the pronunciation of Beria's name, the accent
should fall on the first syllable, and not on the second (a
common mispronunciation among foreigners). I say that the
stress should be on the first syllable because, again, that is
the way Moscow Radio and most educated Russians in
Moscow pronounce the name, and that is the only valid test

. . . . . . nowhere have I heard such music

in such a case. Incidentally, the spelling of Beria's name most commonly accepted in the West is that which is used here (that is, B-e-r-i-a) — but actually, according to the most accurate system of transliterating Cyrillic words with Roman letters, the spelling should be B-e-r-i-y-a. We might as well get this straight now, because the name is going to be in the headlines and in the history books for years to come.

MARCH 25, 1952

Music — it is much more of Moscow than most people realize.

I have now been in almost all of the major capitals of the world — Washington, London, Paris, Berlin, Rome, Vienna, Bern, Brussels, The Hague, Oslo, Stockholm, Copenhagen, Helsinki, Warsaw, Cairo, Manila, Peking, New Delhi, Havana — and nowhere have I heard such music as that which now fills my ears here in Moscow.

I am writing here about two things. First, about the ear-splitting chants of school children packed tight into open trucks, lifting their throats to the sky; about wild, abandoned singing in the streets late at night, as five or six Soviet students or soldiers march through town, arm in arm, with an arm or two loose for an accordion or balalaika. And I am also talking about serious music — classical music of exceptional quality and incredible quantity. Every night, and many afternoons, Tchaikovsky Hall, and the Great Hall and Little Hall of the Conservatory, and the Hall of Columns of Dom Soyuzov, and the Bolshoi Theater, and the Filial of the Bolshoi resound to great music — operas, ballets, symphonic music, choral music, chamber music.

a strange choice . . . .

And throughout the day Moscow Radio provides wonderful music. The best estimate is that music accounts for more than half of all broadcast time for all stations in the Soviet Union — and serious music predominates, standing in the ratio of about four to one in relation to popular music on central broadcasting programs.

It is strange that I have devoted so little space to music in these diary entries, and I think the reason is that all along I have realized that the subject deserves, not a paragraph, but a book.

MARCH 26, 1952

Lest I sound unduly enthusiastic about the musical standards of the Soviet Union today, I should add one note, sour indeed. And that note is that the great works of Western music are being heard less and less, and the great works of purely Russian music (particularly the most melodious) are being heard more and more. That is the trend, that is the direction of the wind of nationalism now sweeping over the steppes. But it does not mean that non-Russian music is completely out — as yet.

There are quite a few Bach programs, and some Mozart — but, all in all, anything written before 1800 has little chance of being heard. Hardly any Wagner is played, and then only occasionally on the radio (no Wagnerian operas are given at the Bolshoi). Almost invariably the Wagner broadcast selections are either the overture to *Tannhäuser* or the overture to *Meistersinger*. Once, however, I did hear excerpts from *Siegfried* on Moscow Radio — and that, it seemed to me, was a strange choice for anti-Hitler Russia. An even stranger

. . . . Every week an anniversary

choice was a program I heard a few nights ago, a broadcast from Leningrad consisting of orchestral excerpts from Richard Strauss's *Salome* — music which even many Westerners consider daring, if not decadent. (The applause in the Leningrad hall was so uproarious that the orchestra had to play all the *Salome* selections over again, and Moscow Radio, too, relayed the entire repetition.)

At the moment, Beethoven is on every program. One hundred and twenty-five years ago today, in the downpour of a terrific thunderstorm in Vienna, Beethoven died — and for weeks now Moscow auditoriums have been echoing in stormy tribute. Actually, these so-called "deathdays" are regular features in the Kremlin's carefully planned calendar of the year's events. Almost every week the Soviet people are told to celebrate an anniversary of one kind or another. So far this year, for example, all of Russia, as well as the entire Communist world, has been instructed to commemorate such assorted anniversaries as the "deathday" of Gogol, the birthday of Skryabin, the birthday of Leonardo da Vinci, and now the "deathday" of Beethoven. Recently, I heard the State Symphony Orchestra of the U.S.S.R., led by one of Russia's most popular conductors, Natan Rakhlin (a Ukrainian Jew), give a performance of the Beethoven Ninth — with the State Chorus of Russian Song sadly singing Schiller's "Ode to Joy" in the fourth movement (the fifty women of the choir were not only dressed exactly alike, but all had identical hairdo's: maidenly braids framing their brows). Also, a few weeks ago, in the Hall of Columns (where Vishinsky conducted the Moscow "purge trials" in the 1930's; and where state funerals are now held in the daytime), I listened to the All-Union Radio Committee Symphony Orchestra, con-

Music in Stalin's image . . . .

ducted by bearded Leo Ginsburg, play the "Eroica." This occasion was really a double "deathday," because the date was January 21, the anniversary of Lenin's death — and the platform was draped with hundreds of yards of black (and red) bunting. And last night the Beethoven commemoration came to a climax. Russia's most celebrated pianist, a short, sandy young artist named Emil Gilels, played, with tremendous force and feeling, four Beethoven sonatas (including the "Pathétique" and "Appassionata") to a sell-out house at the Conservatory. As Gilels bent far over the keyboard (his reddish hair falling over his pale face, covering an ill-concealed expression of disdain, cold and faraway), the audience, too, leaned forward on the edge of their chairs. But, unlike Gilels, the audience was motionless, and listened in deathlike silence.

All of this is beginning to sound as though Moscow heard nothing but great Western music — and I am attempting, of course, to show the opposite. But these examples are only outstanding exceptions to prove the rule.

And, quite aside from this point, I haven't even brought up the fantastic subject of the Kremlin's current campaign to instill "Soviet realism" (an absolutely meaningless phrase — and a misnomer, to boot) in contemporary Russian music — that is, Stalin's drive to purge Soviet music (he even attends secret dress rehearsals of new operas at the Bolshoi), Stalin's personal campaign to force Shostakovich, Khachaturyan, Prokofiev, and all the others to create music in his own image and likeness.

But perhaps an American these days is not in a safe position to carp too much, to moralize about music. I notice from the programs listed in the U.S. newspapers that find their way to the Moscow Embassy that less and less Russian

. . . . craving for culture

music is being heard in America. It is quite apparent that
many of our orchestras are *afraid* to play (because of Mc-
Carthyized public opinion) much of the very same Russian
music which Soviet orchestras are *forbidden* to play (because of Stalinized taste).

MARCH 27, 1952

I noticed the following data on a sign at Tchaikovsky's home
at Klin: in the year 1950 in the Soviet Union the ballet *Swan
Lake* was given in twenty-five cities for a total of four hundred and three performances, with 370,412 spectators.

Moscow is full of such signs and posters, boasting of the
cultural achievements of the Soviet regime and the Russian
people. For example, in connection with the intense, widespread celebration of the one hundredth anniversary of
Gogol's death, a billboard was posted opposite our house stat-
ing the interesting fact that up to 1917 — that is before the
Revolution — six million "books" of Gogol's works had been
published in Russia in five languages, whereas in the years of
the Soviet regime, twenty million had been published in
thirty-eight languages. Also recently I noticed in one of
Russia's many Tolstoy museums a large display poster
proudly pointing out that, up to 1917 only 10,784,000 copies
of Tolstoy's works had been published in Russia (in ten languages), while in the years from 1917 to the present the
Soviet regime had put out the incredible total of 40,337,000
copies (in seventy-one languages).

These figures, of course, don't prove it — but I am positive that the Russians' craving for culture is much deeper,
and more widespread, than our own.

"A work of great blood and great sweat" . . . .

MARCH 28, 1952

Prime Minister Churchill should be interested, I think, in a phrase attributed to Ivan the Terrible. The phrase is repeated in many Russian history books in discussing the career and life work of the Tsar. And the words are these, words used by the Russian Tsar four hundred years ago to depict his reign — *"Delo velikoi krovi i velikovo potu"* (a work of great blood and great sweat).

Perhaps Stalin, too, sometimes thinks of this phrase.

MARCH 29, 1952

There is the Bolshoi Curtain and there is the Iron Curtain — and tonight I had a little look through both, simultaneously. It was just a little crack, a small slit, but it did much to keep me believing in human nature and the goodness of life.

My seat at the theater was in the first level of boxes and my box was the first, the one right next to the proscenium arch. When the performance of *Mirandolina* was over, Lepeshinskaya, the star ballerina of the evening, came out for her curtain calls. In many ways, Lepeshinskaya is the most popular dancer in Russia — even more so than the celebrated Ulanova — which is easy to understand since she has more verve, more enthusiasm, and more technical skill, probably, than any dancer in the world. And her enthusiasm is contagious; it smashes its way throughout the house. So when the final curtain fell, all the audience rushed down to the orchestra pit to give her her usual ovation.

The curtains of the Bolshoi do not fall down from top to

bottom but are drawn together, and so there was a crack between the curtains as one of them was held out in front of the footlights to permit Lepeshinskaya to prance onto the stage to respond to the cheers. And she did prance and she did leap and she did bound from one corner of the stage to the other, back and forth in a frenzy of excitement. Then she went back between the curtains and the applause continued.

From my particular angle, right next to the stage, I could see through the opening in the curtain how she behaved all by herself, backstage, between her curtain calls. The whole time she was behind the curtain she danced from one end of the stage to the other, from the front to the back — she couldn't stop herself. She would swing in circles and leap and spin and then once again she would dash through the opening in the curtain, take her bows, and dance back and then again I could see that alone she continued dancing for herself behind the curtain. This went on for twenty minutes. It was the first time I really saw a Russian off guard and really it was the only gay moment I have had in Moscow.

MARCH 31, 1952

"My ballet weekend":

On the last three successive nights (Saturday, Sunday, and tonight) I saw all the top Russian ballet stars: Lepeshinskaya, Kondratov, and Ermolaev in *Mirandolina* at the Filial of the Bolshoi on Saturday night; Ulanova, Yury Zhdanov, Golovkina, Lapauri, and Farmanyants in *Bakhchisaraisky Fontan* at the Bolshoi on Sunday night; Semenova, Plisetskaya, Struchkova, Tikhomirnova, Bogolyubskaya, Cherka-

April Fools' Day . . . .

sova, Chorokhova, Chikvaidze, and Golubin in a "ballet concert" of Bolshoi artists at Tchaikovsky Hall tonight.

Surely this is a record for anybody — Russian or Westerner.

APRIL 1, 1952

April Fools' Day — and all Russians woke this morning to find a surprise waiting for them, a pleasant surprise, and not a joke. In banner headlines of the country's press, and on the radio, Stalin magnanimously announced to his people: "New Reduction of State Retail Prices for Foodstuffs."

"Surprise," I suppose, is not a completely accurate description. Actually, since the announcement of previous price changes had fallen on March 1 in recent years, the entire country has been stolidly waiting for this news for a whole month. In fact, on the night of February 29, all the foreign correspondents in Moscow stayed glued to the radio, waiting in vain for the story to break. So the surprise, in reverse, really came a month ago. Since the Kremlin spends a lot of time timing things, I imagine there was a good reason for the delay this year. But the reasons for things one is not entitled to know.

Anyway, today the Soviet citizen certainly looked at his morning newspaper with much more interest than usual. Here is a literal translation of what he read under the big headlines:

"In view of the successes achieved by industry and agriculture in 1951, the rise in labor productivity and the lowering of unit costs of production, the Soviet Government and the Central Committee of the CPSU deem it possible, as from

April 1, 1952, to effect another reduction of state retail prices — the fifth in succession — for foodstuffs of general consumption."

Then followed a list of all the foodstuffs affected, with the price reduction in each case given on a percentage basis. Here are key items from this long list:

Rye bread — 12 per cent.

Whole-meal wheat bread — 12 per cent.

Bread made of sifted best-quality rye flour — 15 per cent.

Macaroni, noodles, and other alimentary pastes — 15 per cent.

Yeast — 20 per cent.

Semolina, pearl barley, and oatmeal — 20 per cent.

Millet, buckwheat, rice, sago, and other cereals and legumes — 15 per cent.

Starch — 15 per cent.

Wheat, oats, barley, and other grains — 15 per cent.

Bran, oil cakes, shorts, mixed fodder, hay, and straw — 15 per cent.

Beef, mutton, pork, sausage, fowls, and other meat products — 15 per cent.

Ducks, geese, and turkeys — 20 per cent.

Canned meat and canned meat and vegetables — 20 per cent.

Butter — 15 per cent.

Lard — 20 per cent.

Milk, milk products, and canned milk — 10 per cent.

Cheese (Soviet, Swiss, Dutch, etc.) — 20 per cent.

Arakhisa and seed oil — 30 per cent.

Margarine — 15 per cent.

Mayonnaises — 30 per cent.

Ice cream — 15 per cent.

Eggs — 15 per cent.

Prices cut . . . .

Granulated and lump sugar — 10 per cent.

Wrapped caramels, soft sweets, chocolate, and other confectioneries made with sugar — 10 per cent.

Caramels (unwrapped) — 15 per cent.

Biscuits, wafers, fruit cake, tarts, pastries, honey cakes, rusks, and other confectionery products made with flour — 12 per cent.

Jam and fruit jelly — 10 per cent.

Vitamins — 10 per cent.

Coffee and cocoa — 15 per cent.

Salt — 30 per cent.

Vinegar essence — 15 per cent.

Tea — 20 per cent.

Apples, pears, and grapes — 20 per cent.

Frozen fruits and berries — 20 per cent.

Dried fruits and nuts — 20 per cent.

Canned cucumbers, peppers, green peas, and tomatoes, and frozen vegetables — 20 per cent.

Canned fruit, fruit purée and paste, pickled vegetables, tomato paste, tomato purée, fruit and tomato sauces — 10 per cent.

Grape, apple, plum, and tomato juice — 20 per cent.

In addition to these reductions, it is further "resolved" to lower prices, in accordance with these changes, in restaurants, canteens, and other public catering enterprises. Finally, the new decree ends with two unrelated price decisions. The cost of hotel rooms is to be lowered by an average of 15 per cent, and retail prices for books, including textbooks, will be cut by an average of 18 per cent as of today. In view of the current intensification of ideological indoctrination, the rewriting of history and science, and the rising hysteria of hate-

. . . . **a neat propaganda point**

America propaganda, the reduction in the price of books is not without significance, having the effect of making poison cheaper and so more available to many more millions of people.

All the morning papers devoted at least two entire pages to this news — and, since every Russian newspaper has only four pages in all, that represents 50 per cent of all their space. *Pravda,* for example, published a well-planned round-up of "reactions" from such cities as Leningrad, Minsk, and Kiev. The dispatch from Kiev is typical: "The joyful news of the new price reduction for foodstuffs rapidly spread round the towns and villages of the Ukraine. At meetings and talks, the workers, employees, scientists and arts workers, and housewives are expressing sincere gratitude from the bottom of their hearts to the Party of Lenin and Stalin and the Soviet Government for the enormous concern which they display for the Soviet people daily. . . . "

All of this provides a neat propaganda point for the Kremlin, and today every ounce has been squeezed out of this ready-made opportunity. To illustrate: *Pravda,* in its leading article, the page-one editorial, had this to say, among other things:

The successes in the development of the Soviet economy and the steady advance in the material and cultural well-being of the working people speak more convincingly than any words of the advantages of the Soviet system and its decisive superiority to the capitalist system. . . .

The full weight of preparations for a new war and of the arms race is being cast by the imperialists onto the shoulders of the working people, whose standard of living is falling

those who are not too impressed . . . . . .

sharply. The working man in those countries is under the
scourge of brutal exploitation, he suffers from unemployment, hunger, and poverty, from the uninterrupted rise in
the cost of living and an unbearable burden of taxation.
Even according to the official and clearly reduced statistics
of the Bureau of Labor Statistics of the Department of Labor,
the average price of foodstuffs in the U.S.A. at the end of
December, 1951, was 234 per cent of the average prewar
level from 1935 to 1939 — that is, nearly two and one half
times higher than prewar. Prices have risen many times in
Britain during the last few years. In the first half of 1951
alone, the British Government issued over 60 different
orders for increasing the retail prices of goods vitally important to the population. The increase in prices in Britain
is being accompanied by a reduction in rations, which have
been kept in force since the war.

The working people of Italy, Western Germany, Japan,
Yugoslavia, and other countries that have fallen into
bondage to American imperialism are in an even more im-
poverished condition. . . .

Now, what does all this mean to the Soviet citizen? As the
Kremlin boasts, reductions have taken place here for five
successive years — and, in the case of items affected every
year, the price has fallen considerably, since an article costing 10 rubles at the end of the war would now cost only 5.9
rubles if, for example, a straight 10 per cent reduction had
been applied every year. On the other hand, those who are
not too impressed by these reductions and the accompany-
ing trumpet flourish insist with some validity that the starting point of wartime prices was so much higher than the
prewar level that prices for consumer goods today, even after

. . . . . . **slowly but steadily getting better**

five reductions, are still way out of line. Furthermore, they argue, the currency reform of 1947 involved a radical devaluation of the ruble, with far-reaching consequences — and chief among these was the effect on the peasant, whose purchasing power was largely liquidated.

This is all true, but still, one thing cannot be denied: these reductions have a remarkably good psychological effect. The worker in the factory and his wife in the kitchen see that, in general, things are slowly but steadily getting better, not worse. With respect to their own standard of living, progress may be at a creeping pace, but, still, every year there is improvement. It would be extremely dangerous for us, I think, to dwell only on the fact that Russia's economic level at present is very low in comparison with ours, and to forget the fact that the movement is forward. And it would likewise be dangerous to underestimate the underlying strength this progress must give the regime at home.

APRIL 2, 1952

Yesterday's price reductions focus attention again on the official exchange rate of four rubles to one dollar. If I remember correctly, I wrote here more than a year ago that on the basis of an average retail price index, a more realistic rate for an American living in Moscow would be around twenty-five rubles to a dollar. Since that time, prices in the U.S.S.R. have been reduced on two occasions — and so an index now would probably show that from fifteen to eighteen rubles would be a fair exchange. And, again, if you consider quality as well, then perhaps twenty to twenty-five would be even fairer.

Exchange rates . . . .

It is a complex problem. To straighten myself out on this question, I had a long talk today with the ranking economist in the Embassy. Our conversation, with questions and answers, went something like this:

Q. Is there such a thing as a meaningful exchange rate between the dollar and the ruble, a rate that serves all purposes? And, if so, what standards or measures would you use in your calculations? That is, what is the best system to employ to get valid comparisons and equivalents?

A. The question of what would be a realistic exchange rate between the dollar and the ruble has stumped the best economists and statisticians for a long time. Such an exchange rate, a rate that can do any job you might expect it to do, simply doesn't exist. That's because there are such striking differences between the U.S. and Soviet economies and their respective price structures, because there are such involved questions as the share of national income distributed to the various consumers and returned to the state for future investment. Actually, however, there are several fairly valid answers, depending upon what you want to use the exchange rate for. It all depends on what kind of comparison you're trying to make.

Q. Well, one comparison is to ask what a U.S. employee in our Moscow Embassy should get for his dollar in order to be able to live in the same way as he does in America. Everybody in the foreign colony here seems pretty well agreed that on the basis of an average retail price index, the rate today, following the recent price reductions, should fall close to twenty rubles per dollar. But how about it from another angle? What would a Soviet worker's wage represent in American dollars?

A. If you're interested in this kind of comparison, in fig-

. . . . . **Two to three months' work for a suit**

uring out, for example, what the average monthly wage of about 600 rubles would equal in U.S. currency, then you could do little better than use the figure which the United Nations came up with a year or so ago. The U.N. study, if I recall correctly, calculated the ruble at about ten to the dollar. Perhaps it is more like nine to the dollar today. Now, the important thing here is that this computation is not based merely on retail prices of commodities in the open market, but includes rent, social services, "free" medical care, and other "advantages" Russian workers are supposed to have. As you know, a Rusian worker pays much less rent than a Western worker, although what he gets for his money is quite another matter. It is also questionable just what "free" medical service means, but nonetheless it must be taken into account somehow to get a fully balanced view.

Q. Is it possible to make the computation merely in terms of hours worked — in the U.S.A. and U.S.S.R., respectively — to receive enough money for the purchase of certain goods and services, provided they are available at all in the Soviet Union?

A. The type of computation you mention — that is, comparing what the Soviet worker can buy for a given amount of sweat — does *not* answer the problem of the exchange rate. However, it is probably the most effective means of measuring the comparative standard of living, or at least it translates into some semblance of understandability such concepts as average wages expressed in rubles and the like. For example, a Soviet worker would have to work from two to three months to get enough money to buy a suit, using his rubles for nothing else. If that is all you want to do with this subject — that is, compare what a Soviet worker earns with what other workers earn in other countries — you don't

Taxes . . . .

have to go any further, although you are leaving out "free" services and are probably overlooking rent.

Q. What about the so-called "defense" ruble?

A. There is as yet no well-based answer to the question of what the Soviet Government's total of 96 billion rubles to be spent for "defense" means in dollar terms. It is my guess that the "defense" ruble might be something like six or seven to the dollar, or perhaps even five or six. It is not entirely inconceivable that it is even four to one, although I doubt it. There is one thing I might add here about this entire problem of calculating an exchange rate. You see, Russian retail prices are thrown completely out of line by the Soviet tax system. In our country, if you take jewelry, for example, you may quote the retail price before the 20 per cent tax is added, or you may take the price after it is added. But in the Soviet Union, the only price you have to go on is the price including tax. Now, it's known that many commodities in the U.S.S.R. — including most commodities of mass consumption, like bread, sugar, clothing, shoes, and so forth — carry from 100 per cent to 300 per cent tax. Thus, your price for sugar, purchased in a state store, will be 75 per cent taxes. So, if you're trying to base your exchange of rubles and dollars to estimate *production costs* in the U.S.S.R. in comparison with those in the U.S.A., you don't get very far using this system.

Q. Do national income figures have some bearing on the problem?

A. Some statisticians have tried to arrive at a comparison of U.S.A. and U.S.S.R. economies through elaborate calculations of national income. These calculations are extremely controversial, and there is much disagreement among experts in the field. Most of these surveys, however, do agree that Soviet national income is equivalent to about one third or perhaps one fourth of U.S. national income. One of the steps in calculating such comparisons involves a means of reducing rubles to dollars, and I believe that all such comparisons usually have ended up with something like this: U.S. national income in 1950 was about 240 billion *dollars;* U.S.S.R. national income in 1950 was about 700 billion *rubles.* If U.S. national income is *three* times as great as U.S.S.R. national income, then U.S.S.R. national income in *dollars* would be 80 billion. Thus, 80 billion *dollars* is equal to 700 billion *rubles,* indicating an exchange rate of a little less than nine rubles to the dollar. If U.S. income is *four* times as great as the U.S.S.R. income, then U.S.S.R. national income would be 60 billion *dollars.* Thus, 60 billion *dollars* would be equal to 700 billion *rubles,* or an exchange of nearly twelve rubles to one dollar. Please don't take this figure as absolutely correct, because I just don't happen to have the actual figures with me for either the U.S.A. or the U.S.S.R. — and these are merely approximations to show you the possible range, basing our calculations on different national income statistics.

In all of this, we can be positive about one thing at least: the present official rate of four to one is entirely unrealistic and the least defensible of any. Everybody except the Kremlin agrees about that.

APRIL 5, 1952

This Saturday afternoon I walked the whole way around "B" Circle, the ring of streets encircling Moscow, with few stops and at a brisk pace. It took me four hours.

We left a few moments before three and I returned to the

Around "B Circle" . . . .

same spot on the circle near "Vesnina," at 8.15 — having made four stops en route (taking up about an hour and a quarter in all): at Beer Hall No. 6, at Narodnaya (one of the city's big apartment houses set aside for diplomats), at the Kama Restaurant, and at Sadovaya, another diplomatic ghetto.

I have heard various figures for the whole distance, ranging from fourteen to seventeen kilometers.

APRIL 7, 1952

Tonight I heard Paul Robeson on the Moscow radio — a recording of part of a concert he gave in Tchaikovsky Hall in June 1949 (or at least that was what I thought the radio announcer said).

It is certainly a strange sensation to hear in English such songs as "Ol' Man River" and "Swing Low, Sweet Chariot" on the Russian radio in the middle of the night. Robeson also sang a beautiful lullaby, but mostly his program consisted of a series of more topical songs closer to the Party line — bitter ballads about the exploitation of the working classes, discrimination against Negroes in America, Franco's generals, persecution, etc., as well as a very brief Chinese song, which was extremely popular with the audience, which demanded an encore.

Although he sang in English for the most part, he himself would often introduce and explain his songs in Russian. His Russian was extremely good, although his soft Negro accent made the language sound even stranger than usual.

This recorded program must be popular because I have heard it several times.

In Russia Paul Robeson is an international hero, and a

play built around him has been running on the Moscow stage for two seasons now. The title of the play is *John, Soldier of Peace*. Why they do not call Robeson "Robeson" in the cast of characters, I do not know, but anyway his name is given as "John Robertson," with the note that he is a Negro singer. The whole purpose of the play is to show how the Negroes in America suffer and in what squalor they live. The plot concerns the efforts of the American authorities to keep Robertson from singing at a concert at St. Peter's Mill (read Peekskill).

American gangsters are also involved in this plot and a minor theme concerns the plight of American workers who are on strike. Also prominent in the cast of characters are several Americans who have "seen the light" and are working as local members of "Partisans of Peace Committees."

The sets are extremely realistic, particularly those showing the slum quarters of the Negroes in New York. In contrast to the squalor of these dirty courtyards is the fancy New York apartment of Robertson and his wife, Mary. Mary is always dressed in an elaborate evening dress and quite often caresses a large photograph of Stalin which stands on the grand piano in their palatial living room.

In the play Robertson sings, among other things, "Casey Jones" and "Ol' Man River." The Russian who takes the part has a fine voice and, in comparison with the other actors, his performance is convincing and, at times, moving.

Some of the properties on the sets were quite interesting. In the first scene, for example, which takes place in a government office in Washington, the backdrop is a large American flag which I noted had only forty-two stars. In another scene, the most prominent properties on stage were slogans

Trip to Ryazan . . . .

on the walls which read "We Want Peace," "Ban the A-Bomb," "Stop the War in Asia," and beside them were posters of little American girls releasing peace doves.

APRIL 9, 1952

In addition to Moscow's twenty-odd "legitimate" theaters, the city has more than sixty movie houses. To judge by the lines in the streets waiting to get in, the Tarzan pictures are the most popular fare. I saw one tonight. They are the old American films of Johnny Weissmuller with a German sound track dubbed in. I don't know whether or not the audience knows they are seeing American films, but the Russians do seem to realize there's something extremely odd (as well as exciting) about the whole business.

APRIL 12, 1952

In a holiday mood, two British colleagues and I boarded the Moscow-Karaganda train at the Kazan Station at 9 A.M. yesterday, to take the four and one half hour trip to Ryazan, which is 120 miles southeast of Moscow. In not such a holiday mood, we returned today.

Our first problem on arrival was to find a place in which to stay — and the problem remained unsolved to the very end.

Although Ryazan is the capital of Ryazan Oblast (the latter has a population of close to 2,500,000), and is the only large city in the oblast, it has only two small hotels (the Zvezda and the First of May). The British Embassy had previously telegraphed to both hotels requesting rooms for this one night, and both hotels had replied negatively. Both

. . . . **Search for a room**

replied even more negatively when we applied in person at the reception desk yesterday afternoon. This time, the answer was unpleasantly categorical. During our conversation with the "administrator" of the First of May, we caught a reference to a third hotel, the Moskva. We must have got the tense wrong, because after an hour's search in and out of deserted, dust-covered doorways in the immediate vicinity of the stated address we found that the building in question no longer served as a hotel, but as the headquarters of a local government organ. This building was one of the darkest, dirtiest, and most decrepit structures I have ever seen.

In our next attempt, we traveled across town, far from the center, to the House of the Peasants, a clean-looking community hostel on the edge of a barren gulch, where collective farmers and (presumably) stray travelers can rent a bed for a ruble or two. Two British officers stayed there for a night several months before, but they were evicted the following day, in spite of the fact that cots were still vacant. Here we were received with more sympathy but with equal firmness: "Sorry, but our house is full." Not a soul was in sight. And one soul was out of sight. As we turned away from the makeshift reception desk in the upstairs corridor, a militiaman suddenly appeared from behind an inner door which had been standing ajar, and silently watched our exit.

From our taxi driver we learned that there was another peasant hostel — this one called the House of the Collective Farmers — located near the market. "I don't know where it is, exactly," he said, "but I shall be glad to take you to the market, anyway." In the middle of the market we finally found a rough signboard with an arrow, "To the House of the Collective Farmers." This arrow led us through an in-

A night in the waiting room · · · · · · · ·

teresting series of barnyards, manure piles, garbage dumps, and pigsties — and back again. One log cabin showed signs of life other than that of horses and hens — so we knocked on the door. A woman cooking a stew over a pot, and a man washing his neck over a bowl, politely answered our question: "Yes, there was such a place, but that was years ago."

At this point we decided to spend the night in the waiting room of the station — and to stay up as late as we could, under a roof, before arriving at the station. Accordingly, that evening we managed to go to the theater (from 7.30 to 10.30), then to the last showing of a movie (10.30 to midnight), and finally to a nearby restaurant, where we helped the waitress clean things up at 1 A.M. We arrived at the station at 1.20 A.M. The waiting room was packed, but we found that a good squeeze or nudge, and particularly a push, would provide a surprising amount of bench space and *babushka* warmth. By the end of an hour, however, there was a bit too much of the latter, and one of us (I) began to explore the station in search for something a little less intimate and at the same time slightly more horizontal. There was no need to go far. The adjoining room was absolutely empty of people and filled with beautiful benches. We moved in, and it was only a matter of minutes before the three of us were sound asleep, and then it was only a matter of seconds before the three of us were sound awake. Under the glare of the bare electric light bulb, which hung from the ceiling a few inches over our noses, stood a sturdy station attendant who demanded our immediate withdrawal. A Soviet Army officer appeared at the door at this moment, and then made for a bench, obviously agreeing that our action was logical. The woman station attendant, a virago, stopped him, too, and in the ensuing conversation we learned the

. . . . **"Pay no attention"**

reason for the *nelzya* (impossible): the room was under-going *remont* (repairs). The officer obeyed her command more meekly than we did.

Back in the din and dankness of the waiting room, we settled down again — only to be uprooted by a station offi-cial one grade higher than the vixen. He said, bluntly, that we could not stay in the station at all. At that point we received friendly, but conflicting, advice from peasants on both sides of our bench. One said, "Pay no attention"; the other said, "He'll return." And return he did. When we explained that we could find no hotel room and that we were going back to Moscow early the next afternoon, he made what was unfortunately an unanswerable rejoinder: "This is not a hotel, and there are many trains back to Mos-cow between now and tomorrow afternoon." And so there were: a look at the timetable posted on the wall showed that seventeen trains a day pass through Ryazan en route to Moscow — trains from Rostov, Alma-Ata, Frunze, Penza, Morshansk, Tambov, Kuibyshev, Stalingrad, Ashkhabad, Stalinabad, Voronezh, Baku, Novorossisk, Karaganda, Ke-merovo, Novo Kuznetsk, and Tashkent — and many of these were due before the next afternoon. A few minutes later he returned with two militiamen, and at 2.45 A.M. we were outside on the wind-swept platform.

Earlier in the day, fearing the worst, we had surveyed the park-bench situation. Strangely enough, Ryazan has very few park benches, and pools of water — spring floods having inun-dated many sections of the city — surrounded the few we did notice. Another factor now entered our decision not to try the parks: as we left the station, we suddenly realized how cold it was.

Passing through the gate out onto the street, we caught

A kind old peasant . . . .

sight of a taxi — and then all of us knew at once what the solution was. Our victim, a middle-aged, weather-beaten peasant type, in a greasy sheepskin coat, left the wheel of his old, broken-down Pobeda and gravely listened to our proposition. We asked him to drive us around the city for six hours, or at least until the sun warmed things up. He agreed on hearing we would pay 30 rubles an hour. And so the rest of the night was passed. Our two desires — sleep and warmth — got in each other's way. When we parked the car in a dark alley in order to have a doze, the windows frosted with the cold and the interior was like a deep-freeze. When we kept the car moving in order to warm up the engine, the rough driving along the muddy cobblestone streets made any sleep out of the question.

After two hours, the driver himself got discouraged. Then, in the friendliest fashion, he invited us to his home. "Our house is clean," he said, "very clean, and there is plenty of room. My wife and I would be most pleased to have you." At this point he still did not realize that we were representatives of "enemy" embassies (my British friends were much more vague than I care to be about such matters of identification) and so, for his own protection, we had to decline his warm invitation. Not knowing the real reason for our refusal, this kind old peasant must have thought us rude and superior, if not mad.

Conversation throughout the night could not be described as sparkling — but it did produce many interesting comments from the driver. His curiosity about the West was boundless (but only in material terms). By dawn our identity had at last been established, and the driver peppered us with questions about living conditions in Britain. On asking us whether the British really still had rationing, and on hearing the reply that, yes, some goods were still rationed, he made one of the most significant remarks heard on our trip, particularly when one considers that the words came from the lips of an ignorant, unworldly peasant in a remote, provincial town in the middle of Russia: "Oh, so what we hear on our radio, and read in our papers, is true, after all."

The night finally came to an end, and a few hours later we gave up, and boarded the Moscow train early this afternoon. As we climbed into the car, the loudspeaker system in the corridor was playing, rather appropriately, the last movement of Rimsky-Korsakov's *Scheherazade,* which is entitled, if my memory serves correctly, "The Ship Goes to Pieces on a Rock Surmounted by a Bronze Warrior."

APRIL 13, 1952

More notes on our Ryazan trip:

Ryazan is located on the right bank of the Oka River, in the northwest corner of Ryazan Oblast.

The Oka is the largest right (west) tributary of the Volga, and is navigable for most of its 950-mile length, and is an important artery for lumber and grain. In general, the river flows north and northeast, with several bends, and empties into the Volga at Gorky. At Ryazan the river is north of the city, and then it flows southeast through a level, well-watered area, which is often flooded in the spring.

Ryazan Oblast is chiefly agricultural, with rye, oats, millet, potatoes, and fruits the main crops. The oblast has extensive peat resources, and some peasant industries, especially

Ryazan in history . . . .

textiles and leather and wooden products, but most of the manufacturing is centered in the city of Ryazan, which has many factories for farm machines, textiles, leather and wooden goods, a cannery, and a meat combine.

Before the war Ryazan had a population of almost 100,000 people. In 1939, according to Soviet statistics, 60 per cent of the city's employed population consisted of workers.

On as brief a stay in Ryazan as ours — we were in the city for only sixteen daylight hours — a good point from which to start the visit is the site of the old Kremlin, the highest spot of land in town, where you get an excellent view of both the city and the surrounding country.

From this point, which is at the head of Revolution Street, one of the three main thoroughfares of the city, you can see the valley of the Oka to the north and the industrial areas of the city to the south. At the same time you can see how the Oka serves as a topographical boundary for the entire area — with vast forest lands stretching north of the river, and open, flat, semi-steppe lands, with many lakes, extending to the south. Ryazan once had a reputation of being one of the most picturesque towns in central Russia, but now its numerous gardens have been replaced by bleak factory walls, and the smokestacks outnumber the cupolas.

To an historian, the Ryazan rampart offers a view in time even more interesting than the physical panorama. The town was founded by Slav colonists from Kiev at the end of the eleventh century. The high, grass-covered earthworks on which we stood were constructed in the course of the fourteenth and fifteenth centuries although the earlier section is said to date from 1208, and an elaborate citadel once rose within these walls. These fortifications withstood many Tatar attacks from the south, but in 1517 came the greatest attack of all — this time from a different direction: Moscow. Ryazan has considerable historical significance, because it was the last of the great principalities to lose its independence to Moscow. Under Ivan III and Basil III, all the contenders for dominion had fallen, in rapid succession, under the sway of the new "Tsardom of Moscow." When the Ryazan walls fell, there were no independent political units left. The Russian Middle Ages had come to an end, royal absolutism had replaced feudalism, and the Russian national state was born, for better (in many ways) or worse (in many other ways).

Economic conditions: We visited the market at 8 A.M., and at that time there was no meat or milk for sale. In general, there was very little on display in the half-empty booths, and there were few customers. I noted the following prices for farm products (for which I give the American equivalents at the official rate of exchange): potatoes — 1.25 rubles per kilogram (14¢ per pound); carrots — 4 (45¢); onions — 9 ($1.02); beets — 1.50 (17¢); flour — 1.50 (17¢). Eggs were priced at 17 rubles for ten ($5.10 a dozen); 30 rubles ($7.50) were asked for a live hen, and 35 rubles ($8.75) for a live rooster. I took note of these additional prices outside the main market: in a state vegetable store in the center of town potatoes were marked at 1.90 per kilo (21¢ per pound), and a single lemon cost 6 rubles ($1.50); in the city's best (and only good) restaurant, the Zarya, roast pork was listed on the menu at 5.55 ($1.39), and roast goose at 7.20 ($1.80). Neither, incidentally, was available; nor, for that matter, were eggs or butter.

Long queues were present at every bakery. At Bulochnaya

Culture . . . .

No. 40 and at Bulochnaya No. 42, for example, the lines were so long and so disorderly that many militiamen were on hand to keep things under control when the doors opened at 9 A.M. The near-riots which took place at this time could possibly be explained by the fact that the following day was a traditional church holiday, Pussy-Willow Sunday (our Palm Sunday).

There was little building activity, with the exception of the construction of a central department store, in the city proper. Most of our time, however, was spent in the center of the town, and there is undoubtedly more building going on in the outlying areas, where most of the new industries and housing projects are located.

The local transportation facilities were meager, but nonetheless adequate. Trolley buses traveled along the main streets quite frequently but litle public transportation service was seen anywhere else. In all, there were about twenty taxis in the city, most of them old Pobedas.

Cultural activities: Ryazan has two theaters — the Oblast Dramatic Theater and the Youth Theater. The former, housed in a large, impressive-looking building facing the main park in the approach to the Kremlin, unfortunately had no performance that evening but the bill for the rest of the week was as follows: Gorky's *Vassa Zheleznova,* Ostrovsky's *Light but No Warmth,* and Galan's viciously anti-American play, *Under the Golden Eagle.* The Youth Theater, however, was putting on Solodar's *Star of Peace,* which we attended. This play is called *The Boy From Marseilles* in Moscow, where it was given thirty-two times in 1951, at the Young Spectator's Theater, and more than fifty times so far this year. The action takes place in the port area of Mar-

. . . . **An unruly audience**

seilles in the spring of 1950, and concerns the efforts of a group of Stalin-loving French kids to frustrate the plans of the Americans to ship arms (concealed in champagne cases) to Indo-China in a vessel which had already brought infected potatoes from the U.S.A.

Of considerably more interest than the play was the half-hour lecture given from the platform just before curtain time. The audience consisted of approximately two hundred Soviet children, ranging in age from eight to eighteen (most of them Pioneers and Komsomols), who filled about half the hall. The majority of these must have known about the lecture beforehand, because it was with great reluctance that they left their ice cream, fruit drinks, cigarettes, and sly hand-holding in the lobby and buffet. As a result of the general disorderliness, the evening's entertainment began half an hour late. When the hall finally settled down to relative quiet, a half-frustrated, half-frantic gentleman appeared between the red plush curtains and announced that there would be a lecture on "The Struggle of Youth for Peace Throughout the World." Then, three times, he asked for attention and silence. At that point, a humorless young woman primly walked to the lectern, opened a sheaf of papers, and began to read her lecture hurriedly and monotonously. There was still a great buzz of conversation in the hall, and the master of ceremonies again popped out between the curtains and *begged* everybody to be quiet. Once again the lecturer started, and then, for thirty minutes, took us on a tour of the world, country by country, and, sentence by sentence, repeated the anti-American phrases of the central press and radio. The undercurrent of talk, punctuated by the girls' giggling, continued throughout the lec-

"Tarzan Finds a Son" . . . .

ture — but, at the same time, many of the children listened with wide eyes and frightening credulity. Here, in this small example, as in almost all instances in the U.S.S.R., it was difficult and dangerous to generalize about opinion outside the Kremlin walls: the evidence was contradictory, fifty-fifty.

We — not the play, nor the lecture — were the hit of the evening. The pig-tailed, aproned girls who sat near us knew at once that we were foreigners, and when they found out that two of us were British and one an American, their curiosity was beyond control. At the end of the first act we were surrounded; at the end of the second act we were mobbed. The questions came thick and fast — some childish, some searching and mature. Most of the questions concerned democracy in the West. "Are all people 'equal' in countries outside the Soviet Union?" asked one six-year-old, with wonderful shining eyes and a red ribbon in her hair. When we answered "Yes," the children gravely wondered how that could be so in capitalist countries. As we left the theater, several girls followed us out the door, and warmly begged us to visit their school the next day. For a moment, at least, "The Struggle of Youth for Peace Throughout the World" was being waged in a different way.

There appeared to be only half a dozen movie houses in the city. One of these was showing a revival of Gogol's *Sorochintsy Fair* (a cinema mixture of Musorgsky's opera and Ryabov's operetta), which we attended; all the remaining theaters seemed to be showing *Tarzan Finds a Son*. It is interesting that this particular film, billed as the third in the Tarzan series, has turned up in Ryazan before the showing in Moscow. It is also interesting that at least some of the movie goers of Ryazan displayed the same curiosity as to the source of the Tarzan films as has been encountered in other Soviet cities. For example, one of the first questions of the young Pioneers with whom we talked was: "In what country was the first Tarzan film made, and why is the sound track in German?" They seemed only faintly surprised on hearing that the films were American, and in spite of the obvious absence of such information in the Soviet copies, they showed no disbelief on hearing our explanation.

In pre-revolutionary days, Ryazan had more than twenty Greek Orthodox churches. The shells of them remain, but, in the words of one of our taxi drivers, only two are "working." The services at these two churches, he added, are poorly attended — except on the important days of the church calendar, when the floors are crowded with people of all ages.

At the present time Ryazan has two museums: the I. P. Pavlov Museum (the scientist was born in Ryazan in 1849), and the Ryazan Oblast Museum. The latter lives up to its reputation of being one of the best provincial museums in the Soviet Union. It is located in the center of the old Kremlin, among the ruins and restorations of the ancient churches and monasteries (dating from the fifteenth to the eighteenth centuries), and is housed in the former Archbishop's Palace. There are extensive, well-mounted collections covering all fields of culture and science: art, folklore, history, ethnography, archaeology, botany, zoology, etc., giving a complete picture of the economic and cultural life of the Ryazan area from prehistoric times to the "Stalinist epoch."

Of great personal interest to me was a case of stuffed birds, which explained, at long last, the differences between Rus-

The General Grow incident . . . .

sian rooks, ravens, crows, and jackdaws. For those who, for one reason or another, find themselves in Russian monasteries, or under the Kremlin walls, or in the back court of the British Embassy at Sofiiskaya, and want to know what all the squawking is about, and what is doing it, I submit the following data as authoritative: the *voron* (raven) is the biggest and blackest; the *vorona* (crow) is the next in size, and black and gray in color; the *grach* (rook) is of medium size, black, with a purple neck; and the *galka* (jackdaw) is the smallest, grayish in color, with a black head, breast, and tail.

April 14, 1952

One final word about my Ryazan trip (as described in my last two diary entries):

I am quite proud of this account, I must admit — because all those thousands of words were written entirely from memory, without benefit of notes of any kind. This is why — and the explanation, like everything else concerning our life in Russia, is a bit involved.

It all goes back to the "disclosure" of the supposed diary of General Grow, the American Military Attaché in Moscow. When the Kremlin first "exposed" the diary in the Soviet press a month ago, the rulers of Russia glossed over how they got hold of it (that is, how they stole it), but they certainly didn't gloss over the alleged contents. For weeks now the Moscow papers have been filled with purported entries from what they assert is Grow's diary (of which, they say, they have "photographic" copies in the General's handwriting) — quotes such as these:

. . . . . . **Purported entries in Grow's diary**

Begin war as quickly as possible! Immediately!

The critical year has come. . . . In my opinion, the time is now ripe for the beginning of war.

Poison people's minds by hook or by crook.

The new problem lies in what we must do to fill the vacuum that will be formed after the destruction of the Soviet regime. The new leadership cannot be formed in an improvised fashion, it must be known beforehand.

The Tolstoy Museum [at Yasnaya Polyana] was closed today but this did not trouble us at all since we had no intention of going there. . . . Noted down many license plates of military vehicles. On the road saw some anti-aircraft installations.

The bridge here is best target in South Russia. This, together with bridge over Kuban at Kavkazskaya, would cut off all the Caucasus except for poor line to Astrakhan which could easily be cut. According to our calculations, rail traffic on this main line is the most concentrated in Russia.

Big power plant at Shatura run on peat, of which huge bogs in vicinity. Good target.

Our attack should be directed at enemy weakness. Although the military services are primarily concerned with military weapons and methods, we must understand that this war is total war and is fought with all weapons. We must learn that in this war it is fair to hit below the belt.

Well, anyone can imagine how this incredible incident has complicated the lives (already complicated enough) of other Americans here in Moscow — not only vis-à-vis the Russian authorities, but also vis-à-vis all our Western colleagues now here with us. An example is this trip of mine

there is no Heaven . . . .

to Ryazan. As far as I know, we were the first Westerners in Moscow to travel to another city after the Grow incident. While making preparations for the trip, I learned, in no uncertain terms, how bitter is the bitterness of the British Embassy with respect to the whole business. Since these two British friends of mine had invited me to make the trip with them, and since they had gone to the bother of getting the railroad tickets for me, I had to listen when they explained to me the rules of the game for our journey. Chief among these was the rule against note-taking. "You are not," they said, "to take either pencil or paper." And they meant it.

Hence the memory test. I trust that the results will not bring disgrace either to my government and fellow citizens, or to the British Embassy — or to the Russian people.

April 18, 1952

"There is nothing above Moscow except the Kremlin, and nothing above the Kremlin except Heaven." So says an old Russian proverb. And now the half-dozen men who happen to live inside the Kremlin say there is no Heaven above them. There is just the Kremlin.

Just the Kremlin. Three hours ago I returned from my second visit to this mysterious place — this strange little triangle of good earth at the top of a hill by the bank of a river, this ancient string of battlemented brick walls, with their twentieth-century electric eyes — this pathetic, man-made fortress which has been the seat and symbol of human political power longer than any other single spot of land on earth.

The Kremlin means so much to so many people for so

many different reasons that although I have already set down
my personal impressions on my first visit, today I am going
to try calmly to write what, *exactly,* the Kremlin is. Actually, I was forced to do this, because on the sightseeing tour
this morning the Embassy appointed me as an interpreter
(the Kremlin guide makes a point of speaking only in Russian) — and I boned up in advance, in the likely event I
would fail to catch the machine-gun spatter of dates and
names. Here, roughly, is the lecture I imposed on my
friends:

The Kremlin is located at the joining of the Moscow and
the Neglinnaya Rivers. Basically, the Kremlin for many years
contained all there was of the city of Moscow. It was built
on a small hill, about forty meters high, which was protected
by walls, and almost all the history of Russia, in one way or
another, is involved with these acres. The first mention of
Moscow which survives today is one from the year 1147,
when Grand Prince Yury Dolgoruky (Long-Arm) invited
one of the princes of Novgorod to visit him for a "mighty
feast" in Moscow — that is, the site of the present Kremlin.
Inside the earthen walls there were a few wooden churches
and palaces which a century later housed Daniel (the
youngest son of Alexander Nevsky), who was the first of the
permanent Moscow line of rulers (and so really the first
forefather of Joseph). Around these were built the houses of
some of the court retainers and peasants who lived nearby
for protection. Only about one third of the present area of
the Kremlin was occupied by these buildings. The first
wooden walls were built in 1150.

In 1238, Moscow was captured by the Tatar hordes and
burned. During the period of the Tatar occupation, the city
outgrew its inferior position as a small military trading post.

In 1367 the first stone walls . . . .

Through the efforts of its very clever rulers, who acted as tribute collections for the Tatars, it became the commercial and governmental center of the rising Russian state. In this period, stout oak walls were put up and the wooden churches were rebuilt more elaborately on the very site of the present Kremlin cathedrals.

In 1367, the first stone walls were built. They served not only to defend the Prince of Moscow against potential attackers, but also to prevent his palaces and churches from being destroyed by the fires which swept over Moscow almost every year.

During the reign of Ivan the Great (grandfather of the Terrible) the main stone buildings and higher brick walls were erected.

A second period of building activity took place in the early part of the seventeenth century. By this time, the walls themselves had begun to lose some of their importance as military fortifications. At the same time, the influence of Western European architecture was beginning to be felt in Russia and the tsars of the period brought in a series of Italian architects to decorate and build for them in the Kremlin. It was in this period that the present ornamental, tentlike upper sections of the towers were constructed. Previous to that time the main strong part of the towers had been covered by wooden roofs which gave protection to the archers defending the walls.

During the reign of Peter the Great and his immediate successors, several buildings were added within the walls. As this process of building took place the wooden buildings which had formerly occupied most of the area were demolished.

There was a plan during the reign of Catherine the Great

. . . . . the most important of Russia's shrines

to build a great Kremlin palace which was to stretch the full length of the Kremlin along the brow of the hill facing the Moscow River. This palace was to have been built in the most elaborate European style of the time and was to have cost millions of rubles. In fact, steps toward the construction were taken with the demolition of part of the wall facing the river. However, because of the rising costs of foreign wars, the plan was called off.

When Napoleon conquered Moscow in 1812, he occupied the Kremlin, and when he was forced to retreat from the city, he ordered many of the buildings and most of the walls to be blown up. Later, these buildings were restored and the Great Kremlin Palace of today was constructed.

During the Revolution of 1917, the Kremlin was the center of resistance of the White Guards against the revolutionaries and was conquered only after long fighting in which, again, parts of the wall were destroyed.

From the time Peter the Great moved the capital to St. Petersburg until the return of the government to Moscow after the Revolution, the Kremlin was open to visitors as a state museum. Today the Kremlin, the most important of Russia's shrines, can be visited only by special permit, obtained in the case of diplomats through the Ministry of Foreign Affairs, a privilege which few, if any, ordinary Russians ever receive.

Each person is closely scrutinized as he enters through the Borovitskie Gate, and parties of foreign diplomats are joined not only by a guide, but also by a representative of the Soviet Ministry of Foreign Affairs, an officer of the Kremlin Guard, and also a plain-clothes agent, presumably from the Guard.

Once through the Borovitskie Gate, it is easy to realize that you are on a hill. The area just inside the gate at this point

The Annunciation Cathedral . . . .

is the oldest part of the Kremlin which was occupied by Yury Dolgoruky's clusters of wooden houses and churches.

Visitors to the Kremlin are allowed to see only a limited number of buildings, usually going past the Armory and the Great Kremlin Palace to Cathedral Square, where the main churches are located. On the west side of the square as you enter (to the left) is the Blagoveshchensky Sobor (Annunciation Cathedral), which was built between 1482 and 1490 by Russian architects from the city of Pskov, which was noted for its famous churches. The bronze carved door and the stone carving in the church are magnificent.

The Soviet Government has taken great pains to restore and preserve the interiors of this and the other important Kremlin churches. The icons which were originally painted on the walls and iconostas (altar screen) of the Annunciation Cathedral have been restored by peeling off the successive layers of paint which were added in each century (it was the general practice to repaint the icons, but apparently not to change the subject matter, every time a new tsar was enthroned). The original icons have preserved a beauty of form and color that is amazing. Many of them are the work of the very famous painters Andrei Rublev and Theophanes the Greek. Here also was located the supposedly miracle-working "Virgin of the Don," which was carried by Dimitry Donskoi when he defeated the Tatars at Kulikovo Field. Today this icon is preserved in the Tretyakov Gallery. This church was used by the early tsars for their marriages and christenings.

Opposite and to the right as you enter Cathedral Square, is the Arkhangelsky Sobor (Archangel Cathedral), which was built between 1505 and 1509, on the site of an earlier

wooden cathedral, by a Milanese architect. The portals of
the cathedral are decorated with very beautiful stone carv-
ings. Here were buried most of the tsars who antedated
Peter the Great. The latter and most of his successors are
buried in the church of the Peter and Paul Fortress in
Leningrad, with the exception of Peter II, who is buried in
the Archangel Cathedral, and the last tsar, Nicholas II, whose
body was dumped down a well near Ekaterinburg (now
Sverdlovsk), after his execution by the Reds during the Revolution. The interior of the Archangel Cathedral is being
restored and unfortunately it is not possible to visit the
church at the present time.

Perhaps the most famous and grandiose of the Kremlin
churches is the Uspensky Sobor (Assumption Cathedral),
which was built between 1475 and 1479 by another Italian
architect, Ridolfo Fioravanti. He took as his model the
central portion of the Uspensky Sobor of Vladimir, with its
cupolas which resemble helmets more than the onion-shaped
domes which can be seen on St. Basil's Cathedral in Red
Square. In this church the coronation of all the tsars took
place from the sixteenth century onwards, although the
capital itself was transferred to St. Petersburg. Here can be
seen the carved walnut throne of Ivan the Terrible (which
was later used as the coronation throne) as well as the
thrones of the patriarch (head of the Russian Orthodox
Church) and the tsarina. Many of the patriarchs, and later
the metropolitans, were buried here. The very beautiful
icons of the iconostas and the walls of the church have been
restored; the Soviet Government has left one section of the
eighteenth- and nineteenth-century icons unrestored, which
shows the artistic superiority of the earlier ones.

the oldest part of the Great Kremlin Palace . . .

Just to the west of the square is the oldest part of the Great Kremlin Palace, the so-called Granovitaya Palata, which was the throne room of the earliest tsars. To the north of this is a minor cathedral which cannot be visited, the Cathedral of the Consecration of Priests, built between 1484 and 1486. To the right and opposite the entrance to this cathedral is the outer wall of the Golden Chamber of the tsarinas, a part of the early palace. This wall has three stone arches decorated in carved stone. Above it rise three palace chapels, the Church of "The Redeemer Behind the Golden Railing," the Church of the Crucifixion, and the Church of the Resurrection.

On the northeast side of the square is the great bell tower of Ivan the Great, which is 320 feet high; the upper part of this tower was shot away by the French bombardment of the Kremlin in 1812. To the side of the bell tower is the famous Tsar Kolokol (Tsar Bell), which is said to be the largest bell in the world. It weighs 200 tons and is 26 feet high. It was cast in 1735 and was to have been hung from a wooden bell tower at the present site. While the bell was being hoisted to the tower, a fire swept the Kremlin (1737), burning down the tower and letting the bell drop and embed itself in the earth. A large piece was chipped off. Later the bell was hoisted to a granite platform where it rests today.

To the north of the Ivan the Great bell tower is the Palace of the Patriarch (built from 1655 to 1656), and the Cathedral of the Twelve Apostles. To the east of these buildings on Cathedral Square lie the Kremlin Gardens. The large Voznesensky Nunnery which lay along the wall near the Gate of the Savior was pulled down after the revolution.

. . . . **Two-ton cannon balls**

Walking north from Cathedral Square, you reach the main east-west axis of the Kremlin, Communist Street. On the south side of the street are barracks buildings. At the corner of these buildings is the Tsar Cannon, again supposedly the largest cannon of its time (cast in 1586). It weighs thirty-nine tons and was designed to shoot balls weighing nearly two tons. Apparently this cannon was never shot. Along the barracks walls and the façade of the Arsenal, which can be seen in the far northern corner of the Kremlin, are a number of old Russian and foreign cannon, some of which were captured from the French.

Facing the corner of the barracks near the Tsar Cannon is one of the main government office buildings, part of which is formed by the former Chudov (Miracle) Monastery. This is a large and complex group of buildings, and since it has not been visited by foreigners in recent years, it is hard to say exactly which of the buildings described in earlier Soviet and foreign sources still stand; it is here that Stalin is said to have his apartments.

Between this building and the Arsenal stands the former Senate, now designated merely as the Soviet Government Building, a triangular structure with an interior court which was built by the famous Russian architect Kazakov (1776 to 1784 — roughly the period of the American Revolution). This is where Stalin's offices are said to be located.

Returning to the river side of the Kremlin, visitors are usually shown through the Great Kremlin Palace, which was built by order of Tsar Nicholas I, from 1838 to 1849. Formerly this area was occupied by a number of older buildings as well as the palace of Empress Elizabeth, built by the famous Italian architect, Rastrelli. Entering the palace, you

The Hall of St. George . . . .

ascend the grand stairway to the reception room, from which radiate the state halls. In this anteroom is a massive painting by Repin showing peasants paying homage to Emperor Alexander III.

To the right of the antechamber is the famous Hall of St. George. On its marble walls and under the carved cross of the order are listed the names of each individual knight of the order and of the regiments which received this highest military honor. The floor is made up of inlaid precious woods and the decor of the curtains and chairs is in the black and orange colors of the order, relieved by light gray trimming. In this hall many of the wartime banquets attended by Stalin, Churchill, and other important Allied leaders were held. At the end of the hall nearest the anteroom is the door leading to the Vladimir Hall, decorated with the insignia of the military order after which it is named. To the right is the Sacred Hall, which was the anteroom to the throne and audience rooms — the Granovitaya Palata, built between 1473 and 1491 under Ivan III. Here the tsars received the homage of their nobles after coronation. The walls are decorated with garish nineteenth-century biblical murals. There seems to be no program for the restoration of the early decoration. High on the inner wall of the room is a small window, from which the ladies of the court were allowed to view state functions.

Returning to the Vladimir Hall, one sees its function is to unite the fifteenth-century palace of Ivan III, the seventeenth-century palace, and the nineteenth-century palace, of which only the Hall of St. George has so far been described. On the west side of the hall is a stone stairway that leads to another large hall, which was formerly a terrace outside the seventeenth-century palace. On the east side of the terrace is the Church of "The Redeemer Behind the Golden Railing," the palace chapel of the tsars. Around the terrace itself is a copper ornamental rail, made from coins which were withdrawn from circulation after their decrease in value had caused the "Copper Revolt" of the 1660's. On the west side of the hall is another stairway leading to the fourth story of the Terem. This was the home of the tsars before Peter. It is a five-story building, a curious, barbaric, medieval pyramid. Of the five stories, only the fourth can be visited. A good place to see the whole palace is from across the courtyard in the gallery of the Great Kremlin Palace.

The fourth story of the palace is remarkable because it has preserved to this day a view of the living conditions of the seventeenth-century tsars. The rough wooden floors, the small mica glass windows in rich shades, the elaborately tiled wall stoves, and the stiff furniture are interesting and unspoiled reminders of the art of this period. There are five apartments on this floor which were first used by Tsar Alexis, the second of the House of Romanov. The first room was where the boyars waited to be admitted to audience, while the second was the chamber of the boyar council. The third was the tsar's study where he received persons in private audiences. The fourth was the tsar's bedroom, which still has a bed typical of the time, very hard and very narrow. To the side of this bedroom is a tiny private chapel. Above this floor were the apartment of the tsar's sons and a terrace, where the ladies of the court could promenade. Below the tsar's apartments were the chambers of the royal ladies, and still lower the servants' quarters and kitchens.

The chamber of the Supreme Soviet is to the right of the

The Old Armory . . . .

river end of St. George's Hall. The Supreme Soviet meets in this room a few days a year to hear speeches and the government's plans for the coming period, as well as to give their *pro forma* approval to any laws proposed. This room was formerly two old palace halls, the Alexander Hall (decorated with the symbols of the Order of Alexander Nevsky) and the Hall of St. Andrew, formerly the throne room of the tsars. The place where Stalin and the members of the Politburo sit today is the place occupied by the throne of the earlier rulers of Russia.

To the north of this hall stretches another wing of rooms, which were the state apartments of the tsars, containing the Guard Room, the Hall of St. Catherine (decorated in the red and gray of the Order of St. Catherine), the state drawing room and bedrooms.

On the first floor of the Great Kremlin Palace are the living quarters which the Imperial family occupied when it was in Moscow; they come in the following order: the drawing room, dining room, boudoir and study of the tsarina; the bedroom, dressing room, and study of the tsar. These rooms are richly furnished, but in the gaudy style of the nineteenth century.

Much of the time of a visitor to the Kremlin is spent in the old Armory (or Treasury), now a state museum, containing the crown jewels, the clothing and the carriages of the tsars, old arms and armor, the jeweled robes of the patriarch and other church dignitaries, and tons of gold and jewels, which are so closely displayed and so rapidly seen that the visitor is left chiefly with the impression of lavish confusion.

Impression of confusion? Yes — and during our tour my

party was probably confused by *everything* (as anyone who
reads this may be). But I have done my best — and, as far
as I know, nobody before, Russian or Westerner, has tried
to describe the present-day interior of the Kremlin in such
detail.

APRIL 23, 1952

In the two hours between four and six this afternoon I had
an extraordinary experience. I attended a session of a
people's court. I watched the Soviet legal process in action,
and I watched a Soviet citizen suffer. I use the word "extraordinary" for this experience, because, to the best of my
knowledge, hardly any Americans here take advantage of such
a wonderful opportunity to see and hear Russia in the raw.
Actually, it was simple — I just walked in.

Here is what I saw and heard:

The scene is a dark, musty building at No. 10 Sretenka
Street, in the middle of Moscow — the People's Court for
the capital's Shcherbakov Raion, under the administration
of the Ministry of Justice of the R.S.F.S.R.

On entering the dirty, lightless hallway, the first thing I
notice are several "No Smoking — Penalty" signs, and the
first thing I notice after that are several Russians sitting on
settees under the signs, smoking.

Climbing the unpainted, broken-down stairway, I arrive
on the second floor, and see a deserted corridor, with three or
four tiny courtrooms. There is little sign of activity, so I
grope my way up the dark, gloomy staircase to the third floor.
There is likewise little sign of life here, and I retrace my
steps. Back again on the second floor, I hear voices at the

The accused — bedraggled and bleary-eyed . . . .

end of the corridor on the left. Following in the direction of the sounds, I come to the narrow door of a small courtroom. As I worm my way through the spectators standing in the entrance, I see that the room is packed with people, and with tension. The state prosecutor is making his final charge.

After pushing my way onto a bench, I get a chance to look around over the shoulders of the spectators sitting in front of me.

I see that I am at the back of the room, facing the three judges, who are sitting in high-backed chairs against the opposite wall, under a row of small windows looking out on the street. The room is so small that the judges are only about twenty-five feet away. Immediately in front of the judges is a long bench, over which hangs a single, bare electric light bulb on a wire from the ceiling.

To the left of this bench is a small table for the court stenographer. She is a young, good-looking girl, with very blond hair and a very bright red blouse.

On the side wall to the left of this girl hangs a large photograph of Stalin in a brown wood frame. With the exception of this portrait, the half green, half white walls of the room are bare.

Along this same left-hand wall, between the judges and me, there are two sets of tables and chairs. At one of these, near the judges, sit the defense counsel. At the other, near me, the accused sits alone, motionless. I see at once that the latter is a bedraggled, bleary-eyed man, with a blotchy face, and with his hair cut short. His skull looks like a rat skin.

On the right-hand wall a small door leads into an inner office. The two state prosecutors, with their assistant, walk in and out of this door — and, when they speak, they stand at a table directly in front of me to the right.

. . . .   The unanswered telephone

At this back end of the room, where I am sitting, there are three rows of benches for spectators on each side of the entrance door, with a narrow aisle between. About thirty spectators are packed tight on these benches, and another twenty are standing in the aisle, packed even tighter. Separating these benches from the center of the room are two rows of seats. The row on the right seems to be reserved for witnesses, and that on the left for militiamen. There are three of the latter, one standing and two seated.

Suddenly, while the state prosecutor continues to sum up his case, the telephone in the inner office a few feet away begins to ring — but nobody bothers to answer it. Still standing on his feet and speaking slowly and deliberately (maybe menacingly), the state prosecutor goes on with his charge. Again the telephone begins to ring persistently, but still nobody bothers to answer. Finally the telephone stops. The prosecutor continues.

I learn from this harangue that the crime took place at the end of 1951. Fomin — that, I find, is the name of the pathetic-looking little man sitting in the prisoner's dock in front of me — has been accused of embezzlement. In the words of the prosecutor, Fomin, who previously had served as a storekeeper of a factory restaurant and cafeteria, pilfered 18,000 rubles of state funds. For this alleged crime the prosecutor asks the court to sentence the accused to ten years of "deprivation of liberty" — a euphemism, I think to myself, if I ever heard one.

During all of this, the glamour-girl stenographer in her red blouse sits at her table in the corner, paying little attention to what is going on, and writing hardly at all. From time to time she dips her pen into the inkwell, very slowly

"honorably, honorably, honorably" . . . . . .

and very deliberately. A few minutes later she repeats this operation. Apparently this part of the proceedings is not considered important enough for official recording — in spite of the fact that the trial is rapidly coming to a climax.

At this point the case becomes a bit complicated. Apparently another Soviet citizen is involved in the same trial — but in a minor way. The manager of the factory dining hall has been accused of negligence, with the charge resting on the fact that he permitted such pilfering by Fomin. The manager's surname is Ruchkin, and now I see him sitting in one of the chairs reserved for witnesses, just in front of the first row of spectators (that is, not in the place set aside for "prisoners"). Unlike Fomin, Ruchkin is huge and hulky and dressed in a neat gray suit. And he strikes me as much more sure of himself. Perhaps there is a good reason for all these differences. After all, as Ruchkin's defense counsel keeps emphasizing to the judges, his client has been a member of the Communist Party for many years now. Furthermore, the defense counsel repeatedly, and pointedly, asks Ruchkin about his record in the last war, and Ruchkin, rising to his feet, replies in a deep voice that he served in the Red Army, adding over and over again, *"Chestno, chestno, chestno"* (honorably, honorably, honorably).

A few moments later, shortly before six o'clock, the chief judge announces that there will be a five-minute recess. Then he and the other two judges, one of whom, I forgot to mention, is a large, efficient-looking woman, get up from their high-backed chairs and slowly walk into the inner office, closing the door behind them. I also forgot to say that the judges are not dressed in the traditional black robes of the West (not to mention wigs) — but in ordinary business clothes.

. . . . .   **The verdict will not be given today**

By now the courtroom, which in the course of the last
hour has become jammed even tighter with curious Russians
(who are they?), is intolerably hot, stuffy, and foul. This, I
warn myself, is going to be the first occasion on which I shall
be forced to leave a Russian room because of the sour smell
of dirty, unwashed underwear. Before, I have told myself
that it was, after all, a human smell — and so why should I
object, why should I hold my nose because the Russians,
who, like everybody else, would like to be clean all over, just
don't have enough laundry soap? This time, however, I
give in, and go out into the corridor for a breath of relatively
fresh air. The other spectators have the same idea, and at
once there is a crush at the door. During this brief recess I
learn from those around me (all of whom, incidentally, appear to be extremely down-and-out, as well as dirty) that this
is the final day of this particular trial, much evidence having
been submitted, and many witnesses heard on previous days.
Since the verdict is expected momentarily, we all rush back
into the room when the five minutes come to a close. As we
return to our rough wooden benches, I overhear somebody
say that old Fomin always did take too much vodka, anyway,
and saw to it, in one way or another, that his friends got
too much, too.

The chief judge, who has returned to the center chair,
calls the court to order again. Then we hear from Fomin
himself, making some kind of final statement. But, actually,
we don't hear from him. He stands up and struggles for a
few words — but his mumbling is unintelligible.

And, now, finally, the judge makes a surprise announcement. The verdict of guilty, or not guilty, will not be given
today, but tomorrow at 11 A.M. At this, the three uniformed militiamen immediately leave their seats in front of

I have a hunch what the verdict will be . . . .

me, flank Fomin, and escort him as he stumbles out through the crowd. Where the guards took him, I, of course, do not know — and I do not know, likewise, whether there was a Soviet Dostoyevsky present, peering over the shoulders of the onlookers, gathering material for a contemporary *Crime and Punishment;* or a Soviet Tolstoy, listening and looking, preparing a *Resurrection* courtroom scene. But I doubt it — because this little episode is too inconsequential, hidden and already forgotten.

So the scene closes. Tomorrow, at 11 A.M., I shall have to be at my desk at the Embassy (the Minister would even disapprove of this visit, I am sure, if he knew about it) — and so I, and whoever reads my words, will never hear of Fomin's fate.

But I have a hunch as to what the verdict will be, and I know that tonight, and for the next ten years, I would not want to be in Fomin's boots. His boots, already, are old and cracked and muddy.

APRIL 28, 1952

No private Russian citizen could criticize Stalin or the regime with any great chance of getting away with it. But there is criticism. The papers, from time to time, will be quite severe in denouncing an industry, or a class of Soviet operators such as factory supervisors or automobile manufacturers or some such group. However, since the press is entirely "official," you can be sure that such attacks are planned and purposeful — sometimes, perhaps, they are ordered just to give the people the impression that there is still a remnant of liberty.

. . . . **propaganda at the circus**

Tonight I heard a different sort of criticism — and one perhaps a little harder to explain. I went to the circus, and there Karandash, the famous clown, ridiculed one of the most obvious outgrowths of the all-powerful state — what we would call "empire-building," i.e., the almost limitless multiplication of "management" in factories. Karandash, carrying a briefcase, poses as the manager of an industrial plant and he is followed by a long string of other briefcased "businessmen." When he is asked about them, he introduces them as the directors, foremen, managers, etc., of his factory. Finally one poor bedraggled individual stumbles in. He, Karandash explains, is the "laborer" in the factory. It's all a good gag on officialdom's red tape, and perhaps is allowed in order to let the people laugh openly (which they certainly did) at an aspect of their lives which must annoy and puzzle them daily.

There was also a good deal of anti-American propaganda in the circus. Is this the pill for which Karandash supplies the sugar coating?

MAY 1, 1952

See my diary entry for May Day of a year ago. And read it again, word for word, because everything today was exactly the same — the same red banners of Stalin, the same artificial flowers, the same uproar, the same jet planes, the same blue exhaust from the tanks, the same lack of spontaneity on the part of the Russians in the square as they paraded past our window; the same lack of gaiety on the part of the imprisoned Westerners as they stood behind the window, looking out.

Shostakovich concert . . . .

I have just returned from a great and rare experience — a concert of Shostakovich music played by Shostakovich himself. Since I was the only foreigner present, I am hastening to write down tonight my impressions of this man who, if not the foremost composer in the world today, is certainly among the top two or three, and without any doubt the most bewildered, politically confused, and tragic creator on earth.

Shostakovich is the most celebrated example we have of an artist caught in the trap of totalitarianism, in the trap of a modern, monolithic state, of a genius being forced by a few fellow men to hold back what is pouring through his heart and brain. His is the most tragic example, because the art in question is so great — but the plight of Shostakovich is typical of the general dilemma faced by composers, painters, playwrights, poets, and novelists all over Russia.

Here are some of the fantastic ups and down of the politico-musical career of Shostakovich:

His extraordinary First Symphony, composed in 1925 when he was only nineteen years old, marked the beginning of a career full of spectacular acclaim and equally spectacular denunciation. He was applauded in Russia and abroad until one fateful day in 1936, when the arbiters of Soviet opinion reached the conclusion that his music was politically heterodox. This was a quick, surprising reversal of the Kremlin's previous views and must have occasioned Shostakovich much soul-searching, if not terror. The outstanding Soviet composer of his generation, accustomed for a decade to the honors due a hero of the arts, he awoke one morning to find that all-mighty *Pravda* had sharply criticized "the anti-popular and formalistic distortions" of his music. And further, in the same piece, the editors, who had recently hailed him as the composer-laureate of the Soviet state, now tried to show how "dangerous and pernicious" was the Shostakovich trend for the whole further development of Soviet music. Performances of many of his works stopped at once — and Shostakovich himself, understandably alarmed by the turn of events, hurriedly withdrew still other compositions from circulation. At that moment the manuscript of his Fourth Symphony was in the hands of the Leningrad Philharmonic, which had announced its forthcoming premier presentation. But Shostakovich reclaimed it and to this day it remains unplayed — and unheard, as far as I know, except by the inner ears of Shostakovich himself.

We can only guess what must have been Shostakovich's state of mind during the period of retirement that immediately followed. Long before, he had publicly espoused "orthodoxy" in his political and artistic views, saying in 1931: "I am a Soviet composer, and I see our epoch as something heroic, spirited and joyous. Music cannot help having a political basis — an idea that members of the bourgeoisie are slow to comprehend. There can be no music without ideology. The old composers were bolstering the rule of the upper classes. We as revolutionists have a different conception. . . . Good music lifts and heartens and lightens people for work and effort. It may be tragic, but it must be strong. It is no longer an end in itself, but a vital weapon in the struggle." Having paid his tribute to the "chauvinism of class," Shostakovich must now have asked himself what more he could say.

What he did say he said soon in music: the Fifth Sym-

"The fetters . . . have been torn off" . . . . . .

phony. This had the desired effect. After the first performance, held in connection with the celebration of the
twentieth anniversary of the Soviet state, the press and public
alike took it to heart. However, the fact is that there was
nothing in the Fifth Symphony to indicate an artistic *volte-
face* on Shostakovich's part. As one Western critic has put
it: "The symphony marked a further stage in his development as a composer, but a further stage predictable on the
basis of his earlier works. There was in it more emphasis
on form, on the extended and serious-minded development
of the basic musical ideas, and less emphasis on effects created
by merely harmonic or instrumental means. But this was in
line with tendencies already clearly marked in the succession
of the composer's works, and to sympathetic bourgeois, or
capitalist, ears, it was evidence merely of an expected advance
toward artistic maturity." The Soviet press, however, looked
on the matter quite differently. One Moscow paper wrote:
"The fetters of musical formalism which held Shostakovich
captive for so long, preventing him from creating works
profound in conception, have been torn off. He must follow
up this new trend in his work. He must turn more boldly
toward Soviet reality. He must understand it more pro-
foundly and find in it a new stimulus for his work."

All agree that the massive Fifth Symphony struck a note
of courage and belief in life, and that it sings a noble song
of man's faith in himself and the universe of which he is a
part. And that, under the circumstances, I consider to be a
miracle.

Barely a year after the premier of the Fifth in 1937,
Shostakovich announced plans for his Sixth. For some time
he had considered composing an extensive work in honor of

Lenin, and he decided to make his Sixth a "Lenin" symphony. In an interview in *Soviet Art* of November 20, 1938,
he said: "I have set myself a task fraught with great responsibility, to express through the medium of sound the immortal
image of Lenin as a great son of the Russian people and a
great leader and teacher of the masses. I have received
numerous letters from all corners of the Soviet Union with
regard to my future symphony. The most important advice
contained in these letters was to make ample use of musical
folklore."

For some reason or other, however, the Lenin idea was dis-
carded and the Sixth Symphony emerged as a piece of absolute music without a program.

The work had its first hearing on December 3, 1939, during the two-month Festival of Soviet Music in Moscow. At
that time, it aroused little interest. The festival audiences,
wrote one commentator, were much more excited about
three new cantatas: Prokofiev's *Alexander Nevsky,* celebrating
the victory of the Russians over the Teutonic Knights on the
ice of Lake Peipus in 1242; Shaporin's *On the Kulikovo
Field,* commemorating the Russian victory over the Tatars
in 1380; and Koval's *Emelyan Pugachev,* a musical tribute to
the celebrated rebel who was executed by Catherine the
Great in 1775. In the words of Nicholas Slonimsky: "The
lesson was made fairly clear. What was needed in the year
1940 was the romanticization of Russia *circa* 1240, while
Shostakovich devoted his talent principally to satirizing
Russia *circa* 1840."

The fanfare of praise that followed the Ninth Symphony,
written in the two months between V-E Day and V-J Day,
was nothing new for Shostakovich, since no other composer

"discordant and disharmonious" . . . .

has so consistently made daily headlines — and front-page headlines — during his own life. But, at the same time, after all his previous experiences, he must have been prepared for another reversal. It was not long before *Culture and Life,* which, until its own recent, silent demise, was the organ of the Department of Propaganda and Agitation of the Central Committee of the Communist Party, frowned upon the popular work. In this publication, a Kremlin critic lashed at the composer for writing "a playful and fanciful trifle" and for his failure "to reflect the true spirit of the Soviet people."

On February 10, 1948, the axe really fell. On that date the Central Committee of the Communist Party of the Soviet Union issued a decree "On Muradeli's Opera *The Great Friendship.*" The decree concerned not only this particular opera but Soviet music in general. Here are excerpts from that fateful little document — quotations which show quite clearly what the complicated controversy is all about, and quite clearly what the tragic consequences will be. I cite passages in considerable detail, because these fantastic phrases will help to explain to the West, I think, this puzzling phenomenon:

> *The Great Friendship* does not contain a single melody or air likely to be remembered by audiences. Its music is discordant and disharmonious, built entirely on dissonance and jarring sound combinations. Some parts of the score and some scenes, which aspire to melody, are suddenly interrupted by discordant noises that are absolutely foreign to normal human hearing and have a depressing effect on the listener. . . . The vocal parts of the opera — choral, solo, and ensemble singing — leave a very drab impression. . . .

·　·　·　·　·　·　·　·　· **Soviet musical criticism**

The composer has not drawn on the wealth of folk melodies . . . and dance motives that are so abundant in the folk creations of the peoples of the U.S.S.R. . . .

In his desire to achieve a falsely conceived "originality," Muradeli ignored and disregarded the finest traditions and experience of classical opera, and particularly of Russian classical opera. The latter is distinguished for its rich intrinsic content, wealth and wide range of melody, artistry, refined and clear musical idiom — things that have made the Russian opera, which is rooted in the life of the people, the best in the world, a genre loved and understood by wide sections of the people. . . .

The conference of Soviet music workers convened by the Central Committee has shown that the failure of Muradeli's opera is no isolated instance, but is intimately associated with the present unsatisfactory state of Soviet music, with the fact that the formalistic trend has gained currency among Soviet composers. . . .

The position is particularly unsatisfactory with regard to symphony and opera music. This refers to composers who adhere to the formalistic, anti-popular trend which has found its consummate expression in the works of Dimitry Shostakovich, Sergei Prokofiev, Aram Khachaturyan, V. Shebalin, G. Popov, N. Myaskovsky and others. Formalistic distortions and anti-democratic trends alien to the Soviet people and its artistic tastes are especially evident in the music of these composers. The characteristic features of this music are negation of the basic principles of classical music, advocacy of atonality, dissonance and discord, which are supposed to represent "progress" and "novelty" in the development of musical forms, renunciation of such fundamental principles of musical composition as melody, and preference for confused, neuropathological combinations

mixing music with politics . . . .

that turn music into cacophony, into a chaotic conglomeration of sounds. This music smacks very much of the spirit of the contemporary modernist bourgeois music of Europe and America, which is a reflection of the decay of bourgeois culture and signifies complete negation of musical art. . . .

Every new production by Prokofiev, Shostakovich, Myaskovsky and Shebalin is extolled . . . as a "new victory for Soviet music." They glorify the subjectivism, constructivism, extreme individualism and deliberate complexity of this music, in other words, precisely the things that should be subjected to criticism. Instead of endeavoring to demolish the pernicious views and theories that are foreign to the principles of socialist realism, music critics themselves help to disseminate these views by lavishly praising and proclaiming as "progressive" composers who subscribe to false ideas and canons. . . .

The Committee on Arts and the Organization Committee of the Union of Soviet Composers have not encouraged the realistic trend in Soviet music. The basic principles of this trend are the acceptance of the immense progressive role of the classical heritage, and in particular, of the traditions of the Russian school of music, the utilization of this heritage and its further development, the blending of high standards of idea-content with artistic perfection of musical form, fidelity and realism in music, its profound organic contact with the people and their music and song, and high professional skill coupled with simplicity and accessibility of musical compositions. . . .

This nightmare arrangement of mixing music with politics is still going on — and so is "the problem Shostakovicha." I found that out this evening when a degrading scene took place a few minutes before the concert started.

I noticed on the program that an "introductory address" was to be given by a man named Igor Belza, and the print of his name was almost as big as the letters spelling "Shostakovich." Well, Comrade Belza's opening words took up close to twenty minutes — spanking words, summarizing Shostakovich's sins in the past, but holding out hope for the future (provided the composer continued to see the light), because, after all, Shostakovich was the world's greatest composer, *and* a Russian. At this embarrassing moment, Shostakovich stumbled stiffly onto the platform, as though being called back from the dunce's corner.

The program of the concert tonight (which, by the way, was what the Russians call an "author's evening") consisted of the following Shostakovich works: Sonata in D minor for cello and piano, Op. 40; Trio in E minor, Op. 67; Preludes and Fugues, Op. 87; and, as encores, Prelude and Fugue in D and Prelude and Fugue in A. Shostakovich played at the piano throughout the program; Svyatoslav Knushevitsky was the cellist in the sonata piece; and David Oistrakh, Russia's greatest violinist, joined the other two in the trio.

For the benefit of music lovers in the "outside" world, who assuredly must want to know as much as they can about this mysterious man (as well as his music), and for my own journal, I immediately started to scribble down my impressions of the composer himself while these pieces were being played and applauded. These pencil notes, covering my program in all directions, are now on my desk — and this is how they read:

Concert took place in "Maly Zal" (little hall) of the Conservatory — a tiny, classical room, with white column facings and pediments and capitals; the long, big black grand piano takes up almost half of the oval-shaped stage, at the back of

lukewarm applause .   .   .   .

which is an organ of silver pipes and dark-colored wood; in the center of the proscenium arch over the platform is a simple blue-and-white medallion of Nikolai Rubinstein.

As S. enters, he looks like a confused, absent-minded professor. Younger looking than I had expected. Quite short in stature. Seems ill at ease.

S. dressed in white tie and ill-fitting tails. Wears dark horn-rimmed glasses with thick lenses.

S. of sandy complexion — with light brown hair (cut close in back). As he plays, a short lock of hair falls over his forehead. His whole face extremely pale.

Most prominent features: sharp, aquiline nose; pointed, receding chin; thin, puckered lips. His mouth, with its receding lower jaw (barely orthognathous — I think that's the word), is shaped like a crescent, with the horns turned down. S. nervously bites his lips while bowing jerkily during the lukewarm applause. Quick, stiff bows from the waist, as though he were embarrassed.

S. very serious, tight-lipped, all the time — with worried frown on his forehead. Almost a look of pain.

Seated on very edge of plain wooden chair, with his black coattails sticking out at an angle behind him, S. played his pieces firmly, vigorously, and with feeling (but with no great display). Although S. was performing his own works, he had to have the score on the keyboard in front of him for the sonata and the trio, with an assistant gravely standing by to turn the pages (no score, however, was necessary for the piano pieces). Between the third and fourth movements of the sonata, S. took a long time out to wipe his face with a big white handkerchief.

Not a smile during the whole two hours.

· · · · · · · · · · **Today I was robbed**

MAY 4, 1952

Today I was robbed — in broad daylight, directly under the Kremlin wall. For more than a year now I have been pooh-poohing the countless tales current among Westerners here to the effect that juvenile delinquents are a menace in Moscow. A favorite topic of conversation among diplomats is how so-and-so (usually somebody's wife) had her handbag snatched away in a department store. Now I know that some of those accounts, at least, are not imaginative.

The scene was a bus stop, right off the Red Square. As I look back on the episode, I realize now that I might have been followed for blocks, being considered good game because I had just walked out of a so-called "commission store" (the Soviet version of a second-hand exchange), and so presumably could be carrying a pocketful of rubles. Unfortunately, I *was* carrying a pocketful of rubles — around one hundred. As I approached the bus stop, I saw that there were about eight people ahead of me in the queue, and I took my place at the end of the line. A few seconds later the bus arrived, and the queue moved in strict order along the curb to the open door in the rear of the bus. I was still the last in line when my turn came. Then, just as I was getting ready to leap onto the lower step, there was a sudden commotion, and five or six teen-age boys appeared out of nowhere. Two of them pushed ahead of me, and the rest jostled from behind. In the crush, one of them slipped the roll of rubles out of my pocket. I had a momentary sensation of the withdrawal, but then it was too late. Yelling and shoving, they pushed me onto the steps of the crowded bus and then jumped back to the curb at the last minute as

Early Soviet educational theories . . . .

the doors closed. I looked through the window at their mocking faces, and then the bus started to move slowly down the street. The conductress, a smiling, pink-cheeked peasant girl, asked me for my fare — fortunately, I still had a few kopecks in my pocket — and that was that. There was nothing I could do but sputter to myself, and tell myself that a better planned and executed case of pocket-picking could not be imagined.

Juvenile delinquency has been a problem in Russia ever since the Revolution. This problem has been closely tied to the whole question of education and the role of the family, both of which have been the subject of much theorizing in the Soviet Union. In the early days, the theories were based mainly on the study of Friedrich Engels, *The Origin of the Family, Private Property, and the State*. And many specific programs were carried out to put these theories into effect. With regard to education, the Marxist view in those early days held that education in bourgeois society was a class function to support the ruling classes. Thus it was planned to sweep away the entire bourgeois system of education (because, in the thinking of the Communists, it was oriented toward enslaving students), and to tie education to the needs of the working class. So, in an atmosphere of general distrust of teachers and of the home influence, the Bolshevik leaders, led by Lenin's wife, emancipated the students. In the first years of the Soviet experiment, school children even held their own courts and condemned teachers whom they considered bourgeois. Methods of teaching were changed in the grade schools: visits to factories took the place of a strict curriculum. As the result of this "learning by doing," discipline was weakened. At the same time, discipline was fur-

. . . . **discipline was tightened**

ther weakened by the loss of the control of the family over the child. In an effort to free women from the kitchen and the nursery, the state took over many child-raising functions. The experiments, however, did not work — either in the school or the home.

By the 1930's the Soviet regime itself was only too glad to have the old-time school and the old-time family unit at its disposal to instill the discipline which had been sadly missing in the younger generation. So, to keep the situation from getting out of hand, as had often happened in the first two decades of Soviet rule, many radical and frankly experimental approaches to social institutions were gradually replaced by a more traditional and conservative treatment. In addition to new marriage and divorce laws, and a new attitude toward the church, many fundamental decisions were made in the early 1930's to stabilize education. Textbooks were rewritten, especially textbooks on history; a standard curriculum was adopted; parents became more and more responsible for their children's behavior and upkeep; special children's courts were established.

With the approach of World War II, all these efforts to stabilize Soviet society, many of them diverging widely from the original Marxian position, were intensified. And during the war the backtracking was even more pronounced. In the field of education, for example, a new grading system was introduced, new tests were established in the schools, discipline was tightened in all aspects of school life, with strict rules having the force of law, and coeducation was abolished.

Current textbooks on teaching reflect this still-present emphasis on discipline. For example, one of these books, in referring to the twenty "Rules for School Children" (which

"The New Man" . . . .

were adopted in 1943), says: "In order that they may become immutable law to the pupil, they must be introduced into the daily life of the school by a vast, serious, and systematic effort." And this text says further that discipline must be *conscious, self-initiated, firm, organizational, comradely, resolute.* Here is another quotation: "Before the teacher stands a much deeper task: the cultivation in children of a *state of discipline* as a high quality of Communist morality and one of the most important traits of character. . . . Without discipline one cannot achieve high productivity of labor. . . . Without discipline one cannot conquer in war."

Kalinin, former President of the U.S.S.R., once used the rather unpleasant phrase of "welding" a generation. Now we see the results of that welding — "the new man," as the Soviet press is fond of saying. Today, in spite of the loving care and concern bestowed on children, both by their parents and their Father in the Kremlin, Moscow has thousands of teen-age children whom we at home would call "Dead-End Kids," youth in tattered, dirty clothes who slouch along the streets, boys as young as six or eight who boldly smoke their cigarette butts in dark doorways. Today, in spite of the fact that "Stalin and the Soviet Government watch over every Soviet person" (to use the exact words of a Russian textbook on pedagogy), robbery can take place under the very walls of the Kremlin itself. My experience at the bus stop this afternoon, of course, was not necessarily an every-hour occurrence — but it is highly interesting, nonetheless, that in the most heavily policed city on the face of the globe (with an armed militiaman whistling at every corner and a plain-clothes man lurking in every block) lawless kids are still on the loose. Even Communism can't stamp out crime.

. . . . **Gypsy Theater**

MAY 7, 1952

Tonight, at long last, I went to the gypsy theater. I have
been putting off the visit for months, because I wanted to see
the most celebrated of Moscow's gypsy entertainers, Lyalya
Chernaya, in the best of her roles — Grushenka (in the play
of the same name) — one of the "musts" of Moscow. And
that has been hard to achieve: first, because the leading role
in *Grushenka* is not always given to Lyalya Chernaya (in
the Soviet Union all theaters are repertory companies, and
the roles are rotated); second, because the cast is never
known until the last minute at each performance; and third,
because when it is known that Lyalya Chernaya is going to
perform in *Grushenka,* it is almost impossible to get tickets.

Until this evening, my only direct knowledge of gypsy entertainment in Russia had come from a performance of
Tolstoy's moving tragedy, *The Living Corpse,* which I saw
recently at the Filial of the Maly Theater — and I use the
word "moving" advisedly, because when the final curtain
fell almost everybody, particularly the women, had handker-
chiefs up to their eyes. (I should note here that, in addition
to dramatizations of *Anna Karenina* and *Resurrection,* the
Moscow stage today also includes two of Tolstoy's three great
plays, *Fruits of Enlightenment* and *The Living Corpse,* remarkable works, which for some reason are seldom, if ever,
produced in the West; Tolstoy's third play, *The Power of
Darkness,* which in many respects is the most interesting of
all, is given neither in the West nor in Russia.) Several of
the scenes in *The Living Corpse* have gypsy settings, and in
the most fascinating one of all, Protasov, the hero, is enter-
tained by a gypsy troupe. And what entertainment it is —

five hundred spectators . . . every night . . . . . .

warm, and wild, and incredibly intimate. The scene only
whetted my appetite to see the real thing — and tonight I
did.

Lyalya Chernaya turned out to be all that I had antici-
pated — a wonderful deep voice, wonderful long black
braids, a wonderful bosom, a wonderful big nose, wonderful
flashing teeth, wonderful verve. The play itself (taken from
a well-known tale by Leskov, a popular storyteller of the
nineteenth century — with music by Bugachevsky, whose
works, I hear, form a large part of the musical fare at this
theater) had all the traditional romantic characters: a beautiful gypsy girl, a prince, a gypsy hero, a gypsy horsedealer, an
innkeeper, a uniformed hussar, an animal tamer, a hypnotist,
a police captain. And the plot provided plenty of opportunities for whirlwind gypsy dancing, mournful guitar solos,
and deep vibrant choral singing (with the peculiar arrangement of sitting the singers upright in two straight rows of
straight-backed chairs, like a small country choir singing on
Sunday in a New England church).

But the atmosphere of the theater itself proved to be more
interesting than the play. The theater building, properly
called the Romen, is tucked into a black back alley off
Gorky Street, and is very difficult to find unless you know
the exact spot. Most of the theater is underground — that
is, below the street level — and it has an underworld atmosphere as well. Some five hundred spectators push themselves
into this tiny dark cave every night — and, since the staircase, lobby, wardrobe, and buffet take up most of the
theater's space anyway, the squeeze is tight, once you get
seated. I finally moved up to one of the boxes, and found
that it, too, was full — full of stage lighting paraphernalia,

hissing lamps, colored paper and bulbs, with two young technicians alternately alive at the lamp and asleep on the edge of the balcony rail.

In the long intermissions, thirsty and hungry Russians jammed the dark depths of the buffet. A fascinating feature of this vaulted room was a grand piano beside the bar, a piano so enormous that it filled half of the floor space. There were a few tables, but most of us leaned on the piano and drank our beer in style, with a pedal for a bar rail. And the room was so dark that I hardly knew what I was pouring in my glass.

The whole history of the Romen provides an instructive case study of how the Soviet Government concerns itself with minority problems. The Romen was established in January, 1931, as part of the Kremlin's effort to dissuade the gypsies from their wandering life. (According to Soviet census figures, there were a little more than sixty thousand gypsies in the U.S.S.R. at that time.) In the late 1920's, an alphabet was devised for the gypsy language, Romany, and at least one newspaper and a magazine were published for the gypsies. The Romen, as a gypsy theater, was to provide a cultural focus for the gypsies of the northern U.S.S.R. and particularly the gypsies in and around Moscow.

One of the original purposes of the group which formed the Romen was to preserve the folk art of the *tabor* (gypsy encampment). The original company was recruited in large part from *tabor* gypsies, rather than from the spoiled, citified gypsy colonies.

One of the most important aims of the Romen was to discourage the performance of "cabaret-gypsy" dances and songs, which the Kremlin authorities described as decadent and

Gypsies are dying out . . . .

designed to satisfy the low appetites of the pre-revolutionary nobility and bourgeoise. And today the Romen continues to present only the best gypsy plays, such as *Grushenka, Daughter of the Tents,* and *The Four Bridegrooms.*

One of the women ushers at the Romen, a gypsy herself, recently told a friend of mine that, until about four years ago, the theater had presented its productions in Romany, as it had done from its inception. Soon after the war, however, the Arts Committee of the Council of Ministers issued a decree that Russian was to be the language used henceforth. This usher, a veteran of twenty years at the Romen, said that the theater had not attracted very large audiences during its Romany-language period. At that time non-Romany-speaking spectators followed the action from librettos printed in the Russian language. Since the Romen began working in Russian, however, it has been playing, on the whole, to full houses. Another gypsy present during this conversation added that the lack of interest in Romany-language productions was understandable, after all, since gypsies in the Soviet Union are dying out ("being bred out"). The wandering gypsies have apparently stopped wandering, and have settled down either on collective farms or on state farms (many Russian gypsies are skilled horse breeders and trainers, to mention only two of their specialties where horses are concerned), or are "studying and becoming scholars."

It is evident that younger-generation gypsies are marrying Russians and being absorbed culturally by the majority group. "There are only a few gypsies left," one member of the theater staff lamented. "You don't see the really black gypsies any more."

. . . . **Difficulties of translation**

MAY 8, 1952

Day after day, as I pore over the Moscow newspapers and periodicals and grind out my translation work, I am struck more and more by the fact that underlying the special differences separating the Russian and American peoples — the sharp ideological and political differences, the varied economic and social and cultural dissimilarities — is the common, everyday problem of language. And this language hurdle is not only in the field of semantics, or the science of meanings — for example, what does the word "democracy" mean to the Russians today, and what does it mean to us? It also presents the very urgent and practical question of just what word to select in shifting from Russian to English, and vice versa. We underestimate, I think, the danger of serious spills as we try to leap over this ordinary, but ever-present, barrier.

One of the main reasons for this difficulty, in my opinion, is that the Russian language is not only much more concise than English in sentence structure, but also less precise in the definition of individual words. Take, for example, one of the most common words in present-day Russian, a word which appears at least one hundred times every day in a single four-page edition of *Pravda,* the word *voenny.*

Now that word, used as an attributive adjective, can be translated accurately either as "military" or "war." But what a difference it makes in English whether you say the "military plans of the U.S.A." or the "war plans of the U.S.A." And which meaning does the average Russian give to the phrase when he reads those words in a *Pravda* headline every morning?

Twenty-five translations for one word . . . . .

Or take another important Russian word that fills the columns of the daily press, the adjective *narodny,* from the noun *narod,* meaning "a people," as a collective unit. With different nouns this word should be translated in many different ways — "people's" democracy; "national" economy; "public" education; "popular" masses; "folk" songs.

I have often wondered how interpreters and translators at international conferences, sessions of the United Nations, and meetings of the Foreign Ministers automatically handle the word *otkazatsya,* a verb that is heard on the lips of Soviet diplomats and publicists very frequently these days. To satisfy my curiosity, I have just added up acceptable translations of this key word. The total number of possibilities came to twenty-five. Here they are: to refuse, reject, renounce, decline, disclaim, abandon, retract, forego, desist, resign, eschew, waive, repudiate, surrender, relinquish, foresake, default, abdicate, disavow, renege, abjure, abstain, deny, give up, say "no." In delicate international relations, fine distinctions must be drawn in translating this verb into English — for example: to "reject" the proposals; "decline" the invitation; "retract" the article; "default" on debts; "abdicate" the throne; "foresake" one's principles; "repudiate" the treaty; "waive" restrictions; "forego" food; "relinquish" or "surrender" or "resign" claims; "disclaim" responsibility, "abandon" hope; "eschew" the use of force; "renounce" war as an instrument of policy.

And so the obstacle course stretches on and on.

MAY 11, 1952

On this trip of mine to Vladimir — which is 120 miles east of Moscow — I have had my first good opportunity to see

. . . . **Preparations for a trip**

Russian farming land at close hand. I have received impressions before, of course — from train and airplane windows — but yesterday, on a day-long taxi trip to the village of Suzdal (22 miles north of Vladimir) and back again, I really felt that I was in the country. Furthermore, it was the country of flat plains, low rolling hills, and forest steppes that is so typical of millions of the more than eight million square miles of Russia.

First, perhaps, I should explain the taxi ride itself. The Soviet authorities make it very difficult for foreign visitors to get to Suzdal, even from nearby Vladimir, although it is today only a tiny, hay-strewn village and isolated market place, its only real points of interest being its ancient churches and historical monuments. In the early Middle Ages, Suzdal was one of Russia's most important and celebrated principalities — later absorbed by Vladimir, and then by Moscow.

Accordingly, we (two British Embassy officers and I) were forced to lay our plans carefully — as one must do, anyway, even on the simplest trip.

First of all, we had postponed our trip until the middle of May — that is, after the weeks of spring floods — in the event that the impassible authorities might want to use the excuse of impassable roads, as they have done before.

Secondly, as soon as we checked in at the small hotel in Vladimir, we started making inquiries as to various transportation facilities and the possibility of traveling to Suzdal. A tired old woman in a faded shawl behind the reception window whispered in reply: "Oh, I really don't know. I think there is a bus. Maybe it goes twice a day. But I shall have to telephone." When we asked again a little later, she said: "Yes, I telephoned — and there are two buses a day. But you had better go to the bus station yourselves to make

"Why don't you try a taxi?" . . . .

sure of the exact departure time. The depot is just around the corner and down the hill."

Off we went — to find the station ticket office closed. The schedule posted on the wall, however, showed that it would be impossible to make a good connection for the return trip — and, since there was no place in which to stay overnight in Suzdal, it looked as though we were out of luck. We were disappointed — particularly because few foreigners have such a favorable opportunity to take a cross-country bus ride (an instructive experience in any country). "Why don't you try a taxi?" The words came from a stranger, a tattered Russian lounging on the doorstep.

Looking out over the desolate, deserted courtyard of the bus station, we realized that this might turn out to be a good suggestion — because parked there in the middle of the mud was an old dilapidated Pobeda (one of the few automobiles we had seen in Vladimir), with a driver apparently waiting for stray passengers. We certainly qualified as stray — if not strange — passengers. Our proposal was promptly accepted by the taxi driver, who seemed more than pleased at the prospect of a long trip and a big fare. "Get in," he said, "and we'll start at once. But first I must put in a supply of gasoline." The seats of the car were dirty and springless, but at least we were on four wheels and moving — and all of us, including the old but eager driver, started out in high spirits. After crossing to the opposite end of town to pick up the gas, we returned through the center of the city, and headed for the highway to Gorky (formerly Nizhny Novgorod), from which branches the country road to Suzdal. Then, at the main intersection of Vladimir, a militiaman on the corner suddenly waved our driver to the curb. A mys-

terious conference immediately took place in the middle of
the street — with the policeman, our driver, and a plain-
clothes man, who appeared out of the blue, joining in the
argument, while we remained in the car. Soon the driver
returned, visibly angry and muttering under his breath. But
we started off again, and I thought that all was well. Almost
at once, however, the driver swung around into an open
square, came to a stop, and told us, without explanation,
that he could not take us to Suzdal. As we got out, his low
muttering turned to unmistakable cursing.

At this point, at last, we began to see what it was all about.
There, beside us, stood another taxi, a shiny new car, the
same that, unsolicited, had met us at the railway station in
the darkness of early morning (at 4.49 A.M., to be exact) on
our arrival in Vladimir. And the same chauffeur who had
driven us from the train to the hotel — an agreeable, neatly
dressed young man — stepped out from the driver's seat and
informed us, politely but firmly, that he would take us to
Suzdal.

Such are the devious ways of the Kremlin. Once again I
felt that an unseen hand had reached out from nowhere, and
calmly and silently moved us and everybody else on the chess-
board that is Russia. We felt sorry for the poor old man in
the other taxi — and I, quite suddenly, felt sorry for mankind in general — but, at that point, there was nothing I
could do about either the man or mankind.

Our new car was a very fancy one — each window had silk
curtains with fringe and tassels. This arrangement might be
genteel — but it was not conducive to sightseeing. Throughout the trip I had to push the curtains back at least a hundred times, at every bump, in a very bumpy road. When I

the lonely vastness and potential might . . . .

did look out the window, this is what I saw:

A rough cobblestone road, very narrow — a thin, silver-gray ribbon following the contours of the sloping steppes. Dirt footpaths on each side of the old stones, many of the paths broadening into secondary wheel tracks running through the fields alongside the main roadbed. Broken bridges crossing countless shallow streams. Patches of snow in the gulches — still shining white in the warm sun of May. Piles of wooden fences standing in sections by the side of the road — ready for use in the winter, when the snowdrifts along this route must be tremendous. Big black crows slowly and noisily flapping up from the fields and wheeling into the sky as we drove by. Yellowhammers and wagtails skimming over the edge of flooded meadows. Church cupolas and an isolated tree or two breaking the flat skyline, to the right and left, in front and behind. Here a tractor, there a plow. And everywhere fields rolling to the horizon — some brown and green, some almost lavender in color, as the scattered clouds cast great patches of light and shadow on the earth.

And now, after this long digression about the taxi (but long digressions are necessary in recounting any episode in Russia — because, as you can see in this case, delays in time and detours in space are a part of every event), I must get back to the question of agriculture, to the starting point of this diary entry:

As I looked out over this Russian land that fills half of Europe and half of Asia, the lonely vastness and potential might of the Soviet Union struck me again, harder than ever. While I drove through the endless fields, I was reminded that the Soviet Union has already overtaken the United States as the world's leading producer of wheat, man's most important

food. When will other basic products of economic life —
coal and iron and cotton and oil — follow?

One vital lesson I have learned in Russia: we of the
younger generation in America cannot sit back and safely
assume that we shall always be on top — even in our life-
time. We must grow and conserve and purify, and work and
work, in order to preserve and deserve our place of world
supremacy.

MAY 13, 1952

So far I have seen three Shakespeare productions in Russia:
Twelfth Night, Much Ado About Nothing, and *Othello.*

The performance of *Othello* in Russian was of particular
interest because I saw it in Vladimir, a provincial town many
miles from Moscow, and the whole evening gave me a good
idea of the cultural standards outside the capital.

The production was excellent, and the performances (for
a small town) struck me as being of an unusually high quality. Indeed, this production compared very favorably — although it was much less elaborate — with the Moscow
Othello at the Mossoviet Theater, where Mordvinov, in the
leading part, rants too much, and actually growls and grunts
as he exhibits his animal passions — to the astonishment and
delight of his fascinated audiences.

In the Vladimir production, Othello was played by an ac-
tor named Ivanov, from the Ryazan Oblast Theater, whose acting was just as powerful and more restrained — although he
too growled a bit, and bared his teeth lasciviously in the first
two acts (the whiteness of his teeth and the redness of his
lips showing up against the coffee-colored make-up).

quite moving . . . .

As it turned out, the performance was quite moving because, as we learned from somebody in the audience, these were Ivanov's "last days" of acting for some time, as he had a cancer of the tongue and was about to go to Moscow for treatment and an operation. As a matter of fact, I had noticed in the opening scenes that he appeared to have difficulty in mouthing some of his words — his tongue seeming to get in the way in a peculiar fashion.

Iago, too, acted well — restrained but effective. He was dressed in the customary black — but he was quite stout and short, giving a less conventional appearance.

By comparison, the rest of the cast was much less effective.

The sets and staging were simple and unpretentious by Moscow's standards — and at times the scenery was shaky and tattered, the inner curtain sometimes catching or falling with a bang.

There was a small orchestra in the pit under the stage. The theater itself was barely half full. At times the audience seemed rather restless — although, for the most part, it was silent and attentive and took the whole evening very seriously.

MAY 15, 1952

As in the West, a feature film in a Soviet movie show is invariably preceded by a newsreel. Here is a typical newsreel which I saw in Moscow a few nights ago:

The first item showed a ceremonial meeting in the Great Hall of the Moscow Conservatory in commemoration of the five hundredth anniversary of the birth of Leonardo da Vinci, with shots of prominent Soviet scholars and scientists addressing a large, applauding audience.

. . . .   **Russian newsreel**

Next came a view of a new assembly line in a machine-tool factory, the Red Proletariat Factory in Moscow, with rows of Russians happily working (and obviously even more happy to be photographed).

The third item covered the springtime farm activities of a model collective farm in Moldavia, with many views of far-stretching fields and close-ups of tractors drawing enormous farm machines.

This was followed by a "personality" item, a little feature honoring an Uzbek scientist of the Tashkent Textile Institute.

Then came scenes from the second act of Tchaikovsky's *Sleeping Beauty,* which has just been revived in a tremendous, blazing production at the Bolshoi — and most of the close-ups showed Struchkova, the youngest, fairest, and most exciting of Russia's great ballerinas.

The final portion of the newsreel was marked "Foreign News" — but the only subject presented concerned the new Five-Year Plan in Albania, and here the photographs showed Communist Premier Enver Hoxha making a speech at the dedication of a new factory, against a bleak background of brick walls and white, unsmiling faces.

MAY 19, 1952

Life in the American Embassy in Moscow is an odd business. In a way we are living between two mirrors. There is the actual life we experience day by day and then there is the official Russian description of what we are and how we live. Naturally these two concepts reflect back and forth — to the confusion of everyone caught between.

Tonight all this has been very sharply brought into focus

The House on the Sidestreet . . . .

for me. I am just back from a play called *The House on the Sidestreet* at the Lenin Komsomol Theater. It is one of the most popular anti-American plays and although the United States is never mentioned and the Embassy whose personnel are involved is never identified, it is easy enough to translate "the house on the sidestreet" as Spaso House (which, of course, is on a sidestreet). For instance, the portrait over the fireplace is recognizably of George Washington in Revolutionary uniform. The general theme of the play is very loosely derived from the book *The Truth About American Diplomats* by Annabelle Bucar, who recently worked in our Embassy here and resigned to espouse the Soviet cause — or "went over," as we say.

There are two main threads to the complicated, fantastic plot: the attempt of "Americans" in Berlin to seize incriminating archives of Hitler's "International Intelligence Service," and the efforts of members of the Embassy in Moscow to steal an icon painted by the great fifteenth-century artist Rublev, and worth "200,000 gold."

A young girl who comes to work in the Moscow Embassy, full of hope and high ideals, becomes charmed by the life of the Russians and at the same time bitterly disillusioned at the cynicism, drunkenness, self-seeking, and warmongering of the Embassy officers. These diplomats become more and more hurried in their desperation to start another war before it is "too late," since time is working on the side of the "peace-loving" Russians.

One of the roles, that of a German woman entrusted with vital Nazi secrets, must be among the most fantastic ever played by any actress on any stage. Her make-up was garish to the point of making her look like a buffoon, and her

. . . . **a typical Russian audience**

gestures and tone of voice were in keeping.

The audience seemed particularly pleased when the play portrayed the calm, firm confidence of the Soviet people in the face of the desperate intrigues of the warmongers.

The audience also reacted when the play brought out the dangerous possibilities of even routine Embassy activity. The scene in which the Counselor advises the newly arrived heroine to keep her eyes and ears open in the bus, the streetcar, etc., went over quite well. Nor could the audience fail to note the play's obviously implied warning that if one is a loyal, honest Soviet citizen and always abides by the law, thereby giving the Americans no opportunity for blackmail, it will be possible to stay out of their clutches, and out of serious trouble.

The house was full. I would say it was a typical Russian audience — fairly well dressed — their age, on the average, perhaps in the late thirties. They were very attentive and applauded fairly liberally throughout the play, particularly when Westerners were held up to ridicule and when Russian patriotism was appealed to.

Examples:

Quote of old art worker: "Others conquer with the atomic bomb, but we are winning the world with the light of our national, people's genius."

Quote of correspondent for "Globus" radio network (really a major in his country's intelligence service) while looking out the Embassy window at the illuminated crimson stars on the Kremlin towers: "Some people say they cannot sleep because of the moon, but I can't sleep at night thinking about those stars!"

Quote of Soviet major sitting on Sokolniki park bench and

"... on our Russian soil" . . . .

talking to "Globus" correspondent, who is complaining that the Soviet Union is spreading its ideas beyond its own border: "The wind takes the seed" (this apparently clever response provoked a *big* laugh from the audience); in the same conversation, the correspondent produces a bottle of cognac called the "Atom Bomb," which, he says, knocks everybody over — to which the major replies: "It depends on how strong your legs are!"

Reference is made in the first scene to a performance of Prokofiev's *Romeo and Juliet* ballet — with considerable chagrin among the Embassy personnel, as they reach for cocktails, because they had just reported that it had been banned (reference is also made to another ballet, *Swan Lake*, which actually lasts four hours when performed at the Bolshoi, but which Eva sees in an amazingly short time of ten minutes in Act II, Scene 2).

Park-bench scene at Sokolniki: "Globus" correspondent says to Eva, on seeing a Soviet citizen (actually the Soviet major in civilian clothes) sitting alone on next bench: "Come, we must sit beside him, because we should never lose an opportunity to talk with a Soviet citizen." (You can imagine how *I* felt during this scene, having been guilty of such a crime on so many occasions.)

Eva's Alexander Nevsky quote in the last scene: "Whoever has fallen upon us with the sword has perished by the sword — that is the way it always has been, and always will be, on our Russian soil." Thunderous applause.

MAY 20, 1952

Wherever I have been in Russia, whether in a church in Mos-

· · · · · · · · · · · **A football game**

cow or at a theater in Yaroslavl or in a market square in
Suzdal or under a linden tree at Yasnaya Polyana, I have always felt that I have been doing something wrong.

MAY 21, 1952

This afternoon I went out to the enormous stadium in Moscow to see my first football game in the Soviet Union. Football in Russia, of course, refers to what we know as soccer.

This match was between the Air Force and the local
"Dinamo" team of Moscow. The "Dinamo" outfit was
dressed in two shades of blue and the Air Force wore striped
jerseys. The stadium, which can hold at least one hundred
thousand spectators, was only partially filled. The field was
very muddy.

During the first half of the game it was difficult to see what
was going on because the sun was setting in the west directly
across the field from our seats. The game was divided into
two halves, each lasting forty-five minutes without a stop, and
throughout all that time the players were constantly on the
run.

I would say that their skill and stamina were extremely
high. And so was their politeness to each other. It was a
very neat, gentle match. However, the most striking part of
the afternoon was not the game itself, but these two observations: one, stretching across one end of the stadium was a
giant red banner with letters in Russian, French, and English, reading: "Toiling peoples of all countries, strengthen
the unity of peoples throughout the world in the struggle
for peace"; two, although the stadium was only half full, the
majority of the thousands of people there seemed to be made
up of militiamen, who filled row after row after row.

one million minutes in the Soviet Union . . . .

MAY 26, 1952

I have now spent close to one million minutes in the Soviet Union — and have only a few thousand to go.

In living these minutes — whether standing in the snow with a crowd of silent Soviet citizens at the burial place of Stalin's wife in Novodevichy Monastery; or rushing down the carpet of the center aisle of the Bolshoi to clap for Ulanova during her curtain calls; or paying my bill to a harried Russian waitress; or buying an embroidered Uzbek skullcap called a *tyubeteika,* in the crush of Moscow housewives at the clothing counter of a department store; or listening to Gilels play Skryabin sonatas on the big stage of the Conservatory; or lighting the cigarette of a Soviet stewardess as our plane takes off from Vnukovo Airport on the southwest outskirts of Moscow; or hunting for the grave of Chaadaev in Donskoi Monastery, and thereby disturbing a pair of lovers sitting on the old tombstone (or hunting for the grave of Klyuchevsky in the same churchyard, and thereby disturbing an old peasant woman answering another call of nature); or downing Stolichnaya vodka (one hundred grams a gulp) with a Soviet colonel in Moscow's Beer Hall No. 1; or watching Stalin raise his right hand beatifically on the top of Lenin's tomb; or discussing American democracy and freedom with an ill-clad, wide-eyed peasant at the private altar of Ivan the Terrible in St. Basil's Cathedral — in living all these minutes, I say, I have always had the same underlying thought about the Russian people, the people whose eyes I have tried to read and whose voice I have tried to hear. And the thought is this:

The Russians, underneath, seem to realize that something is going wrong; that something, perhaps, is lacking. They

. . . . **living in defeat**

appear to sense that things are not quite right in their world; that maybe the greatest experiment in man's history has failed, after all. And, at the same time, they are unable, or possibly unwilling, to put their rough, red finger on the cause.

I cannot, of course, prove all this — but I am sure that my final impression of the Soviet Union today will be this unexpressed feeling of defeat.

It is certainly an irony of history that, when the U.S.S.R. has achieved its greatest material and military strength, it appears at that very moment so spiritually weak, to be living with such faint heartbeats. And likewise it is a curious twist of fate that, when the Soviet Union, outside its borders, seems to be at the peak of its prestige and power, when its external reputation of strength is at its height, it appears at the same moment, within its borders, to be living in defeat, sometimes ridiculous, always sad and forlorn.

I often think of Pushkin's comment to Gogol, when Gogol read to him the first part of *Dead Souls,* the great comic epic of the damned. Pushkin had been laughing at the wonderful satire, but then he stopped and said simply: "Oh, God, how sad is our Russia!"

MAY 27, 1952

This afternoon I had my first long interview with George Kennan, who has just arrived as our new Ambassador — the latest of a long line of distinguished Americans to represent the United States in Russia. As I walked up the stairs to his private office in the Chancery, which overlooks the Kremlin and the Red Square, I could not help but think of our first Minister to Russia, John Quincy Adams — and of the vastly

"One always grows a little" . . . .

different situations the two men faced as they took over their post.

I thought, too, of a fascinating and fateful bit of conversation Adams recorded in his diary. On a certain occasion, Adams tried to explain to Tsar Alexander I how the United States in 1810 had happened to take a portion of West Florida from Spain by rather high-handed methods. It is impossible, of course, to say whether or not the Tsar, in his reply, was thinking of the shifting of boundaries in Europe at that time, but in any event, he made a comment that was extremely prophetic then, and extremely pertinent today. Speaking in the French of the diplomatic world, he answered with a smile:

"On s'agrandit toujours un peu, dans ce monde." (One always grows a little in this world.)

Perhaps, after all, the situations are not so completely different. Certainly Stalin today would not converse with Kennan in an informal, man-by-man walk under the Kremlin walls (as Alexander, in those far-off days, frequently met Adams during daily strolls through the parks of St. Petersburg), but Stalin must often repeat to himself at least the words of Alexander — not in high-flown French, of course, but in his own soft-spoken brand of Russian with its odd Georgian accent: "One always grows a little in this world." The immediate circumstances and ways of life have changed in almost every way imaginable — but the same old problem of expansion is still with us.

As I walked up to Kennan's desk and saw there a man already pale and tired after only a few days in Moscow, I realized that the underlying cause of his fatigue was this very problem of Russia's "growing a little." But wan or not,

Kennan immediately inspires confidence and respect. One feels at once that here is a Westerner in Russia who, if anybody, can pluck meaning out of the puzzling phenomena around us, an American who can meet and match the master minds across the street. When I say "across the street," I mean just that. One of the fascinations of sitting at the desk of the American Ambassador in Moscow is that you look through his window directly out onto the Red Square and the red Kremlin walls, with their long rows of windows looking directly back at you, like unblinking eyes. And so, as I watched Kennan lean back and gaze into space, searching for answers, I could picture Stalin and Malenkov, Molotov and Vishinsky, doing the same thing only a few hundred yards away.

Although Kennan has now been here less than three weeks, he is already the acknowledged leader of the entire Western community in Moscow.

From the British and French to the Greeks and Afghans, all seem to realize that Kennan is one of the very few informed people in the non-Communist world who has been in and out of Moscow over a period long enough to give a true perspective to his views. Respecting his years of study of the Russian scene, they crave to know his judgment. And everybody seems to feel, too, that here is a man who combines "modesty of person with dignity of office" — to use the words Kennan himself once wrote down in praising the qualities of such statesmen as John Hay, Elihu Root, Charles Evans Hughes, and Henry Stimson.

Before today, I had watched Kennan on several occasions — mostly at large receptions, in Spaso House and at Western embassies. Tall, thin and dignified, he is conspicuous in a crowd, with his bald head rising high above the shoulders of surrounding guests. But his manner is anything but conspicuous. When Kennan speaks, his thin, tight lips hardly move, and his voice, when heard, is low and subdued. Unassuming and unobtrusive, with a faraway look in his eye, he acts much more like a scholar and aesthete, shy and somewhat sad, than the social lion. Certainly this modest and retiring man does not give the appearance of a person who, as the architect of America's postwar foreign policy, is one of the most influential and powerful human beings in the world today.

At these diplomatic gatherings, the endless small talk and galloping gossip of Moscow are incongruous in the presence of an official of such high seriousness — and Kennan, grave and remote, cannot hide the fact that he is rather ill at ease in these surroundings. Socially, he is a bit stiff — and obviously bored stiff. He is much more like himself at any other time — as, for example, yesterday, when I saw him at the Embassy rushing up two long flights of stairs, two steps at a time, refusing to wait for the elevator in his haste to get to his office.

Working under tremendous pressure, Kennan budgets his days and nights with cold and careful calculation, deliberately making every minute count. This was vividly brought home to me the other day when I happened to run into the Ambassador as he was leaving his outer office. Rushing across the room and putting on his hat before he passed the door, he turned to me with one of his small, infrequent smiles.

"I have just found out," he explained, "that, quite unexpectedly, there is a twenty-minute gap in my list of appointments — and I am going to try to fit in a visit to some of the old-book stores, the shops with the second-hand books. Where are the best ones? They used to be on Kuznetsky Most — on the right-hand side as you go up the hill. That's right, isn't it?"

And he was off with a rush, happy as a child in a school recess. It is at such rare moments that Kennan loses some of his aloofness.

Kennan is still a student at heart — and his heart is still in the Russian problem. One of the reasons for the Ambassador's strict budgeting of his time is his desire to cut out as many of the meaningless social obligations as possible, and thus free himself for more fruitful activity. In this way, he will have more hours to study Russia's past, comprehend Russia's present, foresee Russia's future.

Within a day after Kennan's arrival, the spurt of activities started — and the spurt, incidentally, has enlivened the whole Embassy, reviving our spirits, which drooped considerably after the departure of Ambassador and Mrs. Kirk eight months ago. To illustrate: During the Ambassador's very first week end, he revisited the Tretyakov Gallery, Moscow's most celebrated art museum, with its unequaled collection of icons (including the holiest treasure of ancient Russia, "Our Lady of Vladimir") as well as its equally unequaled collection of vicious anti-American posters; one night recently he attended a public lecture, sitting in the gallery of a Moscow University hall; already in these first few days he has been to the theater several times, including a performance of Ostrovsky's *Ardent Heart* at the Moscow Art Theater. All these activities I happen to know about personally — un-

"What can the real reason be?" . . . .

doubtedly there are many more. All in all, I can safely say that not many heads of missions in Moscow are making every day such an effort in their own person to achieve a better understanding of the greatest problem the world has ever faced.

Today, when I talked alone with Kennan, he not only seemed wistful about the old days in the Embassy — the days in the 1930's when Foreign Service students of Russia were relatively free to follow their pursuits — but also, and more important, he seemed to be worried about the future, worried and wondering. At one point in our conversation, we had been discussing the Russian theater: how the regime appeared to be frankly concerned about the poor state of contemporary Soviet drama; how this open criticism was reflected in the press, where the controversy over the so-called "no conflict" theory is now raging; how the theater always would be a dangerous seat of reaction in the eyes of the Kremlin; how there was very little the government could do about it — except resort to the pathetic expedient of stuffing the stage with worn-out Ostrovsky pieces, as is now being done; how the repertoire of anti-American plays was rapidly increasing in number and virulence. Then, suddenly Kennan clasped his hands behind his head, looked up at the ceiling as though absorbed in something far away and perplexing, and slowly repeated the words: "anti-American, anti-American." Here, once again, I saw that the Ambassador does not bear his heavy responsibilities lightly. "I am particularly puzzled by this anti-American campaign — this extreme case of whipped-up hatred. I don't know, I just don't know, what the Russians are driving at. What can the real reason be?"

Kennan may not know today, but if anybody knows tomorrow, he — I am sure — will be the one.

. . . . . . the hot hatred being coldly built

MAY 28, 1952

As a postscript to my comments on Kennan yesterday, I should point out how surprised I was to realize how surprised he was that the anti-American campaign in Russia had reached such a crude crescendo of abuse, that outrage had turned to rage. The reason for Kennan's astonishment, of course, rests in the fact that the campaign has developed in the postwar years, following his last tour of duty in Moscow. But, nonetheless, the campaign has been going on for many years now — certainly ever since I have been in Russia — and it is strange that the press and people of the non-Communist world, and particularly the citizens of our own country, have not fully appreciated either the extent or the intensity of the campaign, and so have not been aware of the threat in it. Apparently one has to be right here in Moscow, to live and work and walk in what you might call the camp of the enemy, to see and hear and smell the evil manifestations of the campaign every day (almost every hour), and at every turn, in order to comprehend the hot hatred that is being coldly built up against us, as a nation and as a people.

Now at last, however, more and more people in the West seem to be asking for an explanation of this increasingly dangerous development. My guess is that Kennan's newly felt perturbation on this score has already leaked through to informed persons outside Russia — and hence the sudden alarm in Western public opinion, as though a brand-new danger had been detected. I notice that the answers to the question appear to fall into two opposite categories, one encouraging, the other alarming. The more cheerful interpretation, from our point of view, of the anti-American cam-

Reasons for the hate campaign . . . .

paign is made up of several explanations, any one of which is offered as the possible key. One of these is to the effect that American propaganda and the message of the non-Communist world are effectively penetrating the Iron Curtain, and so more ferocious counterattacks are needed by the Kremlin. Another says that the Russian people are so apathetic and indifferent, so skeptical and suspicious, so weary and wary of propaganda, as the result of years of constant shifts in the Party's propaganda line, that the shock treatment is now necessary — and as the people become progressively hardened, ever greater shocks are required. The reasoning of still another explanation is that Russia's internal troubles are so severe that a scapegoat is needed, and the American Government — and now even the American people — can conveniently fill that role.

On the other hand, there is the pessimistic interpretation that the hate-America campaign has been launched to prepare the Soviet people for war on the part of Russia, and to justify any future military move.

Each of these explanations is valid. But the important thing to remember, in my opinion, is that they are not mutually exclusive. It is more likely, therefore, that all of them together form the *raison d'être* of this campaign, a campaign of pure malice which will be studied by historians and psychologists, and the Devil himself, for many years to come.

JUNE 1, 1952

During this stay of ours in Leningrad the main points of interest have related to the degrees and methods of surveillance, to the varying restrictions and limitations to freedom

of movement — all of which, when added together, pass all
understanding.

I have been making this trip in the company of a girl member of the British Embassy, and throughout most of our stay
in Leningrad, each of us has been treated by the authorities
in a different manner. The most important difference has
concerned permission to visit Peterhof, one of the old palaces
of the tsars outside the city. Our respective embassies in
Moscow had advised the Ministry of Foreign Affairs of the
intention of each representative to visit both Peterhof and
Tsarskoe Selo (now called Pushkin). The American Embassy was notified immediately that I could not go to either
place, inasmuch as both are now considered out of bounds
in Leningrad Oblast. The British Embassy, however, received no word of any kind from the Ministry of Foreign
Affairs. Intourist in Leningrad reported that my British colleague could not go to Tsarskoe Selo (no reason given) but
that she was free to visit Peterhof — and they co-operated
completely in arranging her subsequent trip. Moreover two
other British subjects who have been in Leningrad at this
time — one English, the other Canadian — also received
authority from Intourist to visit Peterhof. On the other
hand, whereas I have been permitted to move freely in
Leningrad itself, my British colleague was once stopped by
the militia. The scene was the left bank of the Neva, at the
south end of the former Nicholas Bridge leading across the
river to Vasilevsky Ostrov; she was told by a militiaman, obviously waiting for her, that she could not cross to the island
at this point, nor could she continue straight ahead along
the embankment: she could either retrace her steps or turn
to the left into the city. Another puzzling inconsistency: all

I have often been followed . . . .

the British in Leningrad at this time have been charged 50
rubles by Intourist for a visit to the Golden Treasure in the
Hermitage, and I was charged nothing.

Although I have not been stopped in my wanderings
through the city, I have often been followed. This surveillance has seemed to me to make little sense. For example, I
was closely watched during an obviously innocent and legitimate visit to the Hermitage — particularly when standing in
front of Leonardo da Vinci's "Madonna Benois," in order
to study the painting in the light of the following recent, and
typical, art-criticism comment in the magazine *Bolshevik*
concerning this work: "The painters of the Renaissance . . .
had brought the celestial tsarina down to earth and painted
her as an ordinary town dweller with her son in her arms.
But, perhaps, nobody before Leonardo put in the figure of
the Madonna such a profound revelation of the theme of
happy motherhood . . . as is found, for example, in the so-
called 'Madonna Benois,' which is preserved in the Leningrad Hermitage." I was also closely watched when trying in
vain to get into the room containing Bronzino's celebrated
painting of "Apollo and Marsyas," a mystery canvas which
has never been photographed or reproduced in the West.
On a previous visit to the Hermitage I had located the painting in Room 238, devoted to sixteenth-century Italian art,
to find that the Soviets attributed the work not to Bronzino,
but to Francesco Parmigianino of the Parma School; on this
later occasion, however, the room was completely closed to
the public. On the other hand, there was no indication of
such shadowing when I made a trip to the Russian Museum
to have a last look at the extraordinary fourteenth-century
icon of Boris and Gleb, a strange, realistic painting of the

Suzdal School, which is uniquely Russian, with not a trace of Byzantine influence. Nor was I followed when I went into areas of the city which presumably would be considered more "dangerous." For example, I walked for hours, in what must have appeared to be a suspicious manner, in the out-of-the-way blocks beyond Fontanka Canal and Zagorodny Prospekt, near the Vitebsk station, vainly searching for the old building in which *Pravda* was first published before the revolution. Furthermore, there was no noticeable trailing when I took a long walk through the poor quarter of the city in the neighborhood of the Alexander Nevsky Monastery.

JUNE 2, 1952

My visit to the Alexander Nevsky Monastery brought to light three interesting developments in the Party's present policy with respect to historical monuments, all of which serve to reflect current ideological trends:

1. The first of these questions concerns the whereabouts of the remains of Alexander Nevsky himself. I first became interested in this problem a few weeks ago during a visit to the Cathedral of the Assumption at Vladimir. In spite of the locked doors protecting the extensive restoration work in the interior of this church (the most impressive architectural monument in all of northeastern Russia), I had been fortunate enough to get inside to inspect the recently discovered fresco fragments. While leaning back against one of the central white stone columns to get a better view in the darkness, I accidentally put my foot on an unpainted wooden crate, about the size of a coffin, and then looked down to see

The Cathedral of the Trinity in Leningrad . . .

what I was resting on. Painted in black on the rough boards of this outer case were these words: "Relics of Alexander Nevsky." It is a well-known fact of history, of course, that in 1724 Peter the Great removed these relics from Vladimir, where originally the tomb was in the Church of the Nativity of the Virgin. The bones were brought to Petersburg, where they were placed in a reliquary in the church which Peter, in order to give his new capital the prestige of a national shrine, had built on the banks of the Neva on the spot where, according to tradition, Grand Prince Alexander won his victory over the invading Swedes in 1240 (whence his Nevsky epithet). Up to the Revolution at least, the relics remained in the monastery — in the Cathedral of the Trinity, to the right of the marble iconostas. My object in Leningrad, therefore, was to see whether the bones were still there, or whether the Soviet regime had indeed returned them to Vladimir. Today the Cathedral of the Trinity (which Peter began to build in 1724) is falling to ruins: the central dome is black and rusty, weeds and small green bushes are growing on the edges of the roof, and the laundry of those living in the monastery is hung on the dirty, unpainted porches of the church. When I first tried to get inside, it seemed that all the doors were locked and barred, but I finally found an entry with a rusty, wrought-iron gate which opened into the cold, cavelike interior near the central altar. Then I realized that I was not alone. In addition to the cooing of doves high up under the dome, I could hear human voices, and when my eyes became accustomed to the darkness, I saw five or six peasant women piling sacks in the far corner. The sacks apparently contained sunflower seeds, as the seeds were scattered over the altar floor. Keeping watch over the women workers was a guard with a rifle over one shoulder and a bandage over one eye. As I approached closer, the guard motioned me away, and then told me to get out. Before leaving, however, I noticed that the sacks were piled high under what looked like an elaborate old canopy to the right of the iconostas. Thus, the mystery of the exact whereabouts of Alexander Nevsky's relics remains more or less unanswered — but, as far as I am concerned, the bones of this war hero are no longer on the banks of the Neva.

2. The second question concerns the remains of Field Marshal Suvorov, the "founding father" of modern Russian military might, the man who built the Russian Empire for Catherine the Great. About this, there is no great mystery, but there is great activity. The day before my visit to the Alexander Nevsky Monastery, I had tried to see the tomb of Kutuzov (the great general who beat Napoleon) in the Kazan Cathedral — but with no success. The burial place of Kutuzov (located in the cathedral on the spot where he is supposed to have performed devotions before starting to join the army at Smolensk in 1812) is currently undergoing *remont* (repairs) — and is closed to visitors. To my surprise, I had later exactly the same experience at the Alexander Nevsky Monastery when trying to visit the tomb of Suvorov in the choir of the Church of the Annunciation, where I hoped to learn whether or not the Soviet authorities had felt it fitting to make more elaborate the marble slab with the simple inscription chosen by the Field Marshal himself: "Here lies Suvorov." Suvorov's burial place likewise is now undergoing *remont* (in fact, the whole church is being restored) — and this area, too, is closed to visitors. In view of the current tidal wave of nationalism in the Soviet

Standing before Dostoyevsky's tombstone . . . .

Union, it is not difficult to imagine what the Kremlin intends to do by way of glorifying the memory of these two war leaders.

3. The third development concerns the remains of Dostoyevsky. Here there is less mystery — and no activity at all. The current Party line with respect to Dostoyevsky — the policy of deliberately ignoring, if not suppressing his works — is clear to all who follow the twists and turns of Soviet ideology, and it becomes even clearer on a visit to Dostoyevsky's grave in the Alexander Nevsky Monastery. During two visits last year to the fascinating Dostoyevsky Museum in Moscow — located in the rooms of his boyhood in a wing of the Mariinskaya Hospital, where his father served as staff physician — I had been struck by the almost complete absence of Russian visitors. Not a soul was in sight on either occasion, and very few names had been entered in the visitors' book in recent months — a striking contrast to the hordes who fill, voluntarily or not, the "important" museums of Moscow. On display in this museum was a pathetic photograph of Dostoyevsky's mourning family at his flower-covered grave — and I became curious to see how the Party culture-molders were handling today what must be an awkward problem: the treatment of the grave itself. Now, standing before Dostoyevsky's tombstone in the Alexander Nevsky Monastery in Leningrad, I saw. In the first place, it should be pointed out that although the burial place is very near the main entrance to the monastery, directly behind the wall of the cemetery to the right, before crossing the bridge of a sluggish, moatlike canal, it is nonetheless extremely difficult to find. And the reason that it is difficult to find is that all the signposts indicate the locations of count-

. . . . . the most moving epitaph in Leningrad

less graves of countless celebrated Russians who are still in the good graces (and very much in the good graces) of the regime — with not a word about Dostoyevsky. These guideposts at the very entrance are extremely detailed, listing everybody from Lomonosov and Tchaikovsky to minor, long-forgotten actors and singers of the nineteenth century. And at the various graves themselves are individual signposts in even more vulgar detail, describing at length the achievements and creative works of the Russians resting beneath. In this manner, for example, are treated the graves of Lomonosov and Fonvizin in the eighteenth-century, or so-called Lazarus churchyard, to the left of the entrance walk; and of Krylov, Karamzin, Glinka, Borodin, Musorgsky, Dargomyzhsky, Rimsky-Korsakov, and Tchaikovsky in the nineteenth-century cemetery to the right of the entrance. When I finally found Dostoyevsky's grave, I saw that it too had a sign, but there was only one word: "Writer." This marker is certainly meant as a slight, but in many ways, ways unrecognized by the authorities, it seems to me to be the most moving epitaph in Leningrad.

JUNE 4, 1952

We left Leningrad for Novgorod by train two days ago, departing from the Vitebsk — formerly the Tsarskoe Selo — station at 4.30 P.M., and arriving at Novgorod on time at 10.20 P.M. There is only one train a day from Leningrad, and you have to go via Leningrad to reach Novgorod by railroad from Moscow. Returning a few hours later, the train leaves Novgorod at 12.35 A.M., and arrives at Leningrad at 6.15 A.M. When we made the return trip today, the cars

A mysterious car . . . .

and attendants of the train were exactly the same, and the station master at Novgorod gave us exactly the same places in exactly the same compartment as had been assigned to us by Intourist in Leningrad for the first part of the trip (can it be that this compartment is wired, or can it be that this mind is becoming warped?).

The train itself, made up of ten old cars, seemed as ancient as the original roadbed in this vicinity where Russia's first railroad, from Petersburg to Tsarskoe Selo, was built by private means in 1837. It is no wonder that the trip is always made on schedule, because the train covers the 107 miles between Leningrad and Novgorod in five hours, fifty minutes, averaging the rollicking rate of eighteen miles an hour. One of the ten cars proved to be of considerable interest. It was located near the engine and looked like a boxcar — but it was obviously not carrying freight or mail. High up on the side were four windows with strong steel bars, and even higher up, under the roof, were eight very small barred windows. When the train stopped for any length of time, two armed guards stood on the steps and, in addition to keeping an eye on whatever or whoever was inside, they also kept an eye on the local girls on the platform. All in all, it certainly looked like a prison car: this impression was confirmed by a glimpse of a militiaman through one of the dark windows — but, to complete the picture and to be perfectly honest, I should add that the same glance took in a geranium pot.

Twenty-three kilometers from Leningrad we made a four-minute stop at the forbidden town of Tsarskoe Selo. There was nothing visible from the train windows or the station platform to explain why this area is now out of bounds for

all foreigners. Here, for example, is what I saw: in the foreground, a very modern, clean station, with a militiaman on
the platform successfully keeping an army enlisted man from
entering the "soft" car of our train; beside the station, newly
built ceremonial gates of stone and wrought iron, leading to
the road; in the distance, sun-soaked fields and woods and
dachas, with Catherine's palaces and cupolas poking through
the trees; and, straight ahead, a flock of geese washing in a
brook, and a very old woman flicking flies off a very old cow.

Three hours later, at 8.10 P.M., we made a more interesting stop at Rogavka, the only place en route large enough
to support a station buffet. Although we stayed here only
eight minutes, it was possible to get an impression of this
rather strange "settlement" in the middle of nowhere: most
prominent on the outskirts was a large power grid, and
within the town, most of which looked like a fresh clearing
in a countryside of scrubby evergreens and birches and flat,
open fields, were many brand-new blocks of brick buildings
and wide, empty streets; neither factories nor smokestacks,
however, were in sight. Later in Novgorod, I found out that
Rogavka was what the Russians call a *poselok* — that is, a
village-type settlement, usually of recent construction — and
that it served primarily as a railroad center. The only other
stop of interest was a thirty-minute wait on the outskirts of
Novgorod. From this approach, which is ten minutes from
the Novgorod station, one can get a better view of the city's
scattered factories and plants than from the center of town.

The passengers in our "soft" car were most friendly — and
a few extremely so. The majority were army and navy
officers and railway officials, and two of the former were
most persistent in their invitation to join them in a game of

This spirit of good will . . . .

chess. The pleasantest of all, however, was a twenty-three-year-old student from Novgorod. She had no knowledge of English, her only foreign language being German, which she had studied one or two hours a week in her secondary school, and, in general, she was a very unworldly person. She had spent most of her life in Leningrad (she was there throughout the blockade in the war), and had traveled only as far as Pskov. Thanks to her friendly influence and eager curiosity, and thanks to the vodka-drinking and joking of the chess-playing army officers, the atmosphere in the car was relaxed, and at times hilarious, particularly when the officers hid one of the window curtains, and then complained to the conductress.

This spirit of good will and *joie de vivre* provided quite a contrast to an experience another British colleague, a young woman, recently had on a train trip to Smolensk, an episode worth relating. In the corridor of her car, she was approached by a Soviet Army officer who was obviously, she said, in search of feminine company. However, when this officer, a major, found out that she was English, his manner changed abruptly and he launched into a denunciation of the West in the best agitator's style, with most of the Russian travelers in the corridor for an audience. On leave-taking at Smolensk, the major turned to this British girl, and said: "Perhaps we shall meet again someday — in London."

"Under what circumstances?" she asked in surprise.

"I am sure that the Soviet Army will have to intervene, sooner or later, to save the British from the clutches of the Americans," he replied. "The Russian people cannot stand idly by and watch their comrades suffer."

Although Novgorod gives the appearance of a sleepy district town with a relatively small population, forgotten in the backwash of both time and space, it boasts one of the best small hotels in provincial Russia. This hotel, the Ilmen, is in the center of town on the east bank, or "Commercial Side," of the Volkhov River — with a wide, unobstructed view of the local Kremlin and the Cathedral of St. Sophia to the west directly across the river. The hotel is a modern, three-story building, with close to fifty rooms which are long and narrow — about 27 feet long and 9 feet wide — but clean and adequately furnished. And the price is only 24 rubles a day (12 rubles per person when the room is shared). The plumbing facilities are relatively modern, although on our first night the running water throughout the hotel was turned off until midnight (later it turned out not to be the direct fault of the hotel management). On the ground floor we found a small, stuffy buffet, one of the most popular places in town, with an all-male clientele sitting around the five rough wooden tables.

As the result of a series of unfortunate circumstances, including the negligence of Intourist in Leningrad, I arrived at the hotel without a room reservation. As is the case with all hotels in Russia, this one was full — and the "director," a grim, humorless, middle-aged woman, was none too happy about the situation, so embarrassing for all concerned. She didn't think it proper to fit me into the room which the British Embassy had reserved for my traveling companion — and so I was finally assigned to a back room on the top floor, already occupied by a Russian. When I entered, my roommate was stretched out on the back bed, bent over a bulky book — and there he remained, for the most part, throughout our stay. He was in his middle thirties, and,

A Russian roommate . . . .

with his blond, bushy handle-bar mustache, looked like a Chekhov character: half forlorn, half dashing. He came originally, he said, from southern Russia, but at the present time his home was in Leningrad. He added that he was in Novgorod on business for a few days. On learning that I was an American, my roommate immediately expressed great surprise — almost disbelief — and then was silent for several minutes. From that time on, however, he was as obliging as could be, and, although retiring and reticent by nature (he mingled with nobody else in the hotel, as far as I could see), he bent over backward to be kind to me. He was especially considerate of my comfort and convenience. Almost at once, for example, he asked me whether I objected to his smoking, and when I replied that I undoubtedly smoked more than he did, he immediately arranged to get another ash tray. Next, he worried about the overhead light, wondering whether it would bother me during the night while he continued to read. "I have so much work to do that there is little time to study," he said by way of explanation. As it turned out, I was the disturbing one during the night, because I was suddenly taken sick (that is, I was unable to keep down the goose I had just had in the buffet) — and my roommate did everything but hold my head for me. His main concern was that the trip on a Russian railroad might have been the cause of my condition. Our most extensive conversation, the next day, concerned the book he was constantly reading, Kostylev's fictional trilogy, *Ivan Grozny,* and in this connection he asked me an extremely naïve, but revealing question: "Do you have such books in the West, books about Ivan the Terrible, books about Russia?"

No sooner had we checked in at the hotel desk than the

director asked us whether we would like an official guide the next day. We asked her what the charge would be; when she replied, vaguely and evasively, showing considerable doubt and hesitation, that the service would probably cost about ten rubles an hour, we thanked her and said no, we could not afford a guide.

As we left the hotel after breakfast the next morning, we were formally introduced to a man and a woman who suddenly appeared from nowhere, but who had obviously been waiting for hours in the small lobby. They explained that they were our guides, and when we protested that we could not pay for the service, they answered that it did not matter. We stuck to this agreement, incidentally, and didn't even offer to pay for their meals, which, without invitation, they practically ate out of the same plate with us. By the end of the day, after twelve hours of their minute-to-minute, elbow-to-elbow presence, we had begun to lose patience.

The man was a sick-looking individual, about forty years old. During our first conversation, he stammered considerably, but as the day wore on, this became less noticeable, and it is safe to assume that he was nervous at first. In introducing himself, he said that he was the Museum's Deputy Director for Scientific Work. The girl did not volunteer the nature of her position — and she remained a mystery, as well as a nuisance, throughout the day. She was in her middle twenties, attractive, well dressed, confident — with a rather superior, I-know-it-all-anyway attitude. Most of the time she was absolutely silent, but we did learn from her that she had lived in Leningrad and in the Urals. All in all, unlike our acquaintance on the train, she tried to give the appearance of being a very worldly young lady indeed. Finally I asked

a young Party worker . . . .

her outright what her work was, and she answered, after some thought, and with ill-concealed annoyance, that she was the "representative of the Department of Preservation of Architectural Monuments." If so, she certainly had little knowledge of — and little interest in — her work: she couldn't have been more bored by the celebrated churches of Novgorod, nor more interested in me. It was pretty clear that she was a young Party worker, and that her only purpose probably was to watch both us and the other guide. Also, it was evident that she had some knowledge of English, and so undoubtedly was on hand to overhear the conversations of the two foreigners. Both guides denied that they knew any English at all, but once or twice she made slips indicating her understanding by responding in Russian to stray remarks we had made to each other in English.

The Museum Director proved to be helpful in telling us where the various churches and historical monuments were to be found, in leading us directly to them, and in getting many of the old buildings opened for us, thus saving time for visitors with only a few hours at their disposal, and in giving us the dry facts of archaeological and architectural research, reeling off dates by rote, like a conscientious schoolboy, although the information he supplied did little to supplement the material in good guidebooks. Otherwise, his was a negative role, which took the form of telling us what we could not do, what we could not see. Close to Novgorod there are several great churches which I was most anxious to see: the Church of the Redeemer at Nereditsa, with its famous frescoes; St. Nicholas at Lipno, whose façade shows a novel architectural treatment; the Church of the Redeemer at Kovalyova; the Church of the Transfiguration at Volotovo, with its singular frescoes reflecting the Greek art of the Palaeologi period. When we were told by our guide that these buildings were either too far away or, in most cases, that they had been destroyed during the war, I believe these reasons were undoubtedly sincere. On the other hand, his firm refusal to let us visit the Monastery of St. George seemed hardly justified. In the first place, the high, massive silhouette of the monastery's cathedral was clearly visible across the low meadows on the left bank of the Volkhov to the south — and so was within easy walking distance; we had been permitted, indeed, to walk just as far in the opposite direction to visit the Monastery of St. Anthony. The main reason given for denying us permission, the fact that the cathedral was being restored, made even less sense. It is true, of course, that it was partly ruined by the Germans — but almost all the churches in Novgorod which we were allowed to visit had been partly ruined and were likewise undergoing restoration. The only conclusion we could draw from this situation, therefore, was that the authorities for some reason did not want us to see other projects or activities in this neighborhood — no matter how innocent our request. Another seemingly unnecessary case of *nelzya* (the Russian word for "it is impossible," or "one cannot" — and one of the words most frequently heard in the U.S.S.R. today) concerned our request to take a brief excursion trip on the river. With a straight face, the guide turned this down on the grounds that the season was not on. He did so in spite of the fact that the excursion boat was clearly visible as it ran up and down the river and that the boat's current timetable was posted in our hotel.

Typical of the Museum Director's cultural indoctrination was his flat response to my expression of surprise that Ivan

Watering down Ivan the Terrible . . . . .

the Terrible, nowadays the greatest of heroes in the Stalinist interpretation of Russian history (because of the close similarity between his methods and those of Stalin himself), not only was not prominent, but was not even included among the countless historical figures of Russia's past in Novgorod's celebrated Millennial Monument, which was erected in the latter half of the nineteenth century. On the lower circle alone there are 109 figures in high relief, from Rurik to Nicholas I, from Maxim the Greek to Glinka. By way of explanation, he said: "In the nineteenth century, Ivan the Terrible was considered a psychopathic case — not an outstanding state leader as we look upon him today." Later, as though justifying such an interpretation, the guide maintained that Ivan's cruelty at the time of the Novgorod massacre, in the sixteenth century, had been grossly exaggerated in the old history books. Watering down the traditional account, which relates that Ivan butchered 60,000 of Novgorod's inhabitants, our guide asserted that he killed "barely 6000."

The only other noticeable evidence of shadowing during our stay in Novgorod pertained to the strange activities of a closed-in jeep, which was spotted near us on several occasions. Late last night as we were leaving Novgorod, this jeep accompanied us all the way to the railway station, following closely behind the public bus we took for the two-mile trip.

Novgorod, the capital of Novgorod Oblast, is situated on both sides of the Volkhov River, just north of Lake Ilmen, which is a shallow body of water covering 300 to 700 square miles, whose outlet is the Volkhov, a navigable river 140 miles in length which flows north through Leningrad Oblast to Lake Ladoga.

. . . .   **Ugly traces of the war**

Before World War II, Novgorod had a population of only 31,000 — a far cry from the estimated total of 400,000 in the fourteenth century, when Novgorod was at its peak as the capital of a powerful medieval principality which covered all of northern Russia, from Lake Peipus and Lithuania to the Urals.

During the last war, the city was occupied by the Germans from August, 1941, to January, 1944 — and, as the result of military operations and indiscriminate bombing and artillery fire during this long period, suffered very heavy damage. Ugly traces of the war are still abundant — ragged ruins of buildings, and flat, empty blocks of devastation — but so much of the city has been rebuilt that Novgorod now gives the over-all impression of a new, modern town, clean and open and brightly painted. Even the streets, most of which are of rough, dusty cobblestones, and the old sidewalks, mostly of packed dirt or broken slabs of flagstone, have been given a new look by the planting of rows of slender young trees. This fresh appearance is all the more striking when one recalls the dirty, drab, forlorn face of most Russian towns.

Our guide was quick to point out that "first priority" had been given to the building of new living quarters. This boast was substantiated in one part of town at least: long stretches of Moscow Street, the main thoroughfare in Novgorod, are now lined with new apartment buildings and small blocks of houses, all painted in cheerful pastel colors. "Just one year ago," our guide said with pride, "only three buildings stood on this long street."

Another major change in the town has been the construction of a new bridge across the Volkhov, to replace the old

Novgorod seems dead . . . .

iron bridge which apparently was destroyed during the war. The old bridge was centrally located, connecting the middle gate of Novgorod's Kremlin on the "Sophia Side" with the main square of the "Commercial Side." The new structure, which, as was the case with its predecessors, is the only bridge in the town, is downstream several hundred meters to the north of the old site, at a point where a small, grassy brook runs into the Volkhov on the east bank. This five-trestle bridge is approximately two hundred meters long, and, with the exception of what appeared to be concrete Piers, is made entirely of wood.

Before the war, most of the city's administrative offices were within the ancient red walls of the Kremlin, but now many have been transferred to the "Commercial Side."

On the whole, Novgorod seems dead and deserted. With the exception of white-bloused militiamen (and an occasional sturdy militiawoman), there were very few pedestrians in the city streets or parks or shops — and, actually, there were very few militiamen. Not a single soldier was observed during one whole day — and that is very unusual for Russia.

The cultural life of the people must be stagnant. We noticed only one bookstore in the center of town, and that was scantily stocked. The city does have its own theater, in one of the old buildings of the Kremlin, but a resident of Novgorod whom we met on the train advised us that its productions were not too impressive. While we were there the company was on tour, and variety shows of song and dance by out-of-town companies were advertised from the billboards for future dates. As far as we could find out, Novgorod has three movie houses, and one of these is in the club of the M.G.B. (Secret Police). Of the thirty or forty churches

. . . . **Food prices**

within the precincts of the city, only one, the small, boxlike, twelfth-century Church of St. Nicholas in the Veche Square, has services.

I noticed the following food prices in the inexpensive buffet of the hotel: goose with macaroni, of dubious digestibility (if you remember), 5.20 rubles; cutlets, 2.25; fish (*sudak*), 3; macaroni, 1.60; sour cream, 1.25; cheese *zakuski*, .80; cucumber with sour cream, 1.45. In the best restaurant in town (a rather pretentious, gloomy place on Gorky Street, near the Summer Garden), *borshch* cost 2.60 rubles and fresh *sudak* 3.70. Eggs and fresh butter were not available here, although both were plentiful at the hotel.

We attempted to visit the local market, located on the "Sophia Side," according to the guide, but our escorts, by adroit maneuvering, kept us from the area until 5 P.M., the market's closing time. We did learn, however, that the big "bazaar days" were on Wednesday and Friday every week.

There was some activity on the river, but not very much. Against the background of a few scattered factories and smokestacks on the left bank, one could see five or six tuglike boats and long barges moving slowly up and down the river, and at one point on the right bank a half-dozen log rafts floated against the shore; a dredge was anchored in the river at the site of the old bridge. Within the city likewise there was very little transportation activity: we saw only two or three taxis and with the exception of a few large modern autobuses on the main thoroughfare, the public buses were old and dilapidated, and their service throughout the scattered areas of the town was not very frequent.

One of the most interesting features of Novgorod's economic life is the Moscow-Leningrad highway, which cuts

The Moscow-Leningrad highway . . . .

straight through the town. Inasmuch as this is the main —
and really the only — direct road between Russia's two
largest cities, its economic significance must be considerable.
But you don't see much of this in Novgorod, where through
traffic on the road appears to be nonexistent. Our guide explained this by pointing out that railroads are much more
important than motor highways, and why have competition,
anyway. Originally, this road crossed the river on the old
iron bridge, and as a result, ran straight through the Kremlin. Now, with the new wooden bridge, the route has been
diverted and shortened a bit. The signpost on the road at
the eastern approach to the bridge shows that Moscow is
332 miles away, and that Leningrad is 120 miles to the north.
This section of the highway (a part of Novgorod's Moscow
Street at this point) is macadamized, but the stretches on the
outskirts of the city are not so smooth or well kept — and it
is quite possible that at least part of the road in the countryside turns into the usual cobblestone roadbed, with dirt
footpaths alongside. I received an excellent idea of this
highway on a visit to the Monastery of St. Anthony, two
kilometers north of the center of town. From the side road
turning into the monastery grounds, one can see the Moscow
highway stretching like a narrow ribbon over the flat, endless plains to the southeast.

In view of the fact that rehabilitation of historic monuments and ancient works of art (particularly those which
serve to reflect the greatness of the Russian nation) is a relatively new feature of Soviet life and is occupying a more and
more important place in the Kremlin's scheme of things, and
in view of the intrinsic value and interest of the Novgorod
churches themselves, I visited as many as I could. But I

. . . . **The Cathedral of St. Sophia**

failed to cover the field: in Novgorod and in the surrounding villages there are more than sixty churches. I should add in this connection that whereas evidence of current restoration work — chiefly in the form of scaffolding — is abundant, we did not see a single workman or craftsman or artist in any of the churches we visited.

The Cathedral of St. Sophia, built between 1045 and 1052, is the oldest church in Novgorod, and its renown is so widespread that no description is needed here. Although the cathedral was damaged during the war, such features as the Romanesque exterior, the massive columns of the interior, and the so-called Sigtuna and Khersonian doors, are still intact. In addition to postwar restoration work, new excavations have been started at the floor level. One of the many legends attached to St. Sophia now has an interesting sequel. This legend concerns the fresco of the Pantocrator, in the main cupola, which had the right hand raised, but closed. According to the story, the painters tried in vain three times to show Christ's hand opened in blessing, and three times it was miraculously closed; the third time they heard a mysterious voice saying, "The clenched hand encloses the destiny of Novgorod, which will not fall till it is opened." The sequel concerns the bombing of the cathedral by the Germans during the war. Our guide related that "one bomb fell through the main cupola, destroying the fresco." Thus, the hand was opened forever — and the city fell.

The Church of St. Nicholas, built in 1113, is the second oldest church in Novgorod, and is also, in my opinion, the second most interesting. This simple structure provides an excellent idea of how the standard Kievan six-pillar churches must have looked before their more recent excrescences were

Cathedral of the Nativity of the Virgin . . . .

added. Indeed, in contrast to the chief churches at Kiev, St. Nicholas (like the majority of the Novgorod churches) remains substantially as it was when first erected more than eight hundred years ago. It is this preservation of the primitive appearance of Novgorod's churches which makes the city's monuments so worth while. As I have noted before, this church has the added interest of being the only Novgorod church still in service.

The third oldest church monument in Novgorod is the Cathedral of the Nativity of the Virgin within the walls of the Monastery of St. Anthony. It was built in the second decade of the twelfth century. Since the monastery is located some distance from the center of town on the east bank of the Volkhov, off the beaten track, it is seldom visited by foreigners. But the trip is well worth the effort, because of the frescoes which were found a few years ago on the pillars and on an arch on the right of the apse. They have now been cleaned, and are fine drawings in faded tones of brown and green. The grounds outside the church have a quiet, countryside atmosphere with tall trees high on the riverbank, and big, black nests of rooks swaying in a warm wind, with black-and-white swallows swooping over the monastery walls. Everything must be pretty much the same today as it was eight hundred years ago — and the only incongruity to break the spell during our visit was a fast game of volleyball played by a group of Soviet schoolboys in a clearing under the trees.

Another wonderful experience was a visit to the Church of the Transfiguration, built in 1375. This stark, tiny church provides one of the greatest and rarest sightseeing pleasures in Russia, if not on earth. Hidden high up in the dark, dusty, cobwebby arches under the cupola are a few faint frag-

. . . . a locked church, chill and dark

ments of the impressionistic murals of Theophanes the
Greek, who ranks among the most distinguished and individual artists of the entire medieval world. Very little is
known about Theophanes (in fact, the question of whether
or not he was born on Russian soil is still discussed by art
historians) and very few of his works, which were probably
very few in the beginning, remain today. But we do know
that this mysterious man was the forerunner of Russia's long
line of noted icon painters; that his handful of icons and wall
paintings exerted a tremendous influence on numerous followers, making an especially great impact on his own young
pupil, Rublev, who later turned out to be the most celebrated individual in the entire history of icon-painting. Although Rublev's fame now overshadows that of his master,
the austere, monumental murals of Theophanes have a depth
of character, a weight and import exceeding, in the end, the
intimate, immediate appeal of Rublev.

The hard impact of Theophanes the Greek (and the Gentle) is still there — six hundred years later. And it is still
there even when you look at his faint, feathery work by the
light of a match, leaning on a rickety wooden ladder high up
in the vault of Novgorod's Church of the Transfiguration —
or maybe it is there because of these circumstances. Certainly part of the fascination of finding these masterpieces
is the situation itself: a locked church, chill and dark; an
ancient ladder, with rough steps and no handrail, rising at
an angle of close to ninety degrees; stone dust and bird
dung; the sudden scratch of a match in the solitude of the
dome — and there stonily stares the prophet Melchizedek
(painted in 1378), fierce and remote, although only a few
inches from your nose. In addition to the portrait of Mel-

my mind wandered a bit . . . .

chizedek, there are dozens of other uncompromising old men looking at you from the shadows: Noah, Adam, Abel, Elijah, and John the Baptist — all painted with swift, bold strokes, with the highlights exaggeratedly prominent. And all these venerable patriarchs from the Bible show other features so typical of Theophanes' frescoes: tones of terra-cotta and shades of ocher for the figures, with clothing in pale yellow or gray, with austere backgrounds of silver and blue.

A small church often overlooked in Novgorod is the so-called Nikita Church, on Moscow Street. According to our guide, this church, now neglected, once served as the private chapel of Ivan the Terrible, who paid two historic visits to Novgorod in the 1570's. Our guide also reported that Ivan's palace, which no longer exists, adjoined the church. Today, through the cracks of the high sidewalk fence at this spot, you can see the grounds of the local "Aero Club," with an obsolete Soviet fighter plane on display.

Surely one of the most fascinating bits of land in all of Russia is Novgorod's Veche Square. There, on that history-breathing acre, now covered with green weeds and war rubble, I spent my last afternoon in Russia and saw my last sunset on Soviet soil — and my mind wandered a bit then, as it does here, thinking of the past and the present.

The Past:

Six hundred years ago, when Novgorod was at the height of its power and prosperity, this spot of land was the scene of an absolutely unique development in Russian history. Here, in this square, was practised municipal self-government on a scale never equaled in Russia, before or since. Here the city assembly, an outgrowth of the old Russian *veche* organization, which elsewhere sank into oblivion, came to be supreme. The system was far from perfect: the meetings were ill organized and unwieldy and irregular. The assembly, in fact, was summoned at any moment by the ringing of the town bell, and sessions were hampered by the ancient rule of unanimity. (Here it should be stated parenthetically that the present-day Soviet rule of unanimity does not necessarily have its roots exclusively in this Russian precedent, because the phenomenon has been known in the West as well.) The meetings held in this market-place square, therefore, were invariably turbulent affairs, with free-for-all fights often taking place throughout the efforts to reach agreements. But these difficulties should not becloud the all-important fact that here in Novgorod this city assembly had all-embracing powers: it elected (or dismissed) the prince and the magistrates, it decided foreign policy, it exercised legislative authority, it handled administrative problems, and it maintained control over the supreme court.

There are many interesting points to bring out in connection with Novgorod's past, but the most important is that here in the middle of Russia, in the middle of the ages, a republic did exist in fact — a city republic with many practices containing the seeds of democracy. Furthermore, Novgorod remained a republic in spite of the presence of its local prince. Indeed, the prince was merely the titular head of the government, serving chiefly as a military protector. Here, in the Veche Square, the assembly boisterously elected its prince and forced him to sign a contract to rule according to the ancient customs. Under these customs, the prince could not act without the approval of the magistrates and councilors in regard to administrative and judicial matters.

and to the present . . . .

He could not make appointments at will, he could not alter court verdicts arbitrarily, he could not interfere with foreign trade, he could not own land, nor control an unlimited income — and he could not even reside within the city limits. Eloquent testimony to the spirit of the city is the fact that in the second half of the twelfth century Novgorod changed its prince close to thirty times within a period of fifty years.

The Present:

I sat alone on the ground in the middle of the small square, in a patch of burdock and dandelions, awkwardly trying to hold in my hand a swift which had a broken wing and a fast-beating heart, silently watching the sun set behind St. Sophia.

In many ways the scene I saw was exactly the same as the view of the fourteenth century. In the immediate foreground was the plain, white, boxlike Church of St. Nicholas, with its three semicircular apses and decoration of flat niches. In the distance, across the green meadows and silver surface of the Volknov, rose the white walls of St. Sophia, while the red sun, setting low over the red towers of the Kremlin, caught the gilt of the center cupola. And I could see, as the Novgorodians of the Middle Ages must have seen, how the two churches, viewed from this particular angle, resembled each other — with the four windows of the round cupola of St. Nicholas matching the side cupolas of St. Sophia, and the apses of St. Nicholas matching the center of the eastern façade of the cathedral across the river. Between the churches still stands the conelike Tower of Yaroslav, around which so much of the city's life used to whirl so noisily — as now, in my hour, did flights of swallows and swifts. The only other human beings present (at first, at least) were a handful of

Russians who could have appeared in the square six hundred years ago: a lone bearded priest, in a long, black, greasy robe, getting the evening air, pacing up and down in the shadows of his church; a group of *babushkas* sitting on a nearby row of steps, whispering something to a young peasant woman as she nursed her baby; and, on the other side of the fence, a drunken peasant lurching home down the cobblestone street.

And in many ways the scene could not have been more different. In the place of lusty election brawls, there was the loneliness of a forgotten graveyard. There was no pealing of the town bell, calling for a popular meeting. Weeds grew high on the ruins of nearby churches. To add to the desolation, World War II had left its mark — here was a heap of scrap iron, there was a pile of broken bricks, and directly over my head hung the scarred boughs of a tree which had been sheared in two by German artillery fire. Then, to join the few Russians already present, a white-bloused militia-man suddenly appeared around the corner of the Church of St. Nicholas. He might have come from the M.V.D. Club, a pink-painted building for the secret police which now adjoins the square. From far away across the river came not the song of Sadko, but raucous, rousing chants from the public address system in the Summer Garden, the blare of Moscow Radio forcing gaiety down the ears of the gloomy populace. And finally, instead of the local prince, who in the old days wasn't even allowed to live within the city walls, there was, somehow, the ever-present presence of The Prince in Moscow.

Here one is entitled to ask, I thought to myself at the time, whether Russia's present would not have been far dif-

the last symbol of Russia . . . .

ferent — and far, far, better — if Russia's past, at one precise turning point in history, had been only a little different; if, by a relatively small twist of fortuitous events and
circumstances, all of fifteenth- and sixteenth-century Russia
had fallen under the sway, and followed the traditions, not
of Ivan III and Ivan IV and the new autocratic "Tsardom of
Moscow," but of the democratic city republic of Novgorod
(as Western civilization, in most essentials, followed the traditions, institutions, and ideals of the democratic city republic of Athens); if, as a result, this ancient Veche Square of
Novgorod the Great had turned out to be, in the end, the
Red Square of Russia.

JUNE 5, 1952

It is shortly after midnight, and we are steaming in silence
and darkness northwest through the choppy seas of the Gulf
of Finland, somewhere off the south shore of the island of
Suursaari (Hogland). I am writing this in the small, empty
salon of the *Beloostrov,* the Soviet ship that is taking me
back to a world that I have always loved but have taken for
granted, a way of life I now no longer live as my due, but
as my duty.

A few hours ago we passed the last sign and symbol of
Soviet Russia — a huge, old-fashioned cruiser sitting silently
on the sea, as though anchored forever to the ocean bed,
with its long guns pointing out toward the West. While we
slowly steamed by, there was a flurry of excitement on our
deck as the Russian passengers leaned over the rail to have
a last look. Now all have gone to bed — and what strange
dreams the Russians on board must be dreaming.

. . . . **my farewell ride**

It has been a long day. Early this afternoon, all the *Belo-ostrov* passengers assembled with their luggage in the lobby of Leningrad's Astoria Hotel. I found out there that I was to be the only American passenger on board. There are only thirty of us in all — a rather mysterious Swedish diplomat, and my English friend, who has just finished her assignment at the British Embassy in Moscow, are the only other foreigners; the remaining twenty-seven are all Russians, including seven young children and babies. These Russians are obviously traveling in an official capacity — but what their various missions in the West are to be remains a secret.

For my farewell ride in Russia (a twenty-minute trip from the Astoria to the Customs House — at first through the center of the city, and then through the outlying dock area), the official travel agency proudly provided a Zis. Russia's No. 1 automobile, the Zis is the Soviets' black, bulky, 110-h.p. version of an old American Packard. It was my first ride in a Zis, and I saw that inside, too, it resembled very closely one of our limousines of prewar vintage — except for the fact that the glass was bad in some of the windows, the defects making my last view of Russia even more distorted, perhaps, than usual. (A small point, maybe, but I doubt very much whether any American owner, buying in a capitalist market, would put up with such a deficiency in quality.) The name "Zis," incidentally, comes from a set of initials standing for Russian words that can be translated accurately into English only literally, by the awkward phrase, Factory Named After Stalin — a phrase, by the way, that is typical of the new Soviet, as distinguished from the traditional Russian, lexicon. Our Zis was one of the very few I saw in Leningrad, almost all of the bigger and better cars in

Russian cars . . . .

Russia being concentrated in Moscow. While on the subject
of passenger cars, I should mention that, while the Zis is still
the most impressive car in the U.S.S.R., there is a newer
model, more modern in design, the Zim (here we go again
— this time, Factory Named After Molotov). This six-cylin-
der, 95-h.p. car, which came out last year, has much sleeker
lines than the Zis. In addition, there are two others on
the Soviet production line: the four-cylinder Pobeda (Victory), which is the most common passenger car in Russia;
and the tiny Moskvich, apparently modeled on the German
Opel, which seems to me to be a little larger than a Crosley.
Interestingly enough, the Zis waiting for us at the curbstone
of the Astoria was reserved for the three foreign passengers,
while Intourist loaded the Russian families with all their
baggage in less pretentious vehicles.

We were stopped at the big gates to the dock area by naval
guards, who looked us over — but our Russian chauffeur
quickly and gruffly explained who we were, and brushed the
gaping guards aside. At the customs, I (as the "ranking
diplomat" present, I suppose) was treated with special respect and remarkable efficiency. My eight pieces of luggage
were quickly attended to, and I, first of all the passengers,
was ushered almost at once into an adjoining waiting room.
This large, empty room was bare except for a few wooden
benches along the four walls, and one or two round tables
with pitchers of drinking water and glasses — and the ever-
present portraits of Stalin, Lenin, and a few assorted members of the Politburo hung high on the walls, portraits which
I looked at, with a feeling of satisfaction and relief, for the
last time. The big, locked doors on the far side of this room
gave out directly onto the concrete dock and the gangplank

. . . . **a grim and silent lot**

of the *Beloostrov* a few yards away. There, in this clean but cheerless room, I was able to look the Russian passengers over carefully as they came in one by one, family by family, after the inspection of their extremely small amount of baggage. The baggage, incidentally, was carried by well-dressed dock workers who looked like porters at a fashionable hotel, with clean, white cotton mittens on their hands. The Russians were a grim and silent lot, looking quite unhappy about the whole thing. Instead of behaving as though they were lucky indeed to go on a spree to a free world, they looked and acted as though they were being sent into exile. Perhaps they actually believed the West would corrupt or devour them — and were genuinely afraid, as I, I must admit, was afraid on entering the U.S.S.R. Or perhaps they feared for their future fate on returning to Russia after having been exposed to the influence of the West. The lack of gaiety on the part of the Russians was contagious — if it is possible for something that doesn't exist to spread. In this room you felt as though you should talk in whispers and walk on tiptoe — and we did. Even the babies and small children seemed to catch the spirit of their parents. At the risk of stuttering over an excessively long string of sibilants, I can only say that the Russian kids were silent, sober, somber, stern, and surly. Those, at any rate, are the adjectives that come to mind. One child carried a huge naked celluloid doll. For some reason, it struck me as a gruesome sight — and I won't forget it.

All in all, as you can see, it was far from a gala sailing, a far cry from the traditional shipside scenes at Le Havre or Southampton or on the Hudson. No friends or relatives were permitted to come down and see the passengers off — even

The waterfront, Leningrad . . . .

the Russians apparently were not allowed to have farewell parties. No flags were flying, no confetti was falling, no champagne corks were popping. But I, for one, was in high spirits.

As I ran up the steep gangplank, I got a fleeting impression of a small ship, painted white all over, with a single smokestack (with a red band and a yellow hammer and sickle emblazoned on the side). Once on board, I had a better chance to look at the waterfront. I could see that the *Beloostrov* was docked at the very mouth of the main stream of the Neva on the left (or south) bank — so close to the sea that the hull of our ship was splashed by the choppy waters of Neva Bay, a part of the Gulf of Finland, which at this point stretches blue and open to the west. With its bow facing in toward the city, the ship was tied to the concrete pier of the Customs House, only a few feet away from the nearest rail tracks that lined the bare, empty docks at the end of the harbor. Immediately in front of the bow of the *Beloostrov* two medium-sized freighters rested against the same dock, but here, likewise, there were few signs of life. Beyond these ships, on both sides of the river, the scene toward the center of town was made up mainly of a jungle of motionless cranes, jibs, and derricks stretching at all angles — looking like prehistoric dinosaurs, bending their necks and quietly surveying the water front. Smoke from countless factory chimneys blurred the view a bit, but the gilded dome of Saint Isaac's Cathedral, although far in the distance, stood out bright in the cloudless sky. Several hundred yards to the left upstream a gray destroyer of the Soviet Navy floated at dock, and just beyond it, at an angle, protruded the low, long stern of a larger warship, presumably a cruiser.

. . . . "Your window through on Europe"

As I stood at the rail, and stared at the Neva and the modern skyline of old St. Petersburg, I thought of the opening lines of Pushkin's narrative poem, "The Bronze Horseman," in which he describes how Peter the Great, in the early years of the eighteenth century, built his new capital out of a swamp on the edge of the sea:

> There, by the billows desolate,
> He stood, with mighty thoughts elate,
> And gazed; but in the distance only
> A sorry skiff on the broad spate
> Of Neva drifted seaward, lonely.
> . . . .
> "Here cut" — so Nature gives command —
> "Your window through on Europe; stand
> Firm-footed by the sea, unchanging!"

In many ways the scene seemed as desolate as it must have been on that first day when Peter stood on the bank in the shadows of the forest, took a bayonet from a soldier, cut out two sods, and said: "Here I will build the town" — and when he might have thought: "Thou art Peter and on this rock I will build." But, at the same time, the scene had other old overtones which matched a later line in the same poem:

> Now, city of Peter, stand thou fast
> Foursquare, like Russia; vaunt thy splendor!

Fussing alongside us in the channel were two tugs — the *Nenets* at our bow and the *Iceberg* at the stern — with billows of thick black smoke pouring from their stubby stacks. From the open bridge of the *Beloostrov* the first officer

shouted orders to the tugs through an old-fashioned megaphone, giving loud and precise commands to the wheelhouse
pilots — and then he would put the megaphone to his ear
to get the answer. Finally, at 6 P.M., we began to move
slowly away from the dock — an hour later than the scheduled time of departure.

As the engines started to vibrate and we turned silently
into the stream to enter the Sea Canal, I had my last view
of Russians on Russian soil: a group of three frontier guards
— in their bright green caps, dark green coats with brass
buttons, blue breeches and black leather boots — watching
our sailing without a word or a movement; while above
them, at a higher level of the concrete wall, a blue-coated
sailor stood like a statue silhouetted against the afternoon
sky, guarding his Russia with rifle clutched in hand. This
final impression, I think, was fitting — guns and loneliness.

The Russian coastline beyond the river mouth and the
last stone breakwater, as we approached the Roads of Kronstadt, was flat and green, with the parks and palaces of royal
Peterhof coming down to the sea. By 7.30, we had lost sight
of the tip of the last breakwater in Leningrad Harbor, and
half an hour later we were hugging close to the shore of the
island of Kronstadt. On approaching Kronstadt, our ship
was escorted for twenty minutes or so by a noisy little patrol
craft (with a rickety gun conspicuously mounted on the tiny
bow deck), which roared along beside us only a few feet
away, bouncing over the increasingly rough surface of the
sea.

As we skirted the long, irregular shoreline, I thought of
the many things I had read concerning this historic fortress
— and particularly of the famous Navy revolt in March,

1921, when the Red regime was fighting for its life. Thirty years ago this fortress was held for sixteen days against the forces of the Kremlin. The Russian citizens who rose in revolt wanted to keep the Soviet system — but without the Communists' political and economic dictatorship. They also demanded that the forced food collections should be stopped and that free trade should be started. The interesting thing here is that this dangerous revolt was the last straw for Lenin. The leader of the Soviet state learned his lesson, and the New Economic Policy was his political, as well as economic answer. Thus, at least on one occasion in the turbulent history of the Soviet regime, public opinion backed by arms had an effect.

Tonight, with Kronstadt only a few hundred yards to starboard, I could see that the island with all its defense works was much bigger than I had expected, a far cry from the tiny stone fortress rising in the sea which I had had in my mind's eye. Kronstadt, in fact, is a very large city on a long island, marked by countless piers and docks and jutting breakwaters. From the rail of the *Beloostrov* I could spot all kinds of shipping, ranging from a modern Soviet destroyer, with its gray hull lying low on the water, to two old four-masted schooners, their masts and spars piercing the summer sky. Beyond the long, intricate series of moles and harbors, masses of public buildings of eighteenth- and nineteenth-century architecture rose on the skyline, and in the distance green trees could be seen on low, far-stretching hills. The domes of innumerable churches reflected the sun, which, directly ahead of us, was beginning to sink onto the flat, faraway horizon of the Baltic.

A few minutes later, while our wake washed against the

these menacing fortifications . . . .

last jetty of Kronstadt, we passed the celebrated fortresses themselves — ancient round batteries jutting up all by themselves in the middle of the surrounding sea. Built on small, invisible piles, these odd-looking structures were considered impregnable a hundred years ago, when a combined British and French fleet appeared before Kronstadt during the Crimean War. Today, these menacing fortifications still command one's attention, if not the gateway to Russia.

Several miles west of Kronstadt, early this evening, I suddenly heard a great roaring sound on the port side of the *Beloostrov,* and rushing to the rail I saw fifteen Soviet patrol boats following one another in a long single file, kicking up a great white wake as they thundered home toward their base. I say "patrol boats" — but actually they had little resemblance to the sleek, speedy motorboats of a modern navy. Tubby and top-heavy, they looked more like old trawlers. Perhaps, after all, they were only fishing boats. But if so, why were they strung out in such a perfect straight line, almost as if marching in drill formation. Now that I ask myself this question, I realize that in the U.S.S.R. there is, of course, a possibility that even fishing boats are regimented in ranks — and must not, for a minute, sail out of line.

It was at about this time, around 9 P.M., that the pilot left our ship. The sea had become so choppy that the *Beloostrov* had to slow down almost to a complete stop, while the pilot's small harbor boat tossed alongside, rising and falling with the waves. Quietly riding at anchor to starboard, at the wide, open entrance to the Gulf of Finland, was the pilot ship, which had broad red and white stripes painted the length of its hull — and blocked in big letters,

. . . . The *Beloostrov*

in both Russian and English (!), was the word "Leningrad."

During the few hours I have been on board, I have found out quite a lot about this ship and its service.

The *Beloostrov* originally belonged to Finland, but was transferred to Russia a few years ago as part of Finland's war reparations. Built a few years before World War II, the *Aallotar*, as she was then called, after a sea deity in Finnish mythology, was the pride of the Finnish Steamship Company, running between Helsinki and Hull, carrying passengers and freight (the latter consisted mostly of butter, thousands of tons of which once went to England in the holds of this ship). In view of this history, I wonder what the Finns will be thinking in Helsinki Harbor tomorrow morning (or, rather, late this morning) when we steam into the ship's home port, and they see the hammer and sickle flying at the mast.

As the *Beloostrov* (ironically and pointedly enough, the name of a frontier town on the pre-World War I border between Finland and Russia), the ship is now operated by an organization called the Baltic State Steamship Line — that, anyway, is what my ticket and passage papers say — all of which does not mean, of course, that the ship is not owned and operated by the Soviet State. The captain of the ship — at least on this voyage, I find — is an officer named Shusharin.

During the late spring, throughout the summer, and into the early weeks of fall — that is, the months when Leningrad Harbor is free of ice — the *Beloostrov* shuttles back and forth across the Baltic and North Sea, between Leningrad and London, via Helsinki, Stockholm, and the Kiel Canal. (At London, the ship goes all the way up the Thames

The only sea link with Russia . . . .

to Surrey Docks within sight of St. Paul's.) The one-way trip is usually made in six days, the stopovers in Finland and Sweden being only a few hours each. Under this schedule, the ship manages to sail from Leningrad every three weeks during its brief season. A year or so ago, another, smaller ship, the *Sestroretsk* (likewise a former Finnish coastal steamer taken over by the Russians as reparations — and likewise renamed after a former frontier point), was included in this summer service, but nowadays the *Beloostrov* furnishes the only regular connection by sea between Russia and the Western world.

As I look over the ship tonight, I see why one is enough. The *Beloostrov* was originally designed to carry 150 passengers in comfort — but, as I have already noted, there are only thirty of us now on board. In other words, although the ship is actually tiny, it seems tonight like a big empty barn floating on the Baltic. A few more passengers (Finns, Swedes, and British) are scheduled to join us at Helsinki and Stockholm — but even so the total passenger list, says the purser, will not number more than eighty before the trip is finished. The route, quite clearly, is not much traversed these days — and the demand for tickets is obviously becoming less and less.

However, if you do find yourself traveling between the Soviet Union and Western Europe, it is certainly much cheaper to pitch and list your way through the Curtain on a Soviet ship than to go by train or plane. I don't know why, but the fare is amazingly low — both relatively and absolutely. The whole trip from Leningrad to London is costing me only 451 rubles. Even at the artificial and extremely disadvantageous exchange rate of four to one, the total is only $113. For that small amount, I get a first-class ticket, with a single, outside cabin to myself, and, of course, three meals a day for nearly a week. In comparison, the brief overnight trip by train from Moscow to Leningrad, during which I shared a compartment, cost me almost as much — more than $100.

The officers and crew are keeping to themselves — but seem friendly enough when forced by circumstances to recognize one's presence: for example, when we bump into one another going up and down the narrow ladders, or make way for each other in the hatchways. (Incidentally, unlike American merchant seamen, the members of the crew are all outfitted in neat naval uniforms — with black trousers and the traditional blue-and-white-striped jerseys.) The whole band must be carefully picked — with two major, and difficult, considerations in mind: to see to it that the crew makes a favorable impression on whatever foreigners happen to be on board; and to see to it, in turn, that the impression made by foreign people and foreign ports on the officers and crew is not at all favorable. Only two or three of the entire company know English, but these few seem most anxious to prove that they can speak it well, and understand everything. The second I arrived on board, the young purser, standing at the head of the gangway, immediately greeted me with a warm smile, but with a worried frown on his forehead — a look that revealed some nervousness and extreme conscientiousness. After hurriedly and anxiously scanning the passenger list in his hand, he threw back his shoulders, paused for a deep breath, and then broke forth with the clearest, most precise, and loudest English I have ever heard:

"Meester R-rownts! Your cabin is straight ahead! The

"Is that clear? No, no, no" . . . .

porter takes your baggage! Everything will be all right! Yes, yes."

The food, too, is good — or at least much better than that served today in most public places in the U.S.S.R. Apparently, however, there is to be little, if any, conversation at our meals. At dinner tonight the three of us, that is, the three foreigners on board, quite naturally sat down together with the Russian passengers at one of the few tables that had been set in the large, half-empty dining salon. The meal, lasting almost an hour, passed in complete silence. The Russians didn't even acknowledge our presence by facial expressions or gestures — nor, for that matter, did they say a word to one another. But even this contact of ours turned out to be too intimate — and dangerous. At the close of dinner, the headwaiter (actually the only waiter) said to us in broken English, in a voice quivering with rebuke: "At breakfast, tomorrow, you must not sit at this table — but here." And he pointed to a lone, single table set for three. "Is that clear? No, no, no, you must not sit here where you are now, but there. Do you understand?" We understood.

After dinner I had a walk of exploration throughout the parts of the ship I am permitted to visit — up and down the cabin deck, around the hatches and machinery casings, in and out of the dark, gloomy lounge and card room — and I noted, among other things, the following:

That the chief steward has posted a notice to the passengers saying that breakfast is to be served at 9, lunch at 1, tea at 4, dinner at 7, with the bar open only between 9 and 11 P.M. — and that under no circumstances is smoking permitted at any time in the dining room (this, I know, is just

. . . . **Classes in the classless society**

one more pointless prohibition — but at least it is the very last chance the Soviet authorities, whoever they are, will have to say "No, no" to me);

That the sealed diplomatic pouches of the Swedish courier are left loose and unguarded on the deck;

That the big wooden crate containing a Pobeda (this small Russian car is apparently for export) has finally been lashed down on the open deck, after hours of patient, and rather amateurish tugging and pulling by the crew;

That a sign on my stateroom door reports in English that my "life jacket is keeping in the case";

That Russian vodka at the bar costs the equivalent of only 33 cents a drink (that is, one hundred grams) — and that, strangely enough, the silent, surly barkeeper can make change with a cash drawer full of American pennies;

That there are, indeed, two classes (first and third) on this Soviet ship, with separate dining rooms for the "rich" and "poor" (my last impression, I reflected, of the new classless Communist society).

I have just now returned from the small, glassed-in deckhouse directly beneath the bridge, where I found a chart of our course, and I could see on this map that we have passed a point due south of Vyborg, that soon we shall zigzag first northwest, then southwest as we skirt the coast of Hogland. On my way back from this promenade point, I happened to go by the smoking room (used as a dance floor in the gay old days), where a loud-speaker was blaring forth a strident tune recorded on a scratchy old phonograph record. The singer of this song (a type of tune which the Russians call *estradny* or variety-hall music) recited, over and over again, the evils of the American way of life: billions of dol-

a bright and wonderful question . . . . . .

lars of profits earned out of the sweat and blood of the working people, slums, starvation, corruption, crime, lynching, lying. This theme was followed up when I passed the radio shack further down the deck. The operator had Moscow Radio on full blast, and through the bulkhead I could hear the latest news: "Aiming to start a third world war for the benefit of Wall Street, the vicious American warmongers today carried their plans for world conquest one step further by concluding the so-called general contract with Western Germany."

Fortunately, it was midnight, the Kremlin bells struck the hour — and the program came to an end. Then the day's broadcasting concluded with the slow, thunderous, chantlike bars of the "Hymn of the Soviet Union," which resounded down the deck to the fantail and across the starlit water. The chords of that music, heard so many times in the past year and a half, still beat heavily in my ears. But soon, in a week, I shall hear a different song, asking in an old, familiar way, a bright and wonderful question: "Oh, say, can you see . . ."

INDEX

☆　　☆　　☆

Index . . . .

Index . . . .

Index . . . .

Index . . . .

Index . . . .